Events in the
Semantics of English

Current Studies in Linguistics Series
Samuel Jay Keyser, general editor

Events in the
Semantics of English

Terence Parsons

A Study in
Subatomic Semantics

The MIT Press
Cambridge, Massachusetts
London, England

First MIT Press paperback edition, 1994

© 1990 Massachusetts Institute of Technology

Printed and bound in the United States of America by Maple-Vail, Inc.

Library of Congress in-Publication Data

Parsons, Terence.
  Events in the semantics of English: a study in subatomic
  semantics / Terence Parsons.
    p.   cm. — (Current studies in linguistics series ; 19)
  Includes bibliographical references and index.
  ISBN 0-262-16120-6 (HB), 0-262-66093-8 (PB)
1. English language—Semantics. I. Title. II. Series.
PE1585.P37   1990
420'.143—dc20   90-39273
                                                                CIP

To Anette and Rex and Brent

Contents

Analytical Table of Contents

vestigation in later chapters. The evidence includes the logic of modifiers, the semantics of perceptual statements, the relations between implicit and explicit reference to events, and quantification over events. The chapter concludes by noting the robustness of the major hypothesis: its usefulness in tying together a wide variety of apparently diverse phenomena.

Chapter 3
Event Ontology and Logical Form   20

The tradition in the literature that distinguishes events, states, and processes is discussed and the distinction between events and states is singled out as important (postponing processes until chapter 9). Various ontological assumptions about events and states are articulated: they have participants, they are particular (as opposed to generic), and they culminate or hold. These notions are used in attributing logical forms to sentences of English. The English tense system is discussed, as well as the differences among states, facts, and propositions.

Chapter 4
Modifiers   40

This chapter begins by classifying modifiers in order to isolate "verb modifiers," which are to be construed as predicates of underlying events. The next two sections discuss various issues connected with verb modifiers: attributives, scope, conjunctions of modifiers, and the treatment of group NPs. Section 4 discusses various alternative ac-

counts of the semantics of these
modifiers; most of these accounts
are either incomplete or incorrect.
The chapter concludes with a discussion of modifiers other than verb
modifiers.

Chapter 5

Thematic Roles   68

The theory of thematic roles in linguistics holds that the subject and
the direct and indirect object positions of NPs in sentences are surface clues to underlying relations
between those NPs and the verb.
Within the theory of underlying
events, thematic roles are seen as
relations between events and their
participants, with certain participants seen as Agents of events, others seen as Patients ("Themes"), and
so on. Section 4 extends the account
to some phenomena concerning motion and location modifiers, such as
the relation between 'onto' and 'on',
and the possibility of multiple thematic roles. Objections to the theory
are discussed. The theory is then
extended to an account of the passive. Sections 7 and 8 discuss the
significance of the use of thematic
relations, as well as alternative accounts that are agnostic about thematic roles.

Chapter 6

Causatives and Inchoatives   105

Causatives are certain verbs that are
paraphrasable in terms of 'cause',
such as 'break the window' =
'cause the window to break'. Inchoatives are verbs that are para-
phrasable in terms of 'become' plus
an adjective, such as 'melt' = 'be-

come molten'. This chapter analyzes causatives and inchoatives within the framework of the theory of underlying events and states. Sections 2–4 develop an analysis of causatives, building on early ideas from Generative Semantics. Section 5 discusses and rejects the possibility of a simpler account in terms of thematic roles. An analysis of inchoatives is given, and then the two accounts are combined in an account of causative-inchoatives. Section 8 discusses various complexities of how modifiers relate to causative-inchoatives, including discussion of locutions such as 'hammer the metal flat', 'open the door partway', 'load hay on the wagon'. The last section discusses alternative versions of the account.

Chapter 7
Explicit Discourse about Events   127

English has a wide variety of locutions that are used to refer to and to quantify over events: terms such as 'Mary's singing', 'the destruction of the city', 'the accident that occurred last night', and so on. This chapter links these locutions with simple sentences of English. The first two sections develop an account of NPs that contain explicit reference to events, such as 'the stabbing of Caesar'; the remaining sections discuss sentences in which we use these locutions to say things about events. The last section discusses modifiers of verbs that apply to events.

Chapter 8

Metaphysical Issues   145

This chapter begins by reviewing what the theory tells us about events and states. Section 2 articulates various notions of reductionistic accounts of events and states and explains why such accounts are not given in this book. Sections 3 and 4 summarize issues in the philosophical literature about fine-grained versus coarse-grained accounts of event identity. (Fine-grained accounts distinguish actions finely, with extreme versions holding that "the singing" and "the loud singing" are different actions. Coarse-grained accounts would identify "my handwaving" and "my signaling" when I signal by waving my hand.) The theory developed here falls midway between these extremes. The last two sections discuss and criticize attempts to defend coarse-grained accounts by modifying the underlying event account.

Chapter 9

The Progressive in English: Events, States, and Processes   167

The first goal of this chapter is to formulate an adequate account of the semantics of the progressive aspect in English: the semantics of 'Agatha is making a cake', as opposed to 'Agatha makes a cake'. Some proposals in the literature are reviewed; all have difficulty with the so-called "imperfective paradox", that 'Mary is building a house' might be true even if she is interrupted in her building, so that 'Mary has built a house' is never true. Section 2 contains an account of the progressive in terms of underlying events, an account that is immune to the imperfective paradox. Sections 3 and 4 consider some objections to the analysis as well as other proposals by Dowty, Åqvist, and Michael Bennett. The second goal of the chapter, taken up in the last section, is to refine the notion of a process so as to account for the infamous "category switch" problem: how it is that modification of a verb like 'run' by an adverbial like 'to the store' can turn a Process phrase ('run') into an Event phrase ('run to the store').

how they interact with underlying events. Certain of these (Frame adverbials) set up a "frame of discussion"; they are discussed only briefly. The role of tenses is to constrain certain times at which events and states occur. Some adverbials constrain the same times that the tenses constrain. Certain other temporal modifiers constrain the events themselves. Frequency adverbials quantify various things in the sentence, sometimes constraining times and sometimes constraining events.

Chapter 12
The Semantics of the Perfect and the Progressive in Modern and Old English   229

The perfect (as in 'Mary has eaten') is seen as adding a component to the sentence in addition to the tense. Accounts of the progressive and perfect are given in terms of states associated with events (or with states). Verbs, as usual, pick out events; the progressive is true if the "In-Progress" state associated with the event holds, and the perfect is true if the "Resultant" state associated with the event holds. These correlations explain the equivalence of the present perfect and the simple past when temporal adverbials are absent (e.g., 'Agatha ate' versus 'Agatha has eaten'). There follows a discussion of a popular view according to which the modern forms of the perfect and progressive evolved from certain adjectival uses of participles in Old English. This view is formalized, and the relation between the old and new forms according to the popular view is clarified, and some further problems are discussed. The last section discusses how the perfect interacts with temporal adverbials and provides a slight repair to the theory of the progressive.

Preface

The purpose of this book is to provide a coherent general theory about how events and states relate to language. Most of the ingredients of the general approach have already appeared in the literature, somewhere, in some form. For example, a treatment of German modifiers within a theory of underlying events was developed in detail in Bartsch 1976, expanding on Davidson 1967. The use of thematic roles has been much discussed in the linguistic literature; they are newly amalgamated here into an event framework as are the topics of causatives and inchoatives, where the treatment owes most to Dowty 1979. Indeed, so much of this book is parasitic on Dowty's book that it can almost be seen as an extended commentary on it. The fact that so many of the accounts contained herein are presented as possible improvements on Dowty's proposals should not obscure the common ground between them or the dependence of my accounts on his work. The use of an event framework to analyze bare infinitive perception sentences has been discussed and defended in Higginbotham 1983 and Vlach 1983. The discussions here of the English progressive, of the perfect, and of the use of underlying states to analyze state sentences are mostly mine, as is much of the detailed development of various topics throughout the book. The uniqueness of the book is that it pulls together a wealth of material bearing on the Panini-Ramsey-Davidson hypothesis that English sentences of the simplest sort contain some underlying reference to (quantification over) events or states.

The discussion in this book requires a familiarity with the notation of ordinary predicate logic; otherwise it should be accessible to any philosopher or linguist. Many of the topics discussed are relatively independent. A reader should be able to skip to almost any chapter after reading the first three, though an awareness of the complexities in chapters 4–7 may be helpful in assessing proposals throughout the book. (A useful beginning would be chapters 1 and 2, followed by 3.1–2, 4.1–3, 5.1–3, 6.1–3, 7.1–2.) An analytical table of contents is included to make the survey easier.

This book does not attempt to cover the main issues in the philosophical literature on events. My presentation does not presuppose any of this material, though many will see the justification of my proposals as partly dependent on how they fit with major views in the field. Fortunately, Bennett 1988 appeared while this book was in preparation; it provides a critical presentation of, and commentary on, the mainstream philosophical theories. It can be used to span the gap between this book and much of the philosophical literature.

The topics in this book are related in various ways to a vast literature in both philosophy and linguistics. I apologize to both readers and authors for the enormous quantity of relevant material that is not discussed or even mentioned. Any attempt at an even-handed survey of relevant material would have doubled the size of a book that continually threatened to grow beyond bounds. The goal of this book is neither completeness nor complete accuracy; it is to get some interesting proposals into the public arena for others to criticize, develop, and build on.

I am indebted to many people for help in the production of this book. My principle debts are to Emmon Bach, David Dowty, and Barbara Partee. I received valuable assistance throughout this project from Neil Elliott and Paul Graves. In addition I want to express appreciation for valuable criticism to Carol Gabriel, Edmund Gettier, Roger Higgins, Michael Jubien, Brian Skyrms, Peter Woodruff, and to many graduate students at the Universities of California (Irvine) and Massachusetts (Amherst). I also wish to express thanks to the National Science Foundation for support for this research under grant BNS 8519320, and to the University of California at Irvine for additional research support. Last, I could not have carried out the mechanics of manuscript production without the patience and cheery support of Jean Symonds and Carol Giangola.

PART I
The Basic Account

Chapter 1
Introduction

This book explores a topic in "subatomic semantics," a term I shall shortly explain. The thesis under investigation is that semantics of simple sentences of English require logical forms that are somewhat more complex than is normally assumed in investigations of natural language semantics. In particular, the semantics of a simple sentence such as 'Brutus stabbed Caesar' requires a form of at least the following complexity:

For some event e,
> e is a stabbing, and
> the agent of e is Brutus, and
> the object of e is Caesar, and
> e culminated at some time in the past.

This form, which is typical, is dominated by an existential quantification over events. Since no such quantification is explicitly indicated in the sentence 'Brutus stabbed Caesar', I call it an "underlying" quantification. A main theme of the theory I investigate is that such underlying quantification over events (and states) is ubiquitous in natural language. This is a theoretical hypothesis which is to be justified by its fruitfulness in explaining a wide range of semantic characteristics of natural language. My goal is to describe these characteristics and to articulate a theory that explains them.

1.1 Background

In dictionaries and grammar books we are likely to find definitions such as these:

noun: A word that stands for a person, place, or thing.
verb: A word that expresses an action or state.

That explanations of this sort are so common suggests that they contain some insight. I am interested in giving that insight a useful theoretical characterization.

The semantics of nouns, as opposed to verbs, has received a great deal of scrutiny. We now know that the way in which nouns "stand for things" is a matter of some subtlety and complexity. A proper noun, such as 'Kim' or 'Samantha', refers to its bearer, which is indeed a "thing," but common nouns such as 'table' or 'giraffe' do not stand for things of this sort; they stand for *kinds* of things. We do use common nouns to refer to particular things but only when the nouns are coupled with definite articles or demonstratives: '*the* table', '*that* giraffe'. In addition, and of great importance, we also use them to quantify over things in phrases such as 'some tables' or 'no giraffes'. A large part of the study of modern logic is taken up with the study of complex noun phrases of this sort.

In this book I assume that much the same is true of verbs; ordinary verbs stand for *kinds* of actions or states, and it is a matter of some complexity to formulate a theory of how we use them to talk about particular actions and states.

1.1.1 History of the Idea
The account I shall explore stems originally from the work of Panini, several centuries B.C. According to his account, in a simple sentence such as 'Kim hit the tree with a knife' the verb stands for some particular action, the nouns in the sentence stand for people or things, and the sentence asserts that those things stand in certain relations to the action. For example, Kim is the agent of the action, the knife is the instrument of the action, and the tree is the object of the action. This is very close to the account that I shall discuss, except that my account denies that verbs stand for particular actions. Although the view that verbs, like proper nouns, stand for particular actions can be defended, it is quite awkward when taken seriously in detail.[1]

The proposal that verbs should be related in some way to events and states is found scattered throughout the history of philosophy. It is found, for example, in Plato,[2] and it surfaces in the *Port-Royal Logic*.[3] It was effectively squelched early in this century by Frege's ignoring it, and by Russell's insisting on its secondary importance in semantics.[4]

The version I shall investigate takes verbs to be more like common nouns than proper nouns. On this view, the verb 'hit' in 'Mary hit Fred' does not stand for a particular action (a particular hitting); it stands for a kind of action, a kind that has particular hittings as its instances. The sentence as a whole says that *some* action of that kind took place, an action of the kind that had Mary as agent and Fred as object. A simple sentence using 'hit' says that a hitting took place, one using 'eat' says that an eating took place, and so on. This idea was first articulated, so far as I know, by Frank Ramsey, who said,

'That Caesar died' is really an existential proposition, asserting the existence of an event of a certain sort (Ramsey 1927).

Unfortunately, this is about all that Ramsey said on the subject, and it is not certain that his idea is the same as the one explored here. Hans Reichenbach gave an account (1947) in terms of facts (which he also called events), but it is too complex to profitably duplicate here. His account was then considerably modified by Donald Davidson (1967) into a theory in which verbs explicitly stand for kinds of events, so that a sentence containing such a verb states implicitly that an event of that sort takes place.

Davidson's proposal has had less influence in philosophical semantics than it deserves, for three reasons. First, some saw the proposal as a mere detail in Davidson's attempt to show how to formulate a Tarski truth-definition for English. This particular detail worked fairly well for that purpose, so the controversy quickly shifted elsewhere. Second, others saw the proposal not so much as an account of the semantics of natural language but as a clause in Davidson's metaphysics of events and actions. It was judged therefore by its conformity or lack of conformity with preexisting opinions about actions and events—especially about their "identity conditions." Thus the fruitfulness of the theory in accounting for a broad array of data concerning natural language was missed. Third, the theory failed to impress many workers in the semantics of natural language (including me) because we saw its only virtue as yielding an account of the semantics and logic of adverbial modifiers. And here, the theory fails to provide a *general* account; it works well for 'in the bedroom' but fails for 'in a dream', works well for 'happily' but not for 'necessarily', works well for 'immediately' but seems to fail for 'slowly'—or at least this is what Davidson himself suggested, and most others have taken it for granted. The loss of interest in the theory is understandable but mistaken. No

theory of substance will work for all grammatical modifiers, for these
modifiers occur in different categories, and they behave differently
from one another. And the claim that the account fails for degree
adverbs such as 'slowly' is, when carefully examined, far from obvious. Further, plenty of linguistic constructions in addition to adverbial modification can be well accounted for by positing underlying
quantification over events. That is the view I articulate in this book.

1.1.2 The Theory
The theory to be investigated begins by combining Panini's and Davidson's.[5] The basic assumption is that a sentence such as

Caesar died

says something like the following:

For some event e,
    e is a dying, *and*
    the object of e is Caesar, *and*
    e culminates before now.

In the symbolism of symbolic logic this becomes

$$(\exists e)\,[\,\mathrm{Dying}(e)\ \&\ \mathrm{Object}(e, \mathrm{Caesar})\ \&\ \mathrm{Culminate}(e, \text{before now})]$$

DEFAULT   VERB   SUBJECT   TENSE

The three things blatantly present in the English sentence—subject,
verb, and tense—become separate conjuncts constraining the event of
Caesar's dying. The verb indicates that the event in question is an
event of dying. The subject indicates that Caesar is the object of that
event. (The notion of 'object' is discussed in detail in chapter 5 under
the rubric 'theme'.) The tense indicates that the event in question
culminated before the time of utterance of the sentence. ('Culmination'
is discussed in chapter 3.) Throughout most of the preliminary discussion in these first few chapters I shall ignore tenses; I discuss them
first in chapter 3 and more fully in chapters 11 and 12.

In the absence of other sources of event quantification, the event
variable in question is existentially bound, with scope as narrow as
possible. Other options are discussed in chapter 11.

This analysis of 'Caesar died' is considerably more complex than
the symbolization normally taught in logic books, which (ignoring
tense) is simply

D(c),

where the 'D' represents 'died' and the 'c' represents 'Caesar'. The two proposals are not incompatible, however, for the former can be seen as a more refined version of the latter. If we view the traditional formula 'D(x)' as a crude form that fails to display all the logical structure in question, then a more refined analysis of the logic text formula 'D(x)' is

(∃e)[Dying(e) & Object(e,x)].

Assigning this refined structure to the logic textbook account yields the proposal stated above.[6]

The proposed form is, however, considerably more complicated than the traditional symbolization. The topic of this book is whether, and why, the additional complication is necessary. The answer I propose is that the additional structure provides a nice account of various phenomena concerning language, including

• The logic of modifiers: logical relations among sentences such as 'Brutus stabbed Caesar in the back' and 'Brutus stabbed Caesar' (e.g., that the former entails the latter).
• The semantics of perception statements, including the relation between 'Agatha saw Brutus stab Caesar' and 'Agatha saw the stabbing of Caesar by Brutus'.
• The semantics of causatives and inchoatives: Why, if Mary will open the door, the door will open, and why this in turn entails that the door will be open. (In traditional logic these three uses of 'open' are symbolized as three completely independent predicates.)
• Relations between the explicit ways in which we talk about events and our sentences that do not appear to involve explicit reference to events at all. E.g., between 'A flight over the pole by a Norwegian took place in May 1926' and 'A Norwegian flew over the pole in May 1926'. Or between the NP 'every violent destruction of a city' and the VP 'violently destroyed a city'.[7] Included in this topic is the relation between the semantics of adjectives ('slow') and their corresponding -ly adverbs ('slowly'), and between verbs ('sing') and gerunds used as common nouns ('the singing').
• The relation between "causative" sentences with events as subjects (such as 'Mary's singing broke the window') and the same sentences with agents of events as subjects ('Mary broke the window'). Why, e.g., does the former entail the latter?

These topics, and a host of others, can be addressed by a theory of underlying events and states. There is a wealth of data in our native tongue just waiting to be explained; the hypothesis of underlying events and states explains a great deal of it, provided that that hypothesis is suitably developed. There is also a wealth of data about language in old-fashioned grammar books, couched in terms of 'event' (or 'action') and 'state'.[8] Many observations about language couched in this terminology have been ignored as a consequence of recent advances in the study of syntax that assume syntax to be autonomous from semantics. This may be appropriate for those who work in syntax, since the observations I have gathered are mostly semantical or pragmatic in nature. But since this book is in semantics, they often prove fruitful for my task.

1.2   Subatomic Semantics

In formal logic, formulas are divided into two sorts: *atomic* formulas, from which all the rest are generated, and nonatomic formulas that are generated from the atomic ones, usually by means of quantification (universal or existential quantifiers: '(x)', '($\exists$x)'), or by combination with connectives ('&', '$\vee$', '$\neg$', '$\rightarrow$'), or by the addition of operators (e.g., modal operators representing 'necessarily' and 'possibly'). This idea has generally been carried over to the study of natural language, and there are now fairly firm customs about what things count as atomic formulas of English, so far as their semantics is concerned. These "atomic formulas of English" are phrases like 'x is tall' or 'x stabbed y'. The literature in philosophical logic is full of discussions about how to combine these atomic formulas with other things so as to produce sentences. The "other things" include the English version of quantification with NPs ('Every boy'), modification with sentence operators ('Necessarily', 'Allegedly'), amalgamation with connectives ('and', 'or', 'not'), and embeddings into that-clauses. The topic of this book lies primarily elsewhere. I want to investigate certain aspects of the *subatomic* structure of the atomic formulas of English that these other studies take as their inputs. I do not dispute that 'x stabbed y' is an atomic formula of English, nor do I dispute that it contains two variables and a constant part. I merely want to investigate the structure of the constant part in more detail. This enterprise leaves traditional theories of language mostly untouched and unchallenged. Indeed, I presuppose traditional accounts of quantification, connectives, sentence modification, and so on, as means of getting from the atomic structures I investigate to a more complete theory of English. I do not doubt, for example, that 'Allegedly, every boy dated a girl' has a semantic structure something like

Allegedly $(x)(B(x) \rightarrow (\exists y)(G(y)$ & x dated y)),

Allegedly every-boy   some-girl dated

(where 'Allegedly' is a sentence operator; I ignore tense for the moment). I am interested instead in whether there is some additional structure for 'x dated y', something like

x dates y = $(\exists e)(e$ is a dating & x is the agent of e & y is the object of e).

I believe there is. What this additional structure consists in forms my primary subject matter.

I *will* take issue with one part of the established tradition. The remarkable interest and success in handling portions of the semantics of language in terms of sentential operators, such as in modal logic, have lured people into applying the technique of operators too extensively.[9] In particular, scope-bearing operators have been used to analyze many things that should be handled differently, including verb modifiers, causatives, and the special characteristics of the progressive and perfect aspects. These matters will be addressed in later chapters.

1.3 Methodology

My methodology regarding events differs from that of the main philosophical tradition. Philosophers typically begin with general hypotheses about events, gleaned from intuition and first principles. The principles include views about, for instance, the identity conditions for events. These general principles are then brought to bear on a theory such as the one I investigate to test its adequacy. This usually results in a conflict between the principles and the theory, and in consequence the theory is rejected.

I have reservations about this type of approach. I usually lack the intuitions that others begin with, and I note that the writers in question rarely agree among themselves as to the truth about events. This gives me the courage to ignore their criticisms, at least temporarily, and to pursue a theory having implications for events that would be rejected by many of the main traditions. (Of course the literature contains a host of interesting examples that the theory will have to explain, and so I cannot ignore the discussions, even if I am unmoved by the methodology.)

My approach is different. I begin with a mass of linguistic data to be explained and with the bare outlines of a theory for explaining it. I try to develop the theory in the best way possible to explain the data. Only at the end of the enterprise am I in possession of generalities about events. Conflicts between the resulting theory and views from the philosophical literature are discussed in chapter 8.

What are the linguistic data on which this theory rests? We are examining a semantic theory that tells us that certain sentences are true (or false) in certain circumstances. As native speakers of the language, we are authorities on whether these sentences really are true or false as the theory says, at least for ordinary sentences, such as 'There is beer in the refrigerator', as opposed to sentences such as 'Two events are identical if and only if they have exactly the same causes and the same effects'. I regard judgments about the former type of sentence as data, but not judgments about the latter. Existing theories of natural language tell us that if 'Agatha has a clever boyfriend' is true, then so is 'Agatha has a boyfriend'. A theory that makes many correct predictions of this sort has a claim to being taken seriously as a potentially correct theory of language. The theory I shall be considering makes predictions such as this: If 'Mary runs slowly' is true then so is 'Mary runs'. More ambitiously, if 'Mary fells a tree into the truck' is true then so are 'A tree falls', 'A tree falls into the truck', 'A tree will be in the truck'. (The theory does not say that Mary falls, or that Mary ends up in the truck, though the latter *will* follow from 'Mary climbs into the truck'.) A theory of language needs to explain these data. They should be seen as clear consequences of the theory, and then these consequences, as well as all others not envisioned in the formulation of the theory, need to be tested against further data. If the predictions are widespread and correct, then the theory deserves to be taken seriously. This, in a nutshell, is my method.

Unfortunately, things do not work out so neatly, primarily because most sentences are ambiguous. This fact has two consequences for my enterprise. First, since we, as native speakers, can see the ambiguity in a sentence, we thereby have additional data on which to base our theories. But the "data" also become much less datalike. If a sentence is ambiguous, then it makes no sense to call it "true" or "false" without qualification, but only "true on such and such a reading."[10] We are indeed capable of assessing theories on the basis of their consequences for "truth on a reading," and I rely on this technique. But it is considerably more difficult to articulate the methodology being employed when ambiguity is introduced into the data.

1.4 Logical Form

I seek a theory that describes the semantics of sentences of English, that is, the relations between words of our language and things in the world.[11] One convenient way of accomplishing this is to find a way to associate "logical forms" with English sentences. These "forms" will be sentences of a formal language that has already received a clear semantical treatment. The semantics of the English sentences in question will then be that of their associated logical forms. This intermediate route from the English to its semantics—via logical forms—is for the sake of convenience only. The semantics of the formal language I use (mostly the ordinary predicate calculus) is already widely known, and so I can presuppose a great deal of familiar work in formal semantics. It also allows me to finesse the problem of ambiguity. The semantics of an ambiguous language such as English is cumbersome to state directly; it is easier to assign unambiguous logical forms to sentences of English based on their various modes of generation.[12] For these two reasons alone I employ logical forms. If you prefer to avoid their use, you need only translate the logical forms into stilted English in the usual fashion. You will then be directly (rather then mediately) stating the semantics of the English sentences under study, suitably disambiguated.[13]

When I attribute a logical form to a sentence, part of the significance is that the sentence and the corresponding logical form are true in the same circumstances (ignoring ambiguity, and assuming identical interpretations of the parts of the sentence and corresponding parts of the form). Thus the whole theory might be reinterpreted in entirely different terms. Instead of thinking of L as the logical form of a sentence S, one could think of L as a sentence in a theory of events. The claim made in associating S with L is, as before, that they are true together. The result of the global association of sentences with forms then can be seen as a detailed articulation of a theory of events; the formulation within logical notation makes precise the logical structure of this theory, and its correlation with English sentences makes the consequences of this theory clearly identifiable in our own native tongue.

Other reinterpretations of the logical forms are possible as well. If I am successful in my enterprise, it should be possible to take the results of this work and convert them into several quite different frameworks.

With regard to many of the issues I address, we are still at the stage of needing *some* theory to account for the data. Once we have one, then we can consider formulating others and arguing about which is better. I do little theory comparison here, since we do not yet have the theories to compare.[14] Thus I shall frustrate many readers for not having shown why my approach is the only correct one. Others will have to address this issue when more competing theories are available.

Chapter 2

The Evidence in Favor of Underlying Events

In this chapter I review various kinds of evidence in favor of the underlying event analysis, concentrating on its applications to event sentences, and leaving the issue of state sentences to a later chapter. I begin with no particular preconceptions about the nature of events. My methodology is rather to proceed in a scientific frame of mind: there are data to be explained, and we have in rough outline a theory that might be used to explain it. The final form of the theory will be tailored by the ways in which it meets the test of accounting for the data.

2.1 The First Kind of Evidence: The Logic of Modifiers

The first kind of evidence in favor of the underlying event analysis has to do with the logic of modifiers. Sentences containing grammatical modifiers bear certain logical relations to one another because of these modifiers. The evidence that the underlying event analysis accounts for these relations can be illustrated by the logical relations among these sentences:[1]

A   Brutus stabbed Caesar in the back with a knife.
B   Brutus stabbed Caesar in the back.
C   Brutus stabbed Caesar with a knife.
D   Brutus stabbed Caesar.

The evidence that needs accounting for is that sentence (A) entails the conjunction of (B) and (C), but *not* vice versa, and that either of (B) or (C) alone entails (D). In diagrammatic form, the higher sentences in the following graph entail the lower ones, and not vice versa:

These connections (and lack of connections) are exactly the ones predicted by assigning to the sentences in question the forms described earlier:

A′ (∃e)[Stabbing(e) & Subj(e,B) & Obj(e,C) & In(e,b) & With(e,k)]

B′ (∃e)[Stabbing(e) & Subj(e,B) & Obj(e,C) & In(e,b)]

C′ (∃e)[Stabbing(e) & Subj(e,B) & Obj(e,C) & With(e,k)]

D′ (∃e)[Stabbing(e) & Subj(e,B) & Obj(e,C)]

Notice that it is important that (A) ('Brutus stabbed Caesar in the back with a knife') not follow from the conjunction of (B) and (C) ('Brutus stabbed Caesar in the back & Brutus stabbed Caesar with a knife'). Suppose that Brutus stabbed Caesar in the back with an icepick, and in the thigh with a knife. Then both (B) and (C) are true, but (A) may be false. (This is so even if the stabbings are simultaneous.) The logical forms get this right, and for the right reason: the conjunction of (B′) and (C′) does not require that the two stabbings (the one in the back and the one with the knife) be the same.

The account, of course, needs to be tested against a wide range of data, for it is not obvious that all verb modifiers follow this neat pattern. I cannot survey all the potential problem cases here, but two that are prominent in the literature deserve mention.

First, in many potential counterexamples the modifier in question is actually a sentence modifier. One illustrative example is 'nearly', as in 'Mary nearly hit John'. It is easy to see that if 'nearly' were treated as a predicate of events in this example, then the form would be wrong; it would tell us that if Mary nearly hit John, then there was a hitting of John by Mary that was "near," and this would entail that Mary actually hit John. The solution to this problem is to note that 'nearly' functions here as a sentence modifier, and so the theory under examination does not apply to it. (The distinction between verb-modifiers and sentence-modifiers is discussed in chapter 3.)

Second, the word 'partway' is a classic counterexample in the literature. (See, for example, Stalnaker & Thomason 1973.) If Mary closed the door partway, then it does not follow that she closed the door, as it would if 'partway' were functioning as a predicate of events in the theory under investigation. Yet 'partway' does not appear to be a sentence modifier either. The solution is to see that 'partway' is actually a modifier of other modifiers, not of verbs. This is evidenced by its occurrence in sentences such as 'Mary pushed the door partway closed', in which 'partway' obviously modifies the adjective 'closed'. But a sentence such as 'Mary closed the door' is of a rather well-studied, complex sort; it is a classic "causative-inchoative" sentence, whose meaning is something like

Mary did something that caused the door to become closed.

It then seems plausible to suppose that 'partway' behaves in its usual way in 'Mary closed the door partway', and that the meaning of the whole sentence is something like

Mary did something that caused the door to become partway closed.

If this account is on the right track, 'partway' is not a verb modifier at all, and so it does not provide a counterexample to the theory. (Causative-inchoative constructions and their modifiers are discussed in chapter 6.)

The logic of modifiers affords a rich and complex pattern of inferences that needs explanation. The theory of underlying events does well for verb modifiers, whereas most other theories do not. I take this as some evidence in favor of the view. The evidence is not conclusive—far from it—but it is evidence nonetheless, and it is supportive. Discussion of the logic of modifiers, including critiques of alternative views, occupies most of chapter 4.

2.2 A Second Kind of Evidence: The Logic of Perceptual Idioms

A certain class of idioms has only recently received attention in the philosophical literature. An idiom of this sort is a sentence whose main verb is a perceptual verb that is followed by a clause having the structure of a simple sentence that is missing its tense. Examples are

A   Mary saw *Brutus stab Caesar.*
B   Sam heard *Mary shoot Bill.*
C   Agatha felt *the boat rock.*

Each of the italicized phrases is just like a simple sentence except that the tense is missing.

The semantics of such sentences must be quite different from popular accounts of the semantics of "perceiving-that" constructions. Sentence (A), for example, differs radically from

D   Mary saw *that Brutus stabbed Caesar.*

Not only are (A) and (D) logically independent of one another but their logical behaviors differ. For example, the contents of the that-clause in (D) are in an opaque context, whereas the contents of the italicized phrase in (A) are not. If Caesar is the emperor, then (A) entails that Mary saw Brutus stab the emperor, but (D) does not entail that Mary saw that Brutus stabbed the emperor.

It is fruitless to try to account for such idioms in terms of perception of the *participants* of the events that are perceived. That would be like trying to analyze perception of a melody in terms of perception of the notes constituting it. For example, although it might be plausible to analyze

John saw Mary run

as

John saw Mary & Mary was running (at that time),

the plausibility depends on the fact that 'see' is the perceptual verb and running is the activity.[2] Certainly it is implausible to try to analyze

John felt Mary shuffle her feet

as

John felt Mary & Mary shuffled her feet (then).

This gives neither necessary nor sufficient conditions. On the one hand, one might feel Mary shuffling her feet (for example, in a canoe) without feeling Mary. On the other hand, one might feel Mary (by placing one's hand on her forehead) while she is shuffling her feet without feeling her shuffle her feet. (The proposed analysis incorrectly entails that if John felt Mary shuffle her feet, then he felt her do X, where X is anything at all that she did at that time.)

The underlying event analysis can easily be extended to account for these sentences by construing them as telling us that the subject perceives a certain *event,* an event of the sort picked out by the embedded clause. Thus (A) would have a form that says

There is a seeing whose subject is Mary and whose object is a stabbing of Caesar by Brutus,

or, spelled out in detail

(∃e)[Seeing(e) & Subj(e,Mary) & (∃e′)[Stabbing(e′) &
Subj(e′,Brutus) & Obj(e′,Caesar) & Obj(e,e′)]]].

This is a version of an analysis discussed in some detail by James
Higginbotham (1983) and Frank Vlach (1983) in independent papers;
each argues that it is superior to accounts based on situation semantics.
They both point out that the analysis passes a variety of tests proposed
in Barwise (1981) for any adequate analysis of perceptual idioms.[3]

2.3   Implicit and Explicit Talk about Events

A third kind of evidence in favor of the underlying event analysis lies
in the resources it gives us to explain the relationship between certain
sentences that contain explicit reference to events and those that do
not. For example, sentence (A) contains a phrase that explicitly refers
to an event of singing, the phrase 'the singing of the *Marseillaise*',
whereas there is no explicit reference to any event at all in (B):

$$\overline{\hspace{3cm}} \quad \ulcorner \textit{explicit reference to an event}$$

A   After the singing of the *Marseillaise* they saluted the flag

B   After the *Marseillaise* was sung they saluted the flag.

Yet these sentences convey almost the same information; the main
difference being that a presupposition in (A) seems to be missing in
(B): that there was only one singing of the *Marseillaise*.

   This example also raises the related question of the relationship
between a nominal gerund, such as 'singing', used semantically as a
noun to designate an event, and the verb 'sing' from which it is
derived. The underlying event analysis provides the means for a neat
solution by proposing that nominal gerunds contribute the *very same*
predicates to logical form as the verbs on which they are based.[4] (In
giving English versions of the logical forms of ordinary sentences, I
have already been using such gerunds.) With this assumption, the
definite description in sentence (A) can be symbolized in the ordinary
fashion, assuming as before that the 'of' in 'the singing of the *Marseillaise*' indicates that the *Marseillaise* is the object of the singing in
question. The logical forms are

A′   (∃e)[Saluting(e) & Subj(e,them) & Obj(e,the flag) &
      After(e,SM)],

where 'SM' is '(the e′)(Singing(e′) & Obj(e′,the *M*))'.

["After the event that was a singing of the *Marseillaise*, there was a
saluting of the flag (by them)."]

B′   (∃e)[Saluting(e) & Subj(e,them) & Obj(e,the flag) &
      (∃e′)(Singing(e′) & Obj(e′,the *M*) & After(e,e′)].

["After an event that was a singing of the *Marseillaise* there was a saluting of the flag (by them)."]

On any ordinary account of the logic of definite descriptions, (A′) thereby entails (B′), and (B′) will entail (A′) if supplemented by the claim that there was at most one singing of the *Marseillaise* (by them).

This analysis also accounts for the relationship between certain adverbs ending in 'ly' and the adjectives from which they derive, such as the relationship between 'quietly' and 'quiet' in

C   They sang the *Marseillaise* quietly

and:

D   The quiet singing of the *Marseillaise* (soothed her ears).

Here again, the proposal that the adverb and related adjective contribute exactly the same predicate to logical form seems to give exactly the right results.[5]

These relationships in form between verbs and the nominal gerunds derived from them, and between adjectives and the 'ly' adverbs derived from them, cannot be seen as some gigantic coincidence; a principled theory is needed to account for them. The underlying event theory does so in a natural manner. In chapter 7 I discuss further this additional evidence in favor of the theory.

2.4   Explicit Quantification Over Events

It is a commonplace in philosophical logic that where there is reference there also is quantification. This suggests that we might fruitfully test for implicit quantification over events (in underlying logical form) by looking for inferences linking it with explicit quantification over events at the surface. Here is an example

A   In every burning, oxygen is consumed.
B   Agatha burned the wood.
C   Oxygen was consumed.

Intuitively, sentence (C) follows from (A) and (B); the problem is to account for why this should be so. On ordinary textbook accounts, there is no quantification in (B) or (C), and no reference to events by any phrase in either of them. Yet somehow the quantification over burnings in (A) is logically related to (B) and (C). The mystery dis-

solves in the underlying event approach. Following the recipes given
above, the forms associated with (A) through (C) are

A′ (e)[Burning(e) → (∃e′)[Consuming(e′) & Obj(e′,O_2) & In(e,e′)]]
B′ (∃e)[Burning(e) & Subj(e, Agatha) & Obj(e,wood)]
C′ (∃e′)[Consuming(e′) & Obj(e′,O_2)]

And (C′) follows from (A′) and (B′) in the predicate calculus.

2.5 Robustness

On the basis of the above analyses, it is fair to say that the underlying
event account explains many different kinds of semantically important
phenomena. I take this to be evidence in its favor.

  Each kind of evidence is supportive in its own right, but *the ways
in which these phenomena interact with each other are even more
important.* Part of the pattern of robustness is that the theory accounts
for data in several different epistemically independent domains. The
different domains are then seen to interact in fruitful ways. For example, the domains include the logic of modifiers, the semantics of
perceptual idioms, and relations between explicit and implicit talk
about events. These three applications then interact to explain, for
example, how 'Mary saw Brutus stab Caesar violently' entails 'Mary
saw something violent'. That is the theory's robustness at work.

Chapter 3
Event Ontology and Logical Form

3.1   Events, States, and Processes

A long-standing tradition in the linguistic and philosophical literature divides simple sentences into categories. The most well-known version categorizes sentences into three major groups: "Event sentences," "State sentences," and "Process sentences." Event sentences are often subdivided into "Accomplishment sentences" and "Achievement sentences."

The theory under discussion assumes that there are nonlinguistic things in the world corresponding to the linguistic items classified above: there are, in the world, events, processes, and states. It is convenient to have a generic term to stand for all of them; I shall follow Bach (1986) in referring to them as "eventualities." For many purposes the distinctions among eventualities will not be important, but for a few purposes certain differences will be crucial—that between events and states being most important.

The traditional four-part classification of eventualities is as follows:

Events (Accomplishments)   The sentence 'Agatha made a sandwich' reports an accomplishment type of event. This sort of event may or may not take an extended amount of time, but it is always meaningful to *ask* "how long" it took. Most events have definite culminations. Even if an event lacks a culmination, it still makes sense to ask whether it "finished".

Events (Achievements)   The sentence 'She won the race' reports an achievement. Achievements are events that by their very nature are instantaneous; for this reason it makes no sense to ask how long the event took or how long it lasted.

States   The sentence 'The dress is pink' reports a state. States hold for varying amounts of time. It does not make sense to ask how long a state took (though one can ask how long it lasted), nor does it make sense to ask whether it culminated (finished).

Processes   The sentence 'Mary ran' reports a process. Processes are like events in being "happenings," but they are like states in apparently having no natural finishing points. In the literature, processes are sometimes called "Activities."

Further discussion of how to distinguish among these categories is relegated to section 6 below.

For most of this text, the basic items of investigation are Events and States. I generally ignore the distinction between the two kinds of events, Accomplishments and Achievements. Later (chapter 9) I argue that Processes are analyzable in terms of Events, and so I omit discussion of Processes as a separate case, but nothing in the theory prevents Process from receiving special treatment.

3.2   Ontological Assumptions and Logical Forms

Using Bach's term "eventuality," I make certain assumptions about eventualities in general, as well as certain special assumptions about events in particular.

3.2.1   Participants

Throughout the text I assume that eventualities have participants of various kinds. A stabbing has an agent (the stabber), and it typically has an object (though not always—you can stab and miss, or just stab "at the air"). In keeping with the terminology in the linguistic literature I use the term "theme" for the object of a stabbing, if there is one.

A knowing, on the other hand, typically does not have an agent, since a knowing is not something that is *done* by someone; in such a case the knower will be called the "experiencer," and what is known will again be classified as the theme.

These classifications of participants in an eventuality are difficult. They occupy the whole of chapter 5. However, many of the issues I address are independent of the details of such classifications, and for this reason it is best to keep them in the background. In the next two chapters I therefore follow the policy of using the terminology 'Subject' and 'Object' to stand neutrally for *whatever* appropriate relation relates the (denotations of the) subject and direct object of a sentence to its underlying eventuality. Thus I shall continue to use 'Subject' and 'Object' in writing the logical forms of

Mary sees the tree

and

Brutus stabs Caesar

as

$(\exists e)$[Seeing(e) & Subject(e,Mary) & Object(e,tree)],
$(\exists e)$[Stabbing(e) & Subject(e,Brutus) & Object(e,Caesar)].

A version of the theory (discussed in chapter 5) does not require the classification of participants in this manner. It views the above types of logical forms as odd ways of writing:

$(\exists e)$[Seeing(e,Mary,tree)],
$(\exists e)$[Stabbing(e,Brutus,Caesar)],

(to be read 'e is a seeing by Mary of the tree', and 'e is a stabbing of Caesar by Brutus'). In this form, it does not make sense to ask whether Mary and Brutus participate in their respective eventualities in the same or different ways. I think that this version of the theory is inferior to the version I propose, which selects out kinds of participants, but most of my discussion does not rely on this preference.

On any version of the theory, eventualities are meant to be "small" things linked to simple formulas, not "large" things linked with arbitrary sentences. For example, in some theories there is a semantical entity (proposition, fact, situation) corresponding to the sentence

Mary will run or Henry will quit.

On the underlying eventuality view there is no eventuality corresponding to this sentence. The sentence expresses a proposition, and perhaps it also picks out a unique (propositional) fact, but the sentence *as a whole* does not refer to or quantify over eventualities—only the individual disjuncts making it up do that. It is the disjuncts that have unique participants, not the sentence as a whole. (This is part of what I mean by calling this a study in "subatomic semantics"; the entities studied here apply beneath the level of atomic sentences, and are thus not correlated with molecular sentences.)

3.2.2 Particularity of Events and States

People sometimes distinguish between generic events and states on
the one hand and particular events and states on the other. When we
condemn "murder" and praise "knowledge" we may perhaps be talking
in terms of generic events and states. But when we quantify over
events and states in the theory being discussed, particular events are
at issue. Suppose we say, for example, that Brutus stabbed Caesar
and Laertes stabbed Hamlet; the forms are

($\exists$e)[Stabbing(e) & Subject(e,Brutus) & Object(e,Caesar)],
($\exists$e)[Stabbing(e) & Subject(e,Laertes) & Object(e,Hamlet)].

It is easy to see that these sentences must be satisfied by different
events. If a single event satisfied both, then Brutus and Laertes would
both be subjects of it, and Caesar and Hamlet would both be objects
of it. This event would then satisfy the form attributed to 'Brutus
stabbed Hamlet', which is incorrect. This argument rules out the option that both cases deal with the same "generic" stabbing.[1]

At the outset I do not assume the particularity of eventualities; I
assume only that they should have whatever characteristics they need
so that the theory can be developed into a good account of the semantics of English. Their particularity is, then, a consequence of this
assumption; eventualities need to be particular in order for the theory
to work properly. Because of the structure of sentences such as 'Mary
saw Brutus stab Caesar' (along with 'Mary saw the stabbing of Caesar
by Brutus'), eventualities will turn out to be perceivable, and, because
of examples such as 'Brutus stabbed Caesar in the marketplace at
noon', many will turn out to be located in space-time. I do not cite
these results because they are desirable or undesirable; I cite them in
order to illustrate the ontological character of the theory, and to clarify
how these results flow from the theory. Consequences for the identity
conditions of events are discussed in chapter 8.

3.2.3 Culmination and Holding

The theory employs a basic distinction between an eventuality's *culminating* and that eventuality's *holding*. This distinction is easiest to
explain on a case-by-case basis.

Accomplishment-Events   In the case of ordinary (accomplishment)
events, the subparts having a special significance for the theory are
easy to identify: an event often has both a development portion and a

culmination. For example, if Mary builds a bookcase, then there is a period of time during which the building is going on—the development portion—and then (if she finishes) there is a time at which the bookcase finally gets built, the time of culmination. I do not suppose that every event has a culmination. If Mary begins building a bookcase but is struck by lightning when she has finished three-quarters of the work, then there is an event that is a building, that has her for a subject, that has a bookcase (an unfinished one) as object, and that never culminates. (This view will be important for the analysis of the progressive.)

Achievement-Events I assume that "Achievements," such as 'reaching the summit', are not essentially different from Accomplishment-events. An Achievement culminates when it "happens"; a reaching of the summit by Mary culminates when Mary reaches the summit. The arguable point is whether Achievements have development portions prior to the time of culmination. The popular conception is that they do not; they are, by their very nature, instantaneous events. This is supposed to explain the unacceptability of using Achievement verbs in the progressive, as in

*Samantha is reaching the summit.
*Henry is winning the race.

According to the theory I develop in chapter 9, the progressive version of such a sentence is true during the development portion of the event. If Achievements necessarily have no development portions, the oddity of the displayed sentences would be explained. On the other hand, most speakers treat the displayed sentences as grammatical. They are widely used in colloquial language, and perhaps there is nothing deviant about them at all. If so, Achievement sentences are Event sentences that have development portions, and they are not special in any way that is relevant to the issues I discuss. In either case they may be treated theoretically as other Event sentences are treated. Whether Achievements may have development portions is not relevant to their theoretical classification within the theory.[2]

States I assume that the notion of culmination does not apply to states. At a given time, a state simply holds or it does not.

Processes I discuss processes in chapter 9.

3.2.4 Logical Forms

The two key technical notions I use are those of culminating and holding. I use the notation 'Cul(e,t)' to mean that e is an event that *culminates* at time t. When I say that an eventuality e *holds* (at time t), I mean that either e is a state and e's subject is in state e at t, or e is an event which is in progress (in its development portion) at t. I use the notation 'Hold(e,t)' for 'e holds at t.'[3] The logical forms yielded by the theory of underlying eventualities can best be explained by illustration. The sentence

Mary knows Fred

has a logical form that is, roughly

There is a knowing that
    has Mary as its subject, and
    has Fred as its object, and
    holds now.

In symbols:

$(\exists e)$[Knowing(e) & Subject(e,Mary) & Object(e, Fred) & Hold(e,now)].

The event sentences I discuss[4] will typically deviate from this model in three ways. With intransitive verbs, the object clause is omitted. With past and future tense sentences we add something equivalent to quantification over times; this is taken up in the next section. Third, we need to choose between saying that the eventuality in question *holds* at the time in question, or saying that it *culminates* then. If we want to say that Mary built a bookcase, then we shall need to say that there is a past time (a time before now) at which that building event culminates. If we were to say only that there is a past time at which the event holds, then that leaves it open that she has not yet finished. In such a case the English sentence 'Mary built a bookcase' is not yet true. The logical form of a simple nonprogressive sentence contains 'Hold' if the verb is a state verb; its logical form contains 'Cul' if the verb is an event verb. The logical form associated with:

Mary built the bookcase

will be equivalent to:[5]

$(\exists e)$[Building(e) & Subject(e,Mary) & Object(e,the bookcase) & $(\exists t)$[t<now & Cul(e,t)]].

This essay in "subatomic semantics" has the goal of providing semantical analyses of formulas that other theories normally treat as atomic formulas of English. Its goal is to analyze phrases such as 'x stabs y', 'x stabs y violently', 'x stabs y violently with u', and so on. The primary outputs of this theory are formulas consisting of variables, verbs, and modifiers. So NPs are dealt with by another part of the semantics. NPs contribute to the logical forms of English sentences primarily (perhaps exclusively) by quantification. The syntactic effect of this process is that the NP in question takes the place of the quantified variable (with later occurrences of the same variable being replaced by pronouns); semantically, it is as if the variable is bound by a quantifier contributed by the NP. For example, one of the readings of 'Everyone stabs someone' has the logical form

$(x)(\text{Person}(x) \rightarrow (\exists y)(\text{Person}(y) \ \& \ x \text{ stabs } y)).$

If we start with 'x stabs y' as an atomic formula of English, the sentence can be generated in two steps, first, by combining 'x stabs y' with 'someone' to get 'x stabs someone', and then combining this with 'everyone' to get 'everyone stabs someone'.[6] Semantically, the first step embeds the logical form of 'x stabs y' in the matrix

$(\exists y)(\text{Person}(y) \ \& \ \ldots \ldots \ ),$

and the second embeds the result in the matrix

$(x)(\text{Person}(x) \rightarrow. \ \ldots \ldots \ ).$

This type of process has been familiar ever since Bertrand Russell wrote "On Denoting" in 1905, and although the details may change from theory to theory, something equivalent to it is now commonplace. I take this sort of background for granted. The point of the theory under development is to analyze the inputs to the customary treatment of quantification, so that the structure of 'x stabs y' is analyzed. Since 'stab' is an event verb, the logical form of this part is

x stabs y =
$(\exists e)[\text{Stabbing}(e) \ \& \ \text{Subject}(e,x) \ \& \ \text{Object}(e,y) \ \& \ \text{Cul}(e,\text{now})].$

Accordingly, the whole form for 'Everyone stabs someone' is

$(x)(\text{Person}(x) \rightarrow (\exists y)(\text{Person}(y) \ \& \ (\exists e)[\text{Stabbing}(e) \ \& \ \text{Subject}(e,x) \ \& \ \text{Object}(e,y) \ \& \ \text{Cul}(e,\text{now})])),$

where the theory of underlying eventualities has provided the form for 'x stabs y' that is inserted into the form for the rest of the sentence.

Strictly, then, the subject matter of most of this essay is the analysis of *formulas containing variables,* without regular NPs. But since such formulas are so unnatural to read, I usually give examples in which the variables are replaced by proper names or definite descriptions. I talk as if the theory yielded 'Brutus stabs Caesar', though it actually (directly) yields 'x stabs y'. Nothing of import rests on this. I avoid example sentences containing quantificational NP's (such as 'every dog') wherever possible, in spite of occasional awkwardness in doing so, to spare the reader unnecessarily complex logical formulas.

3.3 Tenses and Times

For a relatively complete account of even the simplest sentences of English, the system of underlying eventualities needs to be amalgamated into a theory of tense, aspect, and temporal modifiers. By 'tense' I mean Simple Past ('Mary left'), Simple Present ('Mary leaves'), and Simple Future ('Mary will leave'). "Aspect" includes the Progressive form of the verb, as opposed to the Simple form: 'be leaving', as opposed to 'leave'; aspect also includes the Perfect form of the verb: 'has left'. Temporal modifiers include such things as 'at noon', 'yesterday', 'during the war', and so on.

Tense, aspect, and temporal modifiers are interrelated topics of great complexity, and I have tried to compartmentalize their exposition for the sake of comprehension. They are ignored throughout the next several chapters (chapters 4 through 8), which are devoted to the issue of underlying eventualities. By employing a simplified version of tense logic (or by ignoring it altogether), and by avoiding examples containing aspects and temporal modifiers, I set these topics aside until chapters 9 through 12. All sentences will therefore be in the Simple Past, Present, or Future and will lack temporal modifiers. These are the simplest examples that constitute full-fledged English sentences. The Progressive has a chapter of its own (chapter 9), as does the Perfect (chapter 12); the details of tenses and of temporal modifiers are covered in chapter 11.

The simplest notation for tenses is the operator notation from standard tense logic. The assumption behind this notation is that ordinary formulas of predicate logic are to be assigned truth-values relative to moments of time. In application, a formula without any tense operator is thought of as being evaluated relative to the present time, so that an unadorned formula such as

Clever(Mary)

means "Mary is clever *now.*" The operator PAST may precede a
formula, in which case the whole formula is construed as being true
now just in case the part following the PAST is true at some previous
time. Likewise, a formula may be preceded by FUT, in which case it
is true now just in case the part governed by FUT will be true at some
time later than now. (In conventional tense logic these operators can
be embedded in one another's scopes, but that never happens in
English, so I shall not use them.)

I shall be working with the following sorts of logical forms:

Brutus stabbed Caesar = PAST($\exists$e)[Stabbing(e) & Subject(e,Brutus)
& Object(e,Caesar) & Cul(e)]

Brutus stabs Caesar = PRES($\exists$e)[Stabbing(e) & Subject(e,Brutus) &
Object(e,Caesar) & Cul(e)]

Brutus will stab Caesar = FUT($\exists$e)[Stabbing(e) & Subject(e,Brutus)
& Object(e,Caesar) & Cul(e)]

(where the 'PRES' is redundant, and could simply be omitted). The
first is true if there is some time in the past when there is a stabbing,
whose subject is Brutus, whose object is Caesar, and which culminates
then. The second is true if there is a stabbing of that sort that culminates now (at the moment of utterance). And the last is true if there
is some time in the future when there is a stabbing of that sort that
culminates then. This account of tenses must be slightly revised (see
chapter 11) in order to correctly accommodate more complex
constructions.

3.4   More Details about Tenses

There are certain objections in the literature to the use of tense operators to symbolize tenses. One is due to Anthony Kenny (1963) who
objects to a certain corollary to the use of tense operators. The corollary is that if Pres(S) is true now, then Past(S) will be true at some
later time. His proposed counterexample is that 'Alf is walking to the
Rose and Crown' does not entail the future truth of 'Alf walked to the
Rose and Crown'. This particular objection is easy to answer, since
the latter sentence is not the past tense version of the former; the
former is in the progressive, and the latter is not. The past tense of
the former sentence is 'Alf was walking to the Rose and Crown', and

this *should* be true at a later time if Alf is now walking to the Rose and Crown.[7]

Since different kinds of simple English sentences behave differently with regard to tense, and the proposed version of tense logic supplies uniform operators to govern all of them, here is how the treatment works in simple examples.

3.4.1 Past

The past tense of an event sentence requires that the event in question culminate at some past time. A sentence such as 'Mary made lunch' starts being true as soon as the culmination of the lunch making has passed. Likewise, the past tense of a state sentence seems to work correctly, since 'Mary knew Fred' is true now if she knew him previously, and is otherwise false. However, an additional dimension of state sentences that this account does not capture is that in certain circumstances it would be odd to say that Mary knew Fred if she still knows him now. This I take to be a matter of conversational maxims, to be accounted for within the study of the pragmatics of language use. It would be incorrect to build into the logical form of 'Mary knew Fred' that she does not know him now, since the implication is not operative in many circumstances, and since even when it is operative it does not make 'Mary knew Fred' false if she still knows him; it merely makes it misleading.

Another relevant phenomenon is the oddity of the past tense sentence's being true just because the eventuality in question holds or culminates *sometime* in the past. As Barbara Partee (1973, 1984) has argued, if we are turning onto the freeway to begin our vacation trip and I say 'I didn't turn off the stove' this may be taken to be a true assertion even though I have in fact turned off the stove at many past times. The point is that context limits the interpretation of the past tense operator to apply only to certain relevant parts of the past. This is an important phenomenon in the pragmatics of language use, but it affects the interpretation of our logical forms, not the forms themselves. The 'PAST' operator should be read 'for some relevant time in the past'.

3.4.2 Present

The logical form of present tense state sentences seems to be unproblematic; 'Mary knows Fred' is true now if the relevant state of knowing holds now. The present tenses of event sentences, however, raise problems. There is something decidedly odd about saying, all by itself, 'Mary builds a house' or 'Agatha wins the race'. Fortunately, our treatment correctly captures this oddity.

In general, verbs can be interpreted in two or more different ways: the so-called "reportive" use, and the "habitual" or "iterative" use. These different uses appear in all tenses. 'Mary drank wine with her lunch' can be construed as reporting a specific incident that took place in the past; this is the "reportive" reading. But it can also be construed as telling us what she habitually did during her years in the corporate world. In the past tense, a simple unmodified sentence taken out of context tends to be taken in its reportive sense, but in the present tense that same construction may almost force the habitual reading. One has to strain to interpret 'Mary drinks wine with her lunch' as a report of a specific drinking. The best examples of the reportive use of present tense event sentences are found in the speech of on-the-scene newscasters, for whom it is not at all odd to say "And the Maryland delegation goes two to one for the Democrats!"

The logical forms proposed above explain these facts perfectly. According to those forms, a present tense event sentence construed in the reportive sense can be true only at one specific instant—the time the event culminates. Such a sentence, then, can be used truly only in certain very special circumstances: the speaker must usually be observing the scene in order to be sure of getting the time right, and the sentence cannot be used in anticipation of the culmination or in the recapitulation[8]—it must be used exactly once and at exactly the right time. Such uses are rare.

My purpose is to capture the reportive readings of sentences, not the habitual or iterative readings, because I suspect that the reportive use is basic. I have not thought through the complexities of the other uses, so my account is limited accordingly, but not in ways that are relevant to the issue of underlying eventualities. Some of my examples of event sentences in the simple present tense (as opposed to the progressive) may therefore look odd. Nonetheless, the logical forms attributed to them will be correct, in spite of the oddity.

3.4.3 Future

The future versions of state sentences share the implication of past tense versions that the state is not going on at present; 'Mary will know Fred' tends to suggest that she does not know him now. The proposed logical forms are not for that reason defective; the account is merely missing a pragmatic component that would explain the implication.

There may be an additional implication in the case of future event sentences. 'Mary will make lunch' may imply that she has not yet started. This implication too is not captured by the proposed logical form, which is true if Mary has already started making lunch and will finish it in the future.

In addition, future tense sentences need their future times limited to "relevant" times, as much as do past tense sentences.

On some views, my appeal to times in logical forms is unduly superficial. Kamp (1980) and Bach (1986) defend the Whiteheadian view that the time-frame itself should be defined or constructed in terms of more basic relations among eventualities. I do not see this as an objection to the theory I am discussing. In appealing to times, I remain neutral on the question of whether they can recovered from an analysis of relations among eventualities. I remain neutral about the issue of ontological priority of times over eventualities or vice versa.

3.5   States, Propositions, and Facts

The purpose of this section is to elucidate the notion of "state" by comparing it with the notions of "proposition" and "fact."

3.5.1   Objects of Belief (Propositions)

I assume that the "objects" of belief are whatever it is that that-clauses refer to when preceded by the verb 'believe', and I use the customary term 'proposition' for these things. I do not try to clarify what propositions are, but I accept a broadly Fregean view of them.[9] Other constructions that behave similarly to that-clauses also refer to propositions; whether-clauses in constructions such as 'Kim wonders whether Sammy loves her' are examples.

That-clauses create opaque contexts; that is, singular terms in that-clauses may not generally be replaced by co-referential singular terms that preserve reference of the that-clause. The proposition that Mary knows Fred is a different proposition from the proposition that Mary knows the king, even if Fred is the king. This must be so, because Agatha might believe the former without believing the latter.

I assume also that it is possible to quantify into propositional that-clauses. I accept the usual view that 'Agatha believes that Mary knows the king' is ambiguous between a *de dicto* reading

Agatha believes the proposition: Mary knows the king

and a *de re* reading

The king is such that: Agatha believes the proposition that Mary knows him.

If Fred is the king, then the *de re* readings of 'Agatha believes that Mary knows the king' and 'Agatha believes that Mary knows Fred' are equivalent. Both the *de dicto* and the *de re* readings are always possible, though context often favors one or the other.

3.5.2 Facts

Although "facts" are discussed a great deal in metaphysics and in philosophical logic, there is a wide variety of views about what they are. I take this to reflect variant usages of the term 'fact'. At one end of the spectrum, facts are seen to be very much like propositions. At the other end, they are seen to be very much like the kinds of states appealed to in this book.

The best illustration of the propositional interpretation of facts is that of Frege (1918), who held that facts simply *are* propositions—they are true propositions. Reflection on the occurrence of that-clauses used in contexts presupposing the truth of the sentence contained in the clause gives rise to this view. An example is

Mary regrets that she insulted Bill

Sometimes these constructions can be paraphrased using the word 'fact', as in

Mary regrets the fact that she insulted Bill.

For this reason it is sometimes assumed that in these contexts that-clauses refer to facts. If so, then these facts must be very much like propositions in at least two respects. First, that-clauses that contain different but co-referential singular terms must be able to pick out different facts. Mary may regret that she insulted Bill without regretting that she insulted the person who is slandering her behind her back, even if Bill is that very person. Second, facts can be found that correspond to complex sentences. Mary may regret the fact that either Bill or Mary stole the gems; if she does not know which of them did it, the object of her regret is a disjunctive fact, just as belief can take a disjunctive proposition as its object.

At the other end of the spectrum, the notion of fact identifies facts in part by their constituents and as corresponding only to simple clauses. On this conception, the fact that Mary insulted Bill and the fact that she insulted the person who is slandering her are the very same fact, if Bill is the person slandering her. And there is no "fact" that either Bill or Mary stole the gems; there is a proposition that either Bill or Mary stole the gems, and either or both of its disjuncts may refer to facts, but the disjunction as a whole is of the wrong sort to pick out a fact.

For clarity I refer to the first type of facts as "propositional facts" and the second as "material facts." There are other conceptions of facts in between, but this contrast will be sufficient for my purposes here. The "states" utilized in the present theory are similar to material facts, and are very unlike propositional facts.

States of affairs are like facts, except that there are "false" states of affairs and no "false" facts. I think that 'state of affairs' covers the same spectrum as 'fact'. States, as used here, are very unlike the propositional conception of states of affairs, but like the material conception.

3.5.3 States

States, if there are any, have different identity conditions than propositions or propositional facts. States have unique "participants." If Agatha's knowing Fred is to be construed as a state, then this is the very same state as the state of Agatha's knowing the king, if Fred is the king. And it is the very same state as the state of the queen's knowing Fred if Agatha is the queen.

States differ from propositions and propositional facts in corresponding only to simple (state) sentences, whereas propositions and facts can correspond to complex ones. Each of the following deals with a single proposition or fact:

Mary believes that either Sam knows Henry or Mary knows Bill.
Mary regrets that either Sam knows Henry or Mary knows Bill.

But if we try to talk about

The state of either Sam's knowing Henry or Mary's knowing Bill,

we do not produce a reference to a disjunctive state; we get instead a disjunctive singular term that refers either to the state of Sam's knowing Henry or to the state of Mary's knowing Bill. (This is on a par with our understanding of a term such as 'Kim or Sammy'. This term, if it refers at all, refers either to Kim or to Sammy; it does not refer to a disjunctive individual composed of the two of them.)[10]

3.6   Tests for Distinctions Among the Categories

A number of philosophers and linguists have attempted to articulate criteria that might allow us to categorize eventualities. The tests I review are all formulated in terms of categorizing linguistic items, not eventualities, though some are convertible into direct tests for eventualities.

The idea of classifying eventualities into events, processes, and states originated with Gilbert Ryle (1949), and was carried on by Anthony Kenny (1963), who attributed the original idea to Aristotle. For this reason, this classification is commonly called "Aristotelian." Kenny proposed various tests, both syntactic and semantic, for classifying eventualities. It is sometimes unclear whether the classification is meant to classify things in the world or pieces of language. When pieces of language are being classified, sometimes verbs, sometimes VPs, and sometimes whole sentences are so classified. I am primarily concerned to classify nonlinguistic things—eventualities. I see a fairly clear distinction between events and states, and I see less clarity (along with less importance) about how processes fit in. Since I assume that verbs pick out basic kinds of eventualities (events and states), the distinction of event and state is also reflected by a corresponding linguistic distinction between kinds of verbs. (Adjectives and nouns, also relevant, are discussed in chapter 10.)

After Kenny, the primary mover in this area was Zeno Vendler (1967), who extended Kenny's ideas. More recently, there has been a great deal of discussion of these notions in the linguistic literature. Dowty 1979, for example, contains a sophisticated development of these ideas, amalgamated into an ambitious program for a semantic theory of English.[11] Bach (1981) and others also discuss these categories.[12]

3.6.1   Use of the Progressive

A test that is supposed to divide Processes and Accomplishment-Events on the one hand from States and Achievement-Events on the other is the felicitous use of sentences in the progressive. Accomplishment-Event sentences and Process sentences are said to occur in the progressive, as in

Sally is making a birdbath.
Sally is running,

whereas State and Achievement-Event sentences are not supposed to occur grammatically in the progressive, as illustrated by

*This book is being pink.
*Martha is reaching the summit.

Some of the problems with this test shed light on the proposed distinction, while others tend to undermine it.

Problem 1 In general it is thought that copular sentences are state sentences, yet some of them easily take the progressive:

John is being silly (. . . being a fool).

This apparent exception to the generalization actually sheds light on the distinction when coupled with the thesis that there exists in English a special use of the verb 'be', sometimes called the 'be' of action. If we are judging John's character, and we say that he is silly, then there is something peculiar about saying in the same vein that he is *being* silly. On the other hand, if we are commenting on his behavior at a party, it is quite appropriate to say that he is being silly. We mean that he is *acting* silly. This interpretation makes it plausible to think of the sentence as reporting an (accomplishment) event or a process, and so this is not a counterexample to the proposed test of classification. The need for a special use of 'be' occurs in several contexts. That there is such a use has a fair amount of plausibility.[13]

Problem 2 Some state sentences occur in the progressive. An example is

You will be wanting to turn right at the next corner.

'Want' is supposed to be a paradigm state verb, one that does not take the progressive. This happens with a small class of state verbs, and it undermines the idea that use with the progressive shows conclusively that a sentence is not a state sentence.[14] However, in those few cases in which a state sentence is used in the progressive, the progressive version differs little in import from the nonprogressive version.[15] Interpreted in this way the test may be helpful in distinguishing state sentences from all the rest.

Problem 3   Paradigm Achievement-Event sentences commonly occur in the progressive. The verb 'win' is supposed to be an achievement verb, but

She is winning

is so common as to suggest that there is something seriously wrong with any test requiring this to be ungrammatical. Our vocabulary may, of course, have two words 'win', one an achievement verb and another a process verb. Perhaps one meaning of 'is winning' is simply 'is ahead'. (But this would be odd, for there is no use of *non*progressive 'win' that means, for example, 'leads'.) Other examples are

Grandpa is dying.
The train is arriving now.

We often seem to use paradigm Achievement verbs as if they were ordinary Accomplishment-event verbs. The progressive test is not terribly helpful in making this distinction.

In summary, the test distinguishing Accomplishment-Event and Process sentences from Achievement-Event and State sentences seems to be helpful in isolating state sentences from the rest. State sentences are unusual in the progressive, and when their progressive forms occur, they differ little in meaning from their nonprogressive counterparts.

3.6.2   How Long?

A second test assisting the categorization is that it makes sense to ask "how long" in connection with a State or Process, but not with an Event. These are supposed to be data:

State: (*OK*) How long was the book pink?
Process: (*OK*) How long did Mary run?
Accomp: (*Bad*) How long did Mary make a birdbath?
Achieve: (*Bad*) How long did Mary win the race?

On the other hand, if we can ask how long something "takes" we get the opposite results:

State: (*Bad*) How long did it take the book to be pink?
Process: (*Bad*) How long did it take Mary to run?
Accomp: (*OK*) How long did it take Mary to make a birdbath?
Achieve: (*OK*) How long did it take Mary to win the race?

Note that it is fine to say "How long did it take Mary to run to the store?", and even "How long did it take Mary to run" if this is elliptical for some thing like ". . . to the store." Except for these peculiarities the test seems to work pretty much as intended.

This test might be convertible into a direct test for eventualities. Events and Processes (as opposed to States) would *take time,* whereas States (as opposed to Events and Processes) would *last* through time. (What to say about Achievement-events, which are supposed to be automatically instantaneous?)

3.6.3 Occurrence with Pseudo-Clefts
A test that perhaps distinguishes State constructions from all the others is the deviance of State sentences that contain constructions linguists call "pseudo-clefts":

State: (*Bad*) What John did was know the answer.
Process: (*OK*) What John did was run.
Accomp: (*OK*) What John did was make a birdbath.
Achieve: (*OK*) What John did was win the race.

This test might be converted into a method for distinguishing States (as opposed to State sentences) from other eventualities: eventualities other than States are things that are *done;* States are not *done.*

3.6.4 Progressive Entails Perfect (vs. Negation of Perfect)
A famous test proposed by Kenny is that Events are supposed to satisfy this formula:

If x is V-ing then x has not V-ed,

whereas Processes are supposed to satisfy the contrary condition:

If x is V-ing then x has V-ed.

For example, these are supposed to be true:

i   Accomplishment-Event: If x is building a birdbath then x has *not* built a birdbath.
ii Achievement-Event: If x is reaching the summit then x has *not* reached the summit.
iii Process: If x is running then x *has* run.

The fascinating thing about (i) and (ii) is that they seem so close to saying something insightful and true in spite of the fact that they are both false. If x has built a birdbath, x may have built many birdbaths before, and if x is reaching the summit x may have reached that summit many times before.[16] The insight lying behind the faulty formulation, as Emmon Bach (1981, 71) points out, is that if x is building a birdbath then *that particular building* is not yet over, and if x is reaching the summit then *that particular summit reaching* is not yet over. It is interesting that we need recourse to events even to state clearly what the test is.

It is questionable whether (iii) is true when x has just started running. What seems to lie behind this test is that the eventualities picked out by process verbs are homogeneous in some sense needing articulation; any given "large" running seems to consist of many smaller runnings. A variety of other tests is discussed in the literature, many of them replete with counterexamples.[17]

3.6.5 Summary of Semantic Tests

I assume that there is a distinction between States, on the one hand, and typical Events, on the other. I accept the "pseudo-cleft" test as a rough guide to distinguishing State sentences from all others, and I accept the "how long" test as distinguishing State sentences from Event sentences. My basic items of investigation are Events and States. For the most part I ignore the distinction between Accomplishments and Achievements and (until chapter 9) the special status of Processes.

What is it *in language* that gets categorized by the traditional list of categories? Sometimes tests that are couched in terms of classifying *verbs* seem better oriented to the classification of VPs (or of simple sentences), for two reasons. First, all the tests make perfectly good sense when applied to these larger phrases. And second, when the tests are applied to VP's, the results do not depend on the verb alone. A well-known sort of example is that the "How Long?" test and the "Progressive Entails Perfect" test both tend to classify 'Mary ran' as a Process:

Grammatical: How long did Mary run?

Mostly True: If Mary is running then Mary has run.

Yet they seem to classify 'Mary ran to the store' as a non-Process:

Ungrammatical: How long did Mary run to the store?

True: If Mary is running to the store, then Mary has *not* run to the store (unless she ran there previously).

The category switch that results from appending modifiers to the verb is a major issue in Aristotelian classification schemes.[18] The theory I develop can solve that problem (see chapter 9). But this shows that the tests articulated are properly seen as classifications of VPs or of simple sentences, not of verbs by themselves. But it is also apparent (by surveying examples) that the basic distinction between State and Event can also be viewed as a classification of verbs—since the addition of other items to their VPs never changes one of *these* to the other.

The semantical theory under development requires that eventualities be divided into States and Events. It is a fundamental assumption of this work that such a distinction makes sense, but whether the assumption is justified depends on how well the theory works overall.

Chapter 4
Modifiers

4.1 Classification of Modifiers

Syntactically, adverblike modifiers take three forms in language:

1. adverbs themselves, single words that occur in modifier position in sentences. Examples are: 'probably', 'gently', 'softly', 'allegedly', 'well', 'foolishly', 'there', 'crosswise', 'partway'.

2. prepositional phrases, consisting of a (one- or two-word) preposition followed by a noun phrase. Examples are: 'in the bank', 'over the river', 'through the woods', 'out of the box', 'after the deluge', 'at the target', 'onto the bus', 'according to the report', 'in her dreams', 'with a knife', 'with hay', 'out of necessity'.

3. subordinate clauses, consisting of a subordinating "conjunction" and a clause. Examples are: 'after Mary left', 'while John slept', 'if Sam doesn't come', 'as we hoped', 'because he perceived the danger to his right flank'.

The third class, subordinate clauses, requires special treatment (see chapter 11). The differences between the first two classes are unimportant from the point of view of their semantic function as modifiers.[1] Although there are semantically different kinds of modifiers, classified in terms of their semantic functions in sentences, the difference between prepositional phrases and adverbs cuts across the semantical distinctions. Prepositional phrases have structure that adverbs lack, but they contribute the same type of items to logical form. A prepositional phrase carries with it a noun phrase position, which typically contributes structure to the sentence by means of NP quantification. Thus, in parallel with the adverbial modification

Mary ran *quickly,*

we have the prepositional phrase modification

Mary ran *into every house.*

The gross logical form of the latter sentence is

For every house, Mary ran *into it,*

that is,

(x)[x is a house → Mary ran *into x*],

in which the 'into x' occurs in the same position as the 'quickly' in the former sentence. The claim, then, is that

'*into x*' (or 'into it')

and

'*quickly*'

have the same modifier roles; the differences in their internal structure do not affect their modifying functions. A prepositional phrase can add considerable complexity to a sentence because of the quantificational structure of the NP that occurs as the object of the preposition; in the example above,

(x)[x is a house → . . . . . .] .

But the part that does the modifying is the remainder of the form—the 'into x'—and this functions no differently than a simple adverb.[2]

Both the adverb and the prepositional phrase in the example just illustrated contribute to logical form a predicate of an underlying event. Not all modifiers do this, but the parallels between adverbs and prepositional phrases carry over to the other functions as well. For example, both 'allegedly' and 'according to Mary' (or 'in a dream') function as sentence modifiers, but they modify sentences in the same way, in spite of the fact that the prepositional phrase introduces the possibility of additional quantification and the adverb does not.

I classify modifiers into five main categories: Speech-Act Modifiers, Sentence Modifiers, Subject-Oriented Modifiers, VP Modifiers, and Other. The VP modifiers turn out to represent predicates of events according to the theory of underlying events. (I also sometimes call them "verb modifiers".) The bulk of this chapter discusses the semantics of verb modifiers.

4.2 Attributives

4.2.1 The Problem

In his original paper, Davidson (1967) suggested that the theory of underlying events might be unable to treat "attributives" such as 'slowly' as predicates of underlying events. Since so many verb modifiers turn out to be attributives, this suggests that the theory has a rather narrow application. Most workers in the field have suspected that Davidson was right to worry about this, but I think their worry is misplaced. Attributives can indeed be treated as predicates of underlying events.

Davidson framed the problem as one involving the identity of events. Suppose that Susan took eighteen hours to cross the Channel. Hearing this, we decide that she crossed slowly. Then we discover that she crossed it by swimming. We judge then that she swam the Channel swiftly. But suppose that the swimming and the crossing are indeed the very same event. Then that event is both slow and swift, an apparent contradiction.

The issue needn't, however, turn on the question of identity of events at all. Suppose we hear that Susan crossed the Channel in eighteen hours, and we judge that she crossed slowly. Then we learn that she crossed it by swimming. Now, thinking of other such crossings, we say that she crossed the Channel swiftly. We have judged in one context that she crossed slowly, and in another that she crossed swiftly. In the first context we are implicitly comparing her crossing with crossings in general. We might even explain: "She crossed slowly because she did it all by herself—she swam!" In the second context we are comparing her Channel crossing with others that are accomplished by swimming, and now we easily say, and without any need to retract our earlier comment, that she crossed swiftly. In the second context, we should even be willing to deny that she crossed slowly. So the verbal forms let us contradict ourselves, yet the remarks are not contradictory. Further, since both remarks use the same verb 'cross', the issue of the identity of events (of swimmings with crossings) does not even arise. We have changed comparison classes for judging slowness and swiftness: crossings in general, or crossings in the water under one's own power.

Two theoretical questions remain. How is the solution to be embodied in a theory of logical form? And what consequences does this solution have for the theory of underlying events?

4.2.2 Two Theories and Their Paradigms

The issue of logical form has been studied in detail for adjectives, so I shall turn for a moment from adverbs to adjectives to survey some of the conventional resources that study has given us.[3] Two ways to analyze adjectives are well-understood in the literature: as predicates or as operators.

A paradigm analysis of an adjective as a predicate is a typical prenominal occurrence of 'red', as in

x is a red house = x is a house & x is red.

This analysis is common in logic textbooks, and indeed such adjectives occur naturally in predicate positions in English sentences: 'This book is red'. This predicative occurrence is used to analyze the prenominal occurrence in 'x is a red house'.

Some adjectives cannot be analyzed as predicates and are treated instead as operators. An example is 'former', as in

x is a former president = formerly(x is president).[4]

Adjectives such as 'formerly' *do not occur* in predicate position, and so predicative meaning is not available for analyzing prenominal occurrences.

4.2.3 The Problem Needing Analysis

In addition to paradigm predicates, such as 'red', and paradigm operators such as 'former', *attributives,* such as 'tall', form a third class of paradigms for adjectives. (It includes most "degree adjectives".) Unlike paradigm operators, attributives occur freely in predicates, but unlike paradigm predicates their predicative analysis seems problematic. 'Clever' seems, *prima facie,* to violate both theories. It violates the predicative analysis since someone can be a clever teacher without being a clever parent; but apparently, if 'clever' is a predicate, then from 'x is a clever teacher' (= 'x is clever & x is a teacher') and 'x is a parent' we should be able to infer 'x is a clever parent' (= 'x is clever & x is a parent'). And it apparently violates the operator analysis in that 'clever' occurs alone in the predicate, as in 'Mary is clever', where there is no argument for the operator to operate on.

The assumption needed that lets either account handle attributives such as 'clever' is that 'clever' always means 'clever for an F', where 'F' is somehow supplied from context. (This F must be supplied both for the prenominal and for the predicate occurrences of the word.) On the predicative treatment, 'x is a clever N' means 'x is an N & x is clever for an F', where F is figured out from context. Sometimes (often, but not always) F is the same as N. In the case of predicative occurrence, we have to guess at the F. On the operator analysis, 'x is a clever N' means 'clever(x is an N that is F)', where this is further analyzed as 'x is N & x is clever for an F'. Often, but not always, F is the same as N. In either case, for predicative occurrences, such as 'Mary is clever' we have to guess at F.

The F cannot always be the same as the noun modified, even in prenominal occurrence. 'He is a tall basketball player' can mean that he is tall for a basketball player *in grade school,* or any of a wide variety of things.[5]

Accordingly, both popular accounts are *equally correct* and *equivalent* in terms of the logical forms they produce. Both accounts need to provide for a parameter, to be fixed by context. Each produces a logical form that is a conjunction, one in which the modifier has an extra place. The "predicative" account displays this directly. The form for the operator account also displays this, but only upon further analysis. When expanded, the operator account turns into the predicative account.

4.2.4 Scope
The operator account is sometimes seen as the more sophisticated of the two, because it allows modifiers to have scope, and so they can take scope over other items in the sentence. This is exactly right in the case of sentence modifiers, such as 'necessarily', since 'necessarily, somebody wins' has a reading in which the necessity takes scope outside the quantifier. But in 'someone is a clever teacher' there is no reading on which the 'clever' takes scope over 'someone'. The introduction of scope is not an advantage of the operator analysis in this context. (See section 4.4.1.)

4.2.5 Attributive Adverbs as Predicates of Events
Since the adverbial analogues of pure paradigm operator adjectives, such as 'formerly', are *sentence modifiers,* they are not at issue in the discussion of underlying events. Attributives are different.

The correct account of 'slowly' within the theory of underlying events is that it is a predicate of events that has a place in it for a contextual parameter. (Or else, it is an operator that has a further analysis as a predicate with a place for such a parameter.) A correct analysis of 'Brutus walked slowly' is

$(\exists e)$[Walking(e) & Subject(e,Brutus) & Slow(e,F)]

where F is the contextual parameter. This gets all of the logic right, so long as we are careful about the parameter. From

Nguyen walked slowly along the quay

we *can* infer

Nguyen walked slowly

provided we keep the contextual parameter fixed. If the former sentence is used to mean

Nguyen walked slowly-for-a-walk-of-his-along-the-quay along the quay,

then when we conclude

Nguyen walked slowly,

this conclusion holds only on the interpretation

Nguyen walked slowly-for-a-walk-of-his-along-the-quay.

In examples throughout this text I suppress the contextual parameter for simplicity, but it should be kept in mind. With its presence, either explicit or implicit, there is no difficulty in treating attributives as predicates of events.

4.3 Group Readings, Scope, and Conjunctions

This section is devoted to a discussion of some miscellaneous issues about the behavior of verb modifiers.

4.3.1 Group Readings and Scope

Certain constructions in English appear to refer to groups. Examples are 'the women' in

The women elected Mary president.
The women were numerous.
The women milled around.

Other NPs do not usually denote groups, but they can do so in certain contexts; examples are 'everyone' in:

Everyone milled around,

and 'Mary and Bill' in

Mary and Bill (together) lifted the piano.

I shall not rehearse the substantial literature on group readings of English NPs. I shall simply assume that sometimes reference to groups is required, and I shall note how this bears on the matter of verb modifiers.

Sometimes reference to groups is an alternative to scope, as an explanation of ambiguity. A classical case is the difference between

Samantha quickly polished each boot,

and

Samantha quickly polished all the boots.

This has sometimes been seen as a scope phenomenon, illustrating the relative scopes of the universal quantifier and the adverb 'quickly', with the proposed readings being

$(x)(Boot(x) \rightarrow QUICKLY(Samantha\ polished\ x))$

$QUICKLY(x)(Boot(x) \rightarrow Samantha\ polished\ x)$.

In the theory under consideration, 'quickly' does not have scope. I see the two readings instead as a contrast between two sentences, one with an individual reading, and one with a group reading:

$(x)(Boot(x) \rightarrow (\exists e)[Polishing(e)\ \&\ Subject(e,\ Samantha)\ \&\ Object(e,x)])$

$(\exists e)[Polishing(e)\ \&\ Subject(e,\ Samantha)\ \&\ Object(e,\ the\ boots)]$.

In the former, there are many polishings, one per boot, and each is said to be quick. In the latter there is a single polishing of the group of boots, and that polishing is said to be quick.[6] Both sentences might be true, but neither implies the other; each individual polishing might be quick without the polishing of the group's being quick, or the polishing of the group might be quick even though one or more individual polishings was not. In each case, the adverb acts as a predicate of single events.

Groups are also sometimes required as the objects of prepositions. The most natural treatment of:

She wandered among the pines

is

$(\exists e)[Wandering(e)\ \&\ Subject(e,her)\ \&\ Among(e,the\ pines)]$,

where 'the pines' refers to the group of trees.

This may also be the correct treatment of 'between', as in

She stood between the boys,

or

She stood between Shem and Shaun.

In the former case the object of 'between' is the (two-person) group of boys. In the latter case the object of 'between' is the group consisting of Shem and Shaun. This analysis explains why 'between' always requires an 'and' if used with singular nouns, and why 'between A and B' is always interchangeable with 'between B and A'.

Conjunctions such as 'Shem and Shaun' may also pick out subjects of events, as in

Shem and Shaun lifted the piano

which has, as one of its readings

($\exists$e)[Lifting(e) & Subject(e,Shem and Shaun) & Object(e,piano)].

In this form, 'Shem and Shaun' denotes the two-membered group of boys.

4.3.2   Groups as Objects of Prepositions

The suggestion that a better analysis of 'She stood between Shem and Shaun' is to see 'between' as taking a single (compound) NP as object raises a more general question. Do prepositions ever take more than one object? Nothing in the theory under examination prevents this, but it is not clear that it ever happens. A nice case to look at is the phrase 'from A to B'. Is 'from . . . to . . .' a single complex preposition that takes two objects, or is it a combination of two prepositions, each of which takes a single object? My suggestion that it is the latter explains some interesting phenomena. For example,

x ran from A to B

entails both

x ran from A

and

x ran to B.

The explanation for this entailment cannot be that the former phrase is the conjunction of the latter two, since if Agatha ran from the house and also ran to the barn it does not follow that she ran from the house to the barn. (She might have run to the barn *before* running from the house.) There are a number of ways in which one might try to analyze these phrases so as to get the right connections. Dowty 1979 (213–16) is the best attempt I know of within a conventional framework (including discussion of problems).

A better treatment may be the most natural one in the theory of underlying events. Both 'from A' and 'to B' are taken at face value as verb modifiers and symbolized in the usual way. The sentence 'x ran from A to B' is symbolized as

$(\exists e)$[Running(e) & Subject(e,x) & From(e,A) & To(e,B)].

This clearly entails both 'x ran from A' and 'x ran to B', without being entailed in turn by their conjunction. The key is that the 'from . . . to . . .' sentence requires that the very same running was both from A and to B, whereas the conjunction does not require this.

4.3.3 Conjunctions of Modifiers
In logical form, iterated modifiers of a single verb give rise to conjunctions of predicates of events, each applying to the same underlying event. What about cases of explicit "conjunctions" of modifiers in the English sentence itself? That is, how are we to symbolize a sentence that contains an explicit conjunction of modifiers, as in

Garfield ran into the room, across the floor, and out through the window?

Is this to be treated as having a single underlying event, modified by three modifiers, or as containing three (possibly distinct) underlying events? That is, does the sentence say that there was a running by Garfield that had these three properties: it was into the room, and it was across the floor, and it was out through the window? Or does it say that there was a running into the room, and then a running across the floor, and then a running out through the window?

Little direct evidence in the example bears on this question. We have not discovered enough about the kind of events this theory needs to know much about their persistence through time, and the sentence itself gives little clue. Evidence will have to come from other cases.

We might be able to appeal to our native understanding of a sentence. If we say

Juanita drove to the store and to the university

we probably have in mind one trip consisting of two or more drivings. This suggests that the sentence should have at least one interpretation with a logical form that does not force there to be only one driving.

More direct evidence for this hypothesis arises from other cases. Consider

x ran from A to B.

This is not entailed by (at least one reading of)

x ran from A and to B.

A natural explanation of this lack of entailment is that the former sentence contains one reference to an underlying event, and the latter contains two; the form of the former is

$(\exists e)[\text{Running}(e) \text{ \& } \text{Subj}(e,x) \text{ \& } \text{From}(e,A) \text{ \& } \text{To}(e,B)]$,

and that of the latter is:

$(\exists e)[\text{Running}(e) \text{ \& } \text{Subj}(e,x) \text{ \& } \text{From}(e,A)] \text{ \& }$
$(\exists e')[\text{Running}(e') \text{ \& } \text{Subj}(e',x) \text{ \& } \text{To}(e',B)]$.

(This kind of test does not apply to the previous sentence because 'Juanita drove to the store to the university' is not grammatical.)

Another example, discovered by John Wallace (1966), depends on a case like this:

Mary hit the 8-ball into the side pocket and the 9-ball into the corner pocket.

If this were construed as containing a single underlying event, then its logical form would contain these conjuncts:

. . . & Obj(e,8-ball) & Into(e,side pocket) & Obj(e,9-ball) &
Into(e,corner pocket) . . .

These conjuncts can be permuted into an equivalent form, which is then the underlying form of

Mary hit the 8-ball into the corner pocket and the 9-ball into the side pocket.

But this sentence is not equivalent to the original, and so the symbolization is incorrect. The solution is to construe the surface English conjunction as indicating conjoined appeals to underlying events, as opposed to conjoined predications of a single underlying event.

I conclude tentatively that explicit surface conjunctions of modifiers (or of fragments of the VP containing modifiers) have readings that permit multiple underlying quantifications over events, as opposed to multiple predications connected to the same underlying quantification.

This leaves open the possibility that surface conjunctions of modi-fiers are ambiguous constructions having readings that require the application of the modifiers to one and the same event. We sometimes interpret sentences as conveying such information, as in

She walked quietly and carefully through the room.

This could naturally be taken to say that there was a single walking that was both quiet and careful (and through the room). On the other hand, it is also possible to hold that surface conjunctions of modifiers never have logical forms that contain multiple predications connected with the same underlying quantification over an event, but that the use of a sentence in context often implies this extra information. I am tempted by this view, but I am not aware of any solid evidence for or against it.[7]

4.4   Alternatives to the Underlying Event Approach

That the underlying event approach correctly captures the logic of modifiers adds to its attractiveness when we survey the known alternatives. Most either yield incorrect inferences, and so are false, or they fail to yield some of the correct ones, and so are incomplete. In almost every alternative account that is correct but incomplete, the underlying event account turns out to be a refinement of it. In this section I survey six alternatives. The "modifiers" I discuss throughout are VP modifiers unless I indicate otherwise.

4.4.1   Unanalyzed Predicates
The simplest alternative is the practice of logic textbooks, which is to treat each complex of verb-plus-modifiers as a single unanalyzed atomic predicate. For example, we might represent each of the following forms by the predicate on the right:

1	x stabbed y	Sxy
2	x stabbed y violently	Vxy
3	x stabbed y with z	Wxyz
4	x stabbed y violently with z	Gxyz

This approach is correct but incomplete. Certainly the English forms on the left yield predicates of the sort displayed on the right. Indeed, from the point of view of the underlying event account, the forms on the right are all definable, as follows:

Sxy = $(\exists e)[Stabbing(e) \,\&\, Subj(e,x) \,\&\, Obj(e,y)]$

Vxy = $(\exists e)[Stabbing(e) \,\&\, Subj(e,x) \,\&\, Obj(e,y) \,\&\, violent(e)]$

Wxyz = ($\exists$e)[Stabbing(e) & Subj(e,x) & Obj(e,y) & with(e,z)]
Gxyz = ($\exists$e)[Stabbing(e) & Subj(e,x) & Obj(e,y) & violent(e) & with(e,z)]

These definitions all yield predicates of the correct form, and they reveal structure that is hidden in the primitive predicates of (1) through (4). So the underlying event account is a refinement of the standard logic-text practice of representing modified phrases. While not incorrect, that practice leaves out a host of good inferences.

Why cannot the logic-text practice be made more adequate by separating out the modifiers themselves as independent predicates? We might represent

2   x stabbed y violently

by

2′   Sxy & Vxy,

where 'Vxy' means something like 'x did something violently to y', and represent

3   x stabbed y with z

by

3′   Sxy & Wxyz,

where now we read 'Wxyz' as 'x did something to y with z'. But this gets the logic wrong; it yields incorrect inferences. For we should now have to represent

4   x stabbed y violently with z

as

4′   Sxy & Vxy & Wxyz.

But now (2′) and (3′) together entail (4′), so this representation tells us incorrectly that if Brutus stabbed Caesar violently and also stabbed him with a knife, then he stabbed him violently with a knife. But this does not follow; Brutus could have stabbed him deftly with a knife and—simultaneously—stabbed him violently with an icepick.

A little tinkering with the various possible uses of predicate logic here should convince the reader that without underlying quantification over something, all the correct inferences will not follow from the assigned logical forms alone unless some incorrect ones are included.

4.4.2   Meaning Postulates

Desired inferences are sometimes accounted for by proposing "meaning postulates." These are sentences of the formal symbolism that, in conjunction with the structurally simple logical forms assigned to individual sentences, yield the desired inference patterns. For example, we might supplement the simple logical forms suggested for (1) through (4) with these principles:

A $(x)(y)(z)[Gxyz \rightarrow Wxyz \ \& \ Vxy]$
B $(x)(y)(z)[Wxyz \rightarrow Sxy]$
C $(x)(y)[Vxy \rightarrow Sxy]$.

By appealing to various combinations of (A) through (C), we can then produce the desired inferences:

$$x \text{ stabbed } y \text{ violently with } z$$
$$\downarrow$$
$$x \text{ stabbed } y \text{ violently } \& \ x \text{ stabbed } y \text{ with } z$$
$$\searwarrow \qquad \swarrow$$
$$x \text{ stabbed } y.$$

This technique yields correct results in individual cases, but it is not clear whether it can be generalized. We needed (A) through (C) to handle two modifiers and one verb: 'violently', 'with x', and 'stab', but every new modifier or verb would require new meaning postulates linking it with all of the others. It is not even clear that the required number is finite, since the number of combinations of modifiers may not be finite.[8]

There is a further difficulty: the constructions under discussion are productive. If a new adverb of manner were to enter the language, it would enter into the same types of inference as those I have been discussing. This fact needs explanation along with my explanation of the inference patterns involving modifiers already in the language. The use of meaning postulates then needs to be supplemented by some further metaprinciple to address the issue of productivity.

I assume that, if this task were carried out, the resulting theory would yield the same inferences involving modifiers as the underlying event theory, and that both would be equally empirically correct in this domain. The remaining issue would be how to relate these modifiers with other constructions in the language, for example, how to connect 'dance slowly' with 'a slow dancing'. My suspicion is that any correct extension of the use of meaning postulates would be parasitic on the underlying event account.

4.4.3 Many-Place Predicates

Another possible use of predicate logic to handle modifiers is worthy of comment. It has been suggested that the basic forms of verbs should contribute many-placed predicates to their logical forms, and that apparently fewer-placed cases should be realized by existentially quantifying the "unused" places.[9] To take an oversimplified example, 'stab' would contribute a four-place predicate

Pxyzw,

which relates x,y,z, and w just in case x stabbed y in z with w. We then represent 'Brutus stabbed Caesar in the back with the knife' by

P(Brutus, Caesar, Caesar's back, the knife).

Then, if we want to say, "Brutus stabbed Caesar in the back," we paraphrase this by 'Brutus stabbed Caesar in the back *with something*':

($\exists$w)P(Brutus, Caesar, Caesar's back, w).

Likewise, the apparently simple 'Brutus stabbed Caesar' would be

($\exists$z)($\exists$w)P(Brutus, Caesar, z, w).

There are three problems with this approach, two of which may be solvable. A potentially solvable problem is determining the actual number of predicate places for the given verb. (This is the so-called "variable polyadicity" problem.)[10] Since we need to be able to say

Brutus stabbed Caesar in the back through his toga with the knife at noon on the bridge under the arch,

'stab' will have to contribute at least an eight-place predicate, and probably many more places are needed. In principle, we may not be able to determine the correct number of places for each verb. But neither is it clear that this is impossible.[11]

A second problem that might be solvable is that the proposal focuses entirely on prepositions, ignoring the question of how to handle adverbs. A possible solution is to construe all adverbs as disguised prepositional phrases, with their object places quantified. Here are some paraphrases that might be useful:

violently = in a violent manner
quickly = in a quick manner
rudely = in a rude manner

Everything I propose throughout this book is neutral with respect to whether adverbs are reducible to prepositional phrases in this way. I have nothing against quantifying over "manners," but I do not see that this either solves or complicates any of the problems I discuss.

The problem I do not see as solvable is that some cases of verbal modification are genuinely optional, and in these cases it is incorrect to quantify over an extra place. For example, it is possible to write a note *to* someone, but it is also possible to write a note that is not written to anyone at all. Likewise, it is possible to stab someone *through* his toga, but also possible to stab him without doing so through anything. It is possible to threaten someone *with* a weapon, and also possible to threaten her simpliciter.[12] This third proposal would require that every note be written to someone, that every stabbing be through something, and so on. It might be advantageous, for all we have seen so far, to associate with verbs many-place predicates, containing places to stand for the objects of prepositions that *must* be present, either explicitly or "understood,"[13] but this will not work as a general solution to the problem of the logic of modifiers.

4.4.4 Operators

Some modifiers modify whole sentences. Examples are 'necessarily', 'allegedly', 'probably', and 'in a dream'. In the tradition of philosophical semantics these have generally been treated as *propositional operators,* that is, they stand for operators (or functions) that map propositions to propositions. For example, 'necessarily' stands for a function that maps the proposition that giraffes are mammals to the proposition that necessarily giraffes are mammals. Although the philosophical analysis of notions such as necessity are replete with controversy, their grammatical status as operators is well entrenched. I do not challenge the received opinion on such modifiers, but they operate on formulas of English, including molecular ones, whereas my enterprise investigates modifiers that work at the subatomic level.

The success of the operator analysis of sentence modifiers of English led some researchers to extend it to other modifiers, treating modifiers such as 'slowly' as operators too.[14] The most popular account treats 'slowly' as standing for an operator that maps properties of individuals to properties of individuals.[15] On this account, the logical form associated with 'Agatha ran slowly' is

[slowly(ran)](Agatha).

'Run slowly' thereby turns out to have the same syntactic role as 'run', that is, it is a one-place predicate.

Using this approach, we must treat operators as acting on the properties expressed by verbs, not on their extensions.[16] If everybody drove if and only if he or she smoked, then the extension of 'x drives' would be the same as 'x smokes', but it would not follow from this that everyone drives slowly if and only if he or she smokes slowly. The solution is to suppose that 'slowly' operates on the properties of driving and smoking, which are different properties no matter how they are manifested in the actual world. This is on a par with the treatment of sentence operators, which take propositions, not truth-values, as their arguments.

The operator account of modifiers appears to say nothing incorrect, but it is not complete. Part of the reason is that this account was intended, historically, to be a special case of a completely general account that includes sentence modifiers as well as verb modifiers. As a general account, it fails to sanction *any* of the inferences under discussion. For example, since the following inference fails

Allegedly, Mary ran   /∴   Mary ran

and since verb operators mimic sentence operators, this inference also fails:

Mary ran slowly   /∴   Mary ran.

The commonest remedy for this recognized inadequacy has been to classify modifiers with respect to this trait. Modifiers such as 'slowly' are called "standard" modifiers because they satisfy the scheme

[OPERATOR(VERB)](x)   /∴   VERB(x).

However, this classification remains inadequate for two reasons. The first problem is that the account is still incomplete. Consider again our sample diagram of inferences:

$$x \text{ stabbed } y \text{ violently with } z$$
$$\downarrow$$
$$x \text{ stabbed } y \text{ violently } \& \ x \text{ stabbed } y \text{ with } z$$
$$\searrow \qquad \swarrow$$
$$x \text{ stabbed } y$$

On the operator approach, whenever there are two or more operators in a given sentence, one must take wider scope than the other. In the top sentence in the diagram, either 'violently' or 'with z' must take wider scope. Let us suppose that it is the latter. Then the logical form of the top sentence is

[with z(violently(stabbed(y)))](x).

By the special rule for "standard" modifiers, this easily entails the logical form of 'x stabbed y violently'

violently(stabbed(y))(x).

But it does *not* entail the logical form of 'x stabbed y with z':

with(z,stabbed(y))(x).

Conversely, if 'violently' is given wider scope, then the inference to 'x stabbed y violently' fails. So an important part of the logic of modifiers is not captured by this proposal.

The second difficulty with the operator account is that there is no evidence that modifiers have scope. According to the operator account, the first sentence

x stabbed y violently with z

is *ambiguous;* it can be read with either modifier taking scope over the other. But no such ambiguity appears in the English sentence.[17] If the operator account is to be viable, then it requires supplementing to neutralize the ambiguity inherent in the use of operators.

If the underlying event account is correct, it offers a natural way to try to do this. The underlying event account may be seen as a refinement of the operator account. Whether this is possible is a somewhat complicated technical issue.

On the underlying event account of verb-phrase modifiers, the correct logical form of 'x stabbed y violently' is given by

$(\exists e)$[Stabbing(e) & Subj(e,x) & Obj(e,y) & Violent(e)].

We can conceive of this form having been produced by inserting 'x' and 'y' into the argument places of a two-place predicate

$\lambda v \lambda w (\exists e)$[Stabbing(e) & Subj(e,v) & Obj(e,w) & Violent(e)].
(This can be read as "being a v and a w such that v stabbed w violently.")

We can think of this two-place predicate as having been produced by some operation from another two-place predicate, the other being

$\lambda v \lambda w (\exists e)$[Stabbing(e) & Subj(e,v) & Obj(e,w)].
("being a v and a w such that v stabbed w.")

This last "input" predicate stands for the type of relation that, according to the operator account, the modifier 'violently' is supposed to operate on, and the "output" predicate given above stands for the type of relation that is supposed to be produced by applying the operator to the verb. It is natural to suppose, then, that there is a function mapping inputs of this sort to outputs of this sort, and that this function is the denotation of the modifier. Then the underlying event account provides an analysis of the operator. The missing inference is supplied by the additional details of the underlying event account. For the same reason, the scope distinctions are neutralized. The underlying event account which is built into the meaning of the operators shows the alternative scope readings to be logically equivalent.

The technical issue is whether it is possible to analyze operators in this way. The operator account requires that modifiers stand for functions. But it is not at all clear that there is a *function* mapping the "inputs" to the "outputs" in every case, as we imagined above. If there is no such function, then the underlying event account is not consistent with the operator account, and we must choose between them on their merits.

Whether there are functions that can serve as the denotata of operators that yield the same results as the underlying event approach depends on the theory of meaning that is presupposed and on additional assumptions about the available choice of verb meanings. For example, if meanings are taken to be intensions, as these are normally understood within possible worlds theory, and if no restrictions are placed on the range of possible verb meanings, then there are possible intensions for verbs and modifiers such that in some cases no function works as I described. Suppose two quite different kinds of event, say stabbings and kickings, are always performed simultaneously in every possible world. Suppose, however, that some stabbings are violent when the contemporaneous kickings are not. Then the property of being a v and a w such that v stabs w would be the very same property as the property of being a v and a w such that v kicks w. And, since 'violently' stands for a function, it would have to map both these properties to the same property (since they are not two properties, but only one). And this would require that anyone who stabs someone violently also kicks that person violently, which should not follow.

It is not true of course that kickings and stabbings coincide in all possible worlds, and a genuine example is hard to come by. It would require two verbs that are necessarily equivalent but that diverge when modified, and I am unaware of any examples of this in natural language. A possible example is the pair 'be bought' and 'be sold', which might be necessarily equivalent even though 'be bought with a credit card' is not synonymous with 'be sold with a credit card'. Such examples might cause trouble for certain versions of the operator approach, but not for others.

In summary, the operator approach may or may not be consistent with the underlying event approach. In its traditional formulation it stands in need of supplementation. It is unclear, for technical reasons, whether the two approaches can be brought into conformity with one another.[18]

I generally ignore the operator account of verb-phrase modifiers because it does not contribute to the issues that remain to be discussed. Operators give no hint of the analysis of perceptual idioms, nor of the relationships between implicit and explicit reference to events, nor of their use in analyzing causative constructions. The underlying event account may possibly be phrased in terms of the operator framework, but this framework does not provide a *better* approach than the underlying event approach.

4.4.5 Iterations of Modifiers

Iterations of modifiers provide a crucial test for theories of their semantics. The unsupplemented operator account does not address this issue. Other approaches are equivalently incomplete. For example, Sally McConnell-Ginet's (1982) analysis is illustrative.[19]

If V is a verb and A is an adverb then the meaning of V+A is obtained as follows:

Let R be the relation expressed by V. Then there is a unique augmentation R^A of R (determined by A) to a relation with one more place than R; and satisfying the constraint that $R^A(x_1, \ldots ,x_{n+1})$ entails $R(x_1, \ldots ,x_n)$. (This is the only constraint that is placed on the augmentation of R relative to A.) Further, there is a one-place property Q^A associated with A. Then the translation of $[V+A](x_1, \ldots ,x_n)$ is given by

$$(\exists x_{n+1})[Q^A(x_{n+1})\ \&\ R^A(x_1, \ldots ,x_{n+1})].$$

For example, using intuitive notation, the analysis of 'x runs quickly' is

There is a [rate] r such that r is quick and x runs-at r (where 'runs-at' is the $n+1$ place relation that augments 'runs' with respect to 'quickly', and 'quick' stands for the one-place property associated with 'quickly').

This is an intuitively natural proposal for analyzing "quickly." To run quickly is to run at a quick rate.[20] The adverb is responsible both for augmenting running to running-at-a-given-rate, and also for restricting the rates in question to the quick ones. (McConnell-Ginet proposes treating prepositional phrases in the same manner as adverbs.)

The iterative challenge comes with simple sentences containing more than one modifier. Here it is natural to apply the analysis twice, once per modifier. When you reiterate the modification you reiterate the analysis, so that the analysis of 'x V's A-ly B-ly' comes out as

$$(\exists z)[Q^B(z) \ \& \ W(x,z)]$$

where W is the augmentation of the analysis of "V-ing A-ly" with respect to B; that is, it augments

$$\lambda x(\exists y)[Q^A(y) \ \& \ R^V(x,y)]$$

with respect to B.

This analysis of the two-modifier case has two drawbacks, both of which it shares with the "operator" approach. First, it is incomplete: it fails to sanction the inference from 'x V's A-ly B-ly' to 'x V's B-ly'. Second, it creates scope distinctions, assigning substantively different meanings to 'x V's A-ly B-ly' and to 'x V's B-ly A-ly'. But 'Brutus stabbed Caesar violently with a knife' does not differ substantively from 'Brutus stabbed Caesar with a knife violently'. The account needs supplementation to produce the missing inference and to neutralize the scope distinctions.

We could try to avoid these problems by using a "conjunctive" approach. Suppose that 'x V's A-ly B-ly' has as its analysis 'x V's A-ly & x V's B-ly', where this is construed as

$$(\exists z)[Q^A(z) \ \& \ R^A(x,z)] \ \& \ (\exists z)[Q^B(z) \ \& \ R^A(x,z)].$$

This avoids the problem cited for the first proposal, but now it is incorrect, because it makes

Brutus stabbed Caesar violently and Brutus stabbed Caesar with a knife

entail

Brutus stabbed Caesar violently with a knife.

There are other ways to try to extend the analysis to reiterated modification, but I will not pursue them here.[21]

In summary, along with the operator approach in general, I find nothing incorrect in McConnell-Ginet's proposals, but I do not see either of them as solving the problems raised.

4.4.6 Reichenbach's Theories

Hans Reichenbach (1947, 301-09) proposes two accounts of the logical forms of sentences containing modifiers. Donald Davidson developed one of these accounts into something like the present version of the underlying events account. Davidson 1967 contains a full discussion of why Reichenbach's original account needs to be modified in various ways and gives the needed improvements. I want to comment on Reichenbach's other account, which Davidson does not discuss.

The gist of the account is that ordinary sentences of English contain underlying quantifications over "specific properties." For example, the logical form of

x moves

is, roughly,

x has some specific motion-property.

In symbols,

$(\exists f)[f(x) \ \& \ M(f)]$,

where 'M(f)' is read as 'f is a motion-property'. Reichenbach uses this proposal to analyze verb modifiers. The statement

x moves slowly

is, roughly,

x has some specific motion-property that is slow.

In symbols,

$(\exists f)[f(x) \ \& \ M(f) \ \& \ S(f)]$,

where 'S(f)' means 'f is slow'. Although Reichenbach does not discuss reiterated modification, the theory can clearly be extended to such cases by treating the additional modifiers as additional conjuncts within the scope of the quantifier over properties.

This theory may be evaluated in terms of its formal adequacy and in terms of its substance. On merely formal grounds, the resulting theory is *formally isomorphic* to the underlying event account. Suppose that the quantifier '$(\exists f)$' is construed as ranging over events, instead of over specific properties, and suppose that 'M(f)' means that f is an *event of moving* instead of a *property of moving*. Finally, suppose that the clause 'f(x)' is shorthand for 'x is the subject of f'. The resulting reinterpretation yields the underlying event analysis. Since the forms of the two theories agree, they must have the same formal consequences. And this entails that they both yield the same "logic of modifiers."[22]

However, on grounds of substance, I see two objections to Reichenbach's account. One, not conclusive, suggests that something is wrong somewhere. His reading of 'S(f)' as 'f is slow' cannot be correct, since f is supposed to be a property, and properties are not fast or slow. The things that are properly said to be slow are either people or motions (or "rates"). The slow-person reading is clearly irrelevant here, and the motion reading forces us to interpret the 'f' as ranging over motions—which are events, not properties. Reichenbach's reading of 'S(f)' thus forces us to interpret his theory as the *same* as the underlying event account, not as an alternative to it.

The more serious objection to Reichenbach's account is that it does not connect with other data of natural language. In contrast, the underlying event theory accounts for other linguistic phenomena, such as perception sentences ('Mary saw x move') and for facts about explicit reference to events ('the singing of the anthem'). If we were to construe underlying events as "specific" properties, we should undercut these additional accounts.

Even this objection is not conclusive. Reichenbach himself seemed to think that the underlying event account was compatible with the underlying specific property account. He explicitly presents the underlying event account as better than the underlying specific property account (1947, 307), but he clearly thought of both as correct. I speculate that this is because the underlying specific property account mirrors the underlying event account at a higher level. Such mirroring is now familiar to us from many applications of higher-order logic; in any such type-theoretic system it is possible to mirror structures of lower type by structures of higher type. And Reichenbach's intent seemed to be to mirror structures involving things of lowest type (events) by things of the next higher type (specific properties). Each event can be mirrored by the "conjunction" of all of that event's properties. Each such "conjunction" is called a specific property, and then individual events can be paired off with specific properties. If this is Reichenbach's intent, then the underlying specific property account is parasitic on the underlying event account, and so its correctness as an "alternative" to the underlying event account supports, rather than casts doubt on, the correctness of the underlying event account.[23]

4.5 Distinguishing Kinds of Modifiers

4.5.1 Classes of Modifiers

Partially on the basis of Jackendoff 1972 and Bellert 1977, I suggest
that modifiers may fruitfully be classified into five main categories:

  I.   Speech-Act Modifiers
 II.   Sentence Modifiers
III.   Subject-Oriented Modifiers
IV.   VP Modifiers
 V.   Other

The VP modifiers turn out to represent predicates of events according
to the theory of underlying events. I shall first characterize the categories. Then I shall turn to the question of how one tells which modifiers fall into which categories.

Speech-Act Modifiers may be subcategorized as[24]

Evaluative: 'fortunately', 'happily', 'surprisingly', 'thanks to God',
. . .

Epistemic Modal: 'perhaps', 'probably', 'certainly', . . .
Conjunctive: 'therefore', 'however', 'finally','in conclusion', . . .
Pragmatic: 'frankly', 'sincerely', 'honestly', 'in my opinion', . . .

Each of these modifiers has the effect of producing a sentence that is
used to make two assertions: a main assertion of a fact that is determined by the rest of the sentence, excluding the modifier, and a
secondary assertion stating that that fact has a certain property. For
example, the sentence

Fortunately, Mary arrived on time.

is suited for making the two assertions:

Main assertion   Mary arrived on time.
Secondary   The fact that Mary arrived on time is fortunate.

In many cases these modifiers carry hidden parameters that need to
be supplied from the speech context. For 'fortunately', we need to
determine "fortunately for whom," and for 'therefore', we need to
determine "follows from what."

The dual assertion nature of these constructions lets them display a
kind of factivity. 'Fortunately, Mary arrived on time' seems to entail
that Mary arrived on time; and 'Therefore, S' seems to entail that S.[25]
(Even 'perhaps' is factive in this sense, though its use indicates that
the speaker takes very little responsibility for the truth of the main

assertion.) Likewise, they display a kind of opacity. From 'Fortunately, Mary arrived' it does not follow that it was fortunate that the
Queen arrived if Mary is the queen. Further, the speech-act orientation
of these modifiers prohibits their being within the scopes of other
adverbs (we do not have 'Quietly, fortunately Mary sang') or of quantificational NPs ('Fortunately, more than five people showed up' cannot mean 'For each of more than five persons it was fortunate that he/
she showed up'). They also cannot take scope inside of negations:
'Fortunately, Mary did not come' cannot mean 'It is false that fortunately, Mary came'.

Speech-act modifiers form a fascinating area of study. For want of
space, I shall not discuss them. The point of including them in this
initial survey is to distinguish them from VP modifiers, which form
my main topic.

Sentence Modifiers include the alethic modalities, that is, the alethic
readings of 'possibly' and 'necessarily' (though not the epistemic readings, which are Speech-act modifiers), as well as certain prepositional
phrases, such as 'according to Agatha' and 'in the story'.[26] Unlike
Speech-act Modifiers, they do not produce dual assertions. They can
take scope inside other modifiers ('Possibly, every deity is necessarily
good') and with respect to quantificational NPs ('Everybody is possibly omnipotent') and negation ('God isn't necessarily good'). They are
not typically factive, though a particular lexical meaning (for example,
of 'necessarily') may override this. They typically produce opacity,
though again a particular lexical meaning (for example, of 'actually')
may override this too.

The semantics of Sentence modifiers is familiar from work in philosophical logic: they stand for properties of propositions. 'Necessarily,
God is good' is true if and only if the proposition that God is good has
the property of being necessary. In my formal symbolism, I precede
a sentence with a caret '^' to form a name of the proposition that is
expressed by that sentence. So if G is the logical form associated with
the sentence 'God is good', the logical form of 'Necessarily, God is
good' is 'N(^G)', where 'N' is a predicate of propositions. The details
of the semantics of such Sentence modifiers are matters of some
complexity and subtlety, as the literature well attests. However, none
of this complexity or subtlety bears in any special way on the theory
of underlying events or on any other aspect of "subatomic semantics,"
since Sentence modifiers operate on structures that are already full-

fledged formulas of English. I shall not comment further on these adverbs, except when I must distinguish them from VP adverbs.

Subject-Oriented Modifiers include adverbs such as 'willingly', 'intentionally', 'deliberately', and certain readings of 'rudely', 'wisely', 'carefully', such as the natural readings of 'Wisely, Mary invested in stocks', or 'Rudely, she spoke in a language that her mother-in-law did not understand'.[27] These modifiers are all factive, and they create opacity, though never in the subject position. They can take scope over quantificational NPs, as in 'Rudely, she insulted everyone'.

Except for their special sensitivity to the subject position, these modifiers resemble Sentence modifiers, and probably similar accounts can be given of each. The common suggestion is that they stand for relations between things and propositions, and that the form, for example, of 'Rudely, x insulted y' is 'Rude(x,"^"[x insults y])', i.e., "It was rude of x that x insulted y."[28] As with earlier classes, Subject-oriented adverbs are not the main objects of study in this book, and I ignore them except insofar as I need to contrast them with VP modifiers.

VP Modifiers include such locutions as 'gently', 'quietly', 'smoothly', 'in the back', 'with a knife', and certain readings of 'rudely', 'wisely', 'carefully', namely, the natural readings occurring in 'Mary spoke rudely', 'Mary invested wisely', 'She ran her fingers carefully along the edge'. These modifiers are all factive, and they do not create opacity. They stand for properties of underlying events or states, according to the theory I am investigating. I have already described their semantics, and I shall continue to examine it in this chapter, and at various points throughout the book.

Other modifiers include such words as 'merely', 'just', 'only'. They have various interesting functions in sentences, but I shall ignore them.

Temporal Modifiers cut across the categories outlined above—the general category that I call "Temporal". It includes phrases such as 'soon', 'at midnight', 'during the afternoon', 'from 2:00 to 3:00', 'usually', 'never', and 'twice'. I discuss these modifiers in chapter 11.

4.5.2 Tests for Classifying Modifiers

A certain amount of literature is devoted to the question of how modifiers may be classified into categories on the basis of their observable semantic effects on the sentences in which they occur.[29] This is a difficult enterprise to carry out. A modifier may not manifest behavior typical of its class because of the special character of its meaning. For example, Sentence modifiers are typically not factive, yet 'Necessarily, S' entails 'S' because of the special meaning of 'necessarily'. It is also tricky to classify modifiers when they may be homonymous. It is especially difficult to tell, in operational terms, whether the difference in meaning between

Happily, the war ended.

and

The war ended happily.

is due to an ambiguity in 'happily' or to its occupying different positions in the two sentences, or whether the differences between

The dolphin swam swiftly

and

The baby with the innertube swam swiftly

are due to homonymy in 'swiftly', or to a contextual shift in the relevant standards of swiftness that are appropriate, or possibly to its taking scope over the subject of the sentence. It is especially difficult to formulate *theory-neutral* versions of such tests.

I shall not try to develop such operational tests. Perhaps the best that can be done is to articulate a theory that covers the various kinds of modifiers that are posited and then to view a proposed classification of each modifier in each construction as an hypothesis that is subject to test, given the rest of the theory. Perhaps a fully developed theory will, in hindsight, yield some operational tests.

Instead, I offer some rules of thumb that may be helpful in classifying modifiers into the categories given above.

Test #1 Sentence Position   Jackendoff 1972 distinguishes three positions in which an adverb may appear in a simple sentence: in initial position (optionally with a comma), in Aux position—that is, between the subject and the main verb—and inside the VP. The positions are illustrated in

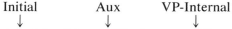

Initial   Aux   VP-Internal
   ↓   ↓   ↓
Fortunately Mary willingly ran swiftly to the store.

The following rules of thumb help to classify adverbs in terms of their occurrences.

1. Any adverb that can occur only in Aux position is in the category "Other"; examples are 'merely', 'nearly' and 'only'.[30]

2. Any adverb that occurs in Initial or Aux position but not in VP-internal position is a Speech-act modifier, or a Sentence modifier, or a Subject-oriented modifier. Examples: 'fortunately', 'possibly'.

3. Any adverb that occurs in Aux or VP-internal position but not in Initial position is a VP modifier. Example: 'easily'.

4. Any adverb that occurs in all three positions, but is ambiguous in Aux position, is homonymous between a VP adverb and a Speech-act modifier or Sentence modifier or Subject-oriented adverb.[31]

This homonymy is quite important. The classic illustration is 'happily', which occurs as a Speech-act adverb in initial position, as a VP adverb in VP-internal position, and is ambiguous between these two readings in Aux position. Other examples are 'carefully', 'wisely', 'rudely'.[32]

Test #2 Factivity   This is simple if homonymy is not at issue: all modifiers except Sentence modifiers are factive.

Test #3 Opacity   Speech-act modifiers, Sentence modifiers, and Subject-oriented modifiers are all capable of producing opacity, unless this is ruled out by their special lexical meaning.

Test #4 Presupposition Under Negation   If the modifier occurs with a simple negated sentence, then

1. If the modifier is a Speech-act modifier, the sentence is unambiguous, and the "main assertion" is a negation. E.g., 'Fortunately, Mary did not show up' is unambiguous; the main assertion is that Mary did not show up, and this is what is said to be fortunate.

2. If the modifier is a Sentence modifier then it can take scope either inside or outside of negation. Although word order or choice of determiner ('everyone' versus 'each one') often helps disambiguate, a sentence with a Sentence modifier can be ambiguous because two different orderings of the scopes of the modifier and the negation are possible. An example is 'I didn't fly in my dream', or 'That isn't required according to the church'.[33]

3. If the modifier is Subject-oriented, then the sentence is unambiguous; the negation goes with the "content" sentence, not with the

modifier. 'Rudely, Mary didn't answer' can mean only "It was rude of Mary not to answer," not "For Mary to answer was not rude." 4. If the modifier is a VP modifier, then the negation is of the whole sentence, including the modifier; an example is the reading of 'Agatha didn't run quickly' to deny that Agatha ran quickly, which could felicitously be followed by 'She didn't run at all'.

Presupposition and Focus A factor that interacts with the negation tests has to do with what is called "focus" and its effect on presupposition. To take an example without negation, if the sentence 'Agatha and Fred arrived late' is pronounced with emphasis on 'and Fred', a natural account of this speech act is to say that the speaker presupposes that Agatha arrived late, and asserts that Fred did too:

Asserted   Agatha and Fred arrived late
Presupposed   Agatha arrived late

It is a subtle matter to formulate an adequate account of this phenomenon, but one cannot deny its reality, and it must be taken into account when testing modifiers for status. For example, for VP modifiers this phenomenon produces an additional reading when coupled with negation: in addition to the reading of 'Agatha didn't run quickly', which merely denies that she ran quickly, there is another reading that presupposes that she did run and asserts that she did not do so quickly. This gives the appearance of the negation's somehow applying to the 'quickly' by itself, but this is no more accurate than to suppose that the negation applies to 'and Fred' in 'Agatha *and Fred* didn't run'.[34] This phenomenon also occurs with Sentence modifiers and with Subject-oriented modifiers when they occur in the VP (or in Aux position following the negation); witness 'Mary didn't *willingly* run' (which presupposes that she ran) and 'God isn't *necessarily* good' (which presupposes that God is good). Phrases other than negation can be "limited" in this way to a single part of the sentence. In 'She allegedly stabbed him *with a knife*', the allegation is in some sense limited to *with a knife*. This works the same as above:

Asserted   Alleged by z: x stabs y with knife
Presupposed   x stabs y

(where z is supplied from context). Thereby, no special logical form is required for 'allegedly' in order to capture its "limitation" to only part of the sentence.

Chapter 5
Thematic Roles

5.1 Thematic Roles in Grammatical Theory

In contemporary syntactic theory it is common to relate simple sentences to structures consisting of a verb and a tense plus some NPs marked for "deep cases" (Fillmore's term) or "thematic roles" (the contemporary term). These thematic roles can affect the surface position of the NPs (as in Modern English), their inflections (in inflected languages), and the choice of prepositions that precede them. All these are surface clues to the semantically significant thematic roles of the NPs. In the version of Fillmore 1968, a typical thematic structure from which we might generate a sentence has this pattern:

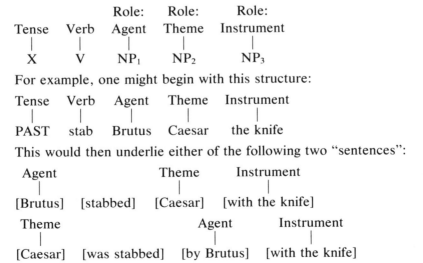

For example, one might begin with this structure:

This would then underlie either of the following two "sentences":

In the first (active) sentence the Agent is identified by being in subject position, the Theme is identified by being in direct object position, and the Instrument is "marked" by the preposition 'with'. These are the surface clues that let us figure out the thematic roles of the NPs in the sentence, given the lexical meaning of 'stab'. (Other verbs might require a different set of correlations between surface clues and thematic roles, and other languages would use a different system of clues to identify the roles. For example, in Old English, word order has little significance; inflections on the nouns and their modifiers provide the clues.) In the second sentence the passive is indicated by the verb's being marked with its passive form; the subject now indicates the Theme, and the Agent is marked with the preposition 'by'.

The general pattern correlating surface clues and thematic roles is this. Lexical information about the verb determines which thematic roles it may combine with. Then general information about the language, supplemented by particular information about the verb in question, determines which sentences may be formed using this verb plus thematic roles. English, in particular, is subject to some of the following principles (in which "double-object" verbs are ignored for simplicity).

Assumptions Not Referring to Thematic Roles:

1. A past or present tense verb by itself indicates an "active" sentence; a verb preceded by the copula and in the past participle form indicates a "passive" sentence.

2. Each simple sentence must have a subject. (In English, the subject is an NP that precedes the verb.)

3. Some sentences have direct objects. (In Modern English these are NPs that immediately follow the verb.)

Assumptions Involving Thematic Roles:

4. In an active sentence, if an Agent is present it must be the subject; in a passive sentence, if an Agent is present it is marked with 'by'.

5. If a Theme is present with an Agent, the Theme must be the direct object in an active sentence and the subject in a passive sentence.

6. If an Instrument is present, it is marked with 'with' (unless it is the subject, in which case it is unmarked).

Using the structure indicated above, if we wish to make an active sentence, then the sentence must begin with a subject and a verb, and, by one, two, and four they must be

Agent   Verb
 | |
Brutus   stab

Then, by five and three, the sentence may continue:

Agent   Verb   Theme
 | | |
Brutus   stab   Caesar.

Finally, by six, the Instrument appears with 'with'; since all earlier positions are occupied, it goes at the end:

Agent   Verb   Theme   Instrument
 | | | |
Brutus   stab   Caesar   with the knife.

The assumptions need not be "applied" in any given order. Any structure that satisfies all of them is supposed to yield an acceptable English sentence.

   If, instead, we wish to make a passive sentence, rules one, two, and five require the sentence to start with

Theme   Verb
 | |
Caesar   was stabbed.

Then, by four, the sentence may continue,

Theme   Verb   Agent
 | | |
Caesar   was stabbed   by Brutus

And then 'with the knife' again appears on the end, by six:

Theme   Verb   Agent   Instrument
 | | | |
Caesar   was stabbed   by Brutus   with the knife.

In the last example, the Agent need not be placed before the Instrument; if we do things in reverse order we get instead

Theme   Verb   Instrument   Agent
 | | | |
Caesar   was stabbed   with the knife   by Brutus.

   If we start with different underlying structures, other sentences are generated. For example, beginning with

```
Tense    Verb    Agent    Theme
  |        |       |        |
PAST     stab    Brutus   Caesar
```

and using the same assumptions, we produce the simpler sentences

Brutus stabbed Caesar

Caesar was stabbed by Brutus.

Beginning with the still simpler structure

```
Tense    Verb    Theme
  |        |       |
PAST     stab    Caesar
```

we get

Caesar was stabbed.[1]

The assumptions also permit a structure that may be impossible for 'stab', though possible for other verbs. If we begin with

```
Tense    Verb    Instr.    Theme
  |        |       |          |
PAST     stab    knife     Caesar,
```

then the assumptions allow the sentence

```
Instrument      Verb      Theme
    |             |          |
 The knife     stabbed    Caesar,
```

where 'the knife' is missing its 'with' because it appears as subject. This sentence may be unacceptable in English (this is arguable); if so, this is a special fact about 'stab' since various other verbs permit the structure. For example, we have

The hammer hit the nail,

which should follow from 'John hit the nail with the hammer'. If 'the hammer' is the Instrument in both sentences, then the two sentences have related underlying thematic structures:

John hit the hammer with the nail:

```
Tense    Verb    Agent    Instrument    Theme
  |        |       |           |           |
PAST     hit     John     the hammer    the nail
```

The hammer hit the nail:

Tense	Verb	Instrument	Theme
PAST	hit	the hammer	the nail

The latter sentence is like the former, except that it is missing its Agent.

5.2 Thematic Roles with Underlying Events

The theory described above fits nicely into the grammatical framework of Panini that I alluded to in chapter 1. This framework provides three levels: the semantic level, containing an event and a number of objects related to the event by distinctive relations; a "surface structure", containing a verb and a number of NPs, all with a specified order and/or marked with inflections or prepositions, depending on the language in question; and the actual sentence itself, in phonological form or in written form.

The theory described in the previous section can implement this account, provided that we attribute *semantic* significance to the classification of NPs in terms of their roles. As it stands, the theory merely describes how sentences are related to certain structures that contain NPs classified by thematic role. What is missing is how all of this is correlated with the semantic realm—how the roles relate to the world. The version of the theory that I shall explore correlates the thematic roles in a one-one fashion with distinctive relations that hold between objects and events at the semantic level.[2]

This is in fact a description of the theory of underlying events, with one addition: that the 'Subj' and 'Obj' relational symbols are now regarded as placeholders for more specific "deep" thematic relations such as Agent and Theme. The logical form of the sentence

Brutus stabs Caesar,

which was formerly

$(\exists e)[\text{Stabbing}(e) \& \text{Cul}(e) \& \text{Subj}(e,B) \& \text{Obj}(e,C)]$

is now replaced by

$(\exists e)[\text{Stabbing}(e) \& \text{Cul}(e) \& \text{Agent}(e,B) \& \text{Theme}(e,C)]$.

The old 'Subj' relation is now seen as short for 'whatever relation ends up being relevant to the surface subject of the sentence' (in this case, Agent), and similarly for the 'Obj' relation.

The precise ways in which surface syntactical forms are related to thematic relations in logical forms is described in detail in chapter 13. The more important issue has to do with the principles on which I base that description. The main questions of principle to be faced are: (1) what thematic roles are there? and, (2) how do we tell which NPs have which thematic roles in a given case?

In answering the first question, I shall not be concerned with possible relations to events that show up at the surface only as prepositional phrases. For example, the prepositional phrase 'through x' will appear in a great many sentences, and correlated with it in logical form will be the relational formula 'Through(e,x)'. I shall not count this as a "thematic role". Since the same word 'through' is used in both the surface form and logical form, I shall not be concerned with discovering *which* relation is at play. This oversimplifies a major issue, since such questions arise whenever a preposition is ambiguous. And most prepositions appear to be highly ambiguous.[3] Rather than focusing on the ambiguity of prepositions, which is worth a book of its own, I address only the issue of which semantic relations between events and things are sometimes indicated by a variable for the thing that occupies the position of subject, direct object, or indirect object.[4]

Which thematic roles of this sort are there? There is certainly no agreement in the literature on this issue, and so any answer I give will be idiosyncratic. Sections 5.2 through 5.6 describe a particular version of the theory of thematic roles. My discussion is neutral among various frameworks for syntactic theory; none of my proposals require thematic roles to play a significant part in the purely syntactic principles of sentence formation (assuming that there are such principles). Section 5.7 discusses the feasibility of dispensing with thematic roles within the theory of underlying events.

5.3 The Basic Account

A simple version of the theory of thematic roles assumes that six such roles can appear in English unmarked by prepositions:

Role	Typical Position in Active Sentence
Agent	Subject
Theme	Direct Object; subject of 'is'
Goal	Indirect object, or with 'to'

Benefactive	Indirect object, or with 'for'
Instrument (=Performer)	Object of 'with'; subject
Experiencer	Subject

Each of these roles relates an event (or a state) and a thing. No event stands in one of these relations to more than one thing; thus, each event possesses at most one Agent, at most one Experiencer, and so on.[5]

Most of the names chosen here for thematic roles are awkward at best. By their very nature, the roles combine with a wide variety of verbs, and any English word chosen to name the role will be odd in some cases. That apology made, I turn to explaining how to identify the roles in general, relying heavily on paradigms.

Use of the Agent relation in a sentence indicates agency on the part of the thing picked out. It indicates not only that the thing in question is a doer but also that it is responsible for what is done. This relation may also be used in nonhuman cases of agency, as when we say 'GM is now offering rebates on its new models'. (A popular test for the Agent role in the linguistic literature is whether it makes sense to precede the NP in question with 'persuade'. For example, we can say felicitously "We persuaded GM to offer rebates on its new models.")

In an active sentence of English, if there is an Agent NP in the sentence, then it must be the subject. The Agent relation is used in subject position in these sentences:

Brutus stabbed Caesar.
Mary walked to school.
Sam sliced the salami.
Mary looked at the buffalo.

The use of Theme ("Patient") is often called the "leftover case," since so little can be said about it in general. The direct object of a (noncausative) transitive verb in English is always a Theme,[6] and the subject of a copula plus an adjective or prepositional phrase is almost always a Theme. Examples are the italicized phrases in

Brutus stabbed *Caesar.*
John hit *the nail* on the head with the hammer.
Mary saw *the woman.*
The book is red.
Brutus is under the tree.

'Goal' is the usual term for indirect objects that are paraphrasable with 'to'. Thus we have

'Benefactive' is the usual term for indirect objects that are para-phrasable with 'for':

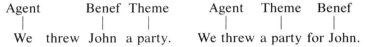

Use of the Experiencer relation does not indicate agency, but it does indicate sentience in a broad sense. We sometimes speak of institutions or mechanisms in terms appropriate to sentient beings; these things can also fill the Experiencer role. The Experiencer relation is used for the subjects of these sentences (all of which fail the "persuade test"):[7]

Mary knows that there are spotted giraffes.
Mary likes roses.
Mary sees the buffalo.
The government thinks I owe it back taxes.
The computer understands the first command but not the second.

Use of the Instrument relation includes the objects of instrumental 'with', and it sometimes surfaces as the subject. The italicized NPs in the following examples all use the Instrument relation:

John opened the door *with the key*.
The key opened the door.
They loaded the wagon with hay *with large pitchforks*.
John carried the piano upstairs with Gertrude *with a handtruck*.

(Use of the nonitalicized 'with' in the third sentence is sometimes called the 'ornamental use' to distinguish it from the instrumental use. The nonitalicized 'with' in the last sentence is the 'with' of joint action, discussed in section 5.5.)

Over and above the contribution of the thematic roles, the whole sentence or the context in which it occurs may indicate agency, or experiencer, or instrument. Thus, in

Brutus stabbed Caesar,

we might naturally assume that Caesar is a normal human being, and thus an agent and an experiencer, but these are not implied by the thematic role of 'Caesar' in the sentence. The word occurs simply as the Theme. Brutus could have stabbed his pillow as well, and it is neither an agent nor an experiencer.

Even without clear criteria of classification, which NPs play which roles is easy to discern in most sentences. Here are some illustrative samples with comments:

She slapped me with her hand; I just stood there.
I see you; stop yelling!
She gave him the book, but he didn't read it.
I looked for days, and finally I found it.

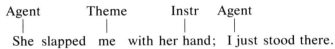
Agent   Theme   Instr   Agent
  | | | |
She slapped   me   with her hand;   I just stood there.

Although one can guess from the whole sentence that 'me' refers to an experiencer, its role as object of 'slap' does not tell us this; anything can be slapped. The classification of 'I' as Agent indicates that agency includes intentionally "doing nothing." There may also be a nonagentive reading of this sentence.

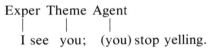
Exper Theme Agent
  | | |
 I see you; (you) stop yelling.

It is tricky to classify the subject of 'see', which seems to be borderline between Agent and non-Agent.

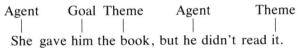
Agent   Goal Theme   Agent   Theme
  | | | | |
She gave him the book, but he didn't read it.

Although the last sentence says that he did *not* read the book, which is consistent with his lacking agency, the classification of 'he' depends on the verb, not the whole sentence. The subject of 'read' will be agentive, no matter what the whole sentence says. In this case, the whole sentence denies that a certain person is agent of a certain reading.

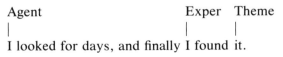
Agent   Exper Theme
  | | |
I looked for days, and finally I found it.

5.4   Enhancements

Theories of thematic relations appear in various forms in the literature. Two enhancements of the system just described are extending and relabeling the Instrument role, and allowing NPs to have multiple roles in the same occurrence.

5.4.1   Extension and Relabeling of the Instrumental Role

A classic objection to the roles described above stems from sentences like

The wind opened the door.

In 'Mary opened the door', it appears that 'Mary' should be Agent and 'the door' should be Theme. But then what is 'the wind' in 'The wind opened the door'? It cannot also be Theme, because then the logical forms of 'The wind opened the door' and 'The door opened the wind' would be equivalent. The wind cannot be an Agent, at least not without personification (which is not at issue here), and it is certainly not Experiencer. This leaves only Instrument. But if the wind is an instrument in this sentence, where is the agent that uses the instrument?

This sort of case is much more widespread than has been recognized in the literature. The classic use of Instrument as subject of a sentence is illustrated by examples such as

The hammer hit the nail.

But even here there need not be an agent to use the instrument. Granted, if Mary hit the nail with the hammer, then the hammer is an instrument. But what if the hammer just materialized out of thin air, and fell to the ground, hitting a nail on the way? The sentence does not *itself* require a user of the hammer. And thus even here the use of Instrument as a role seems misguided. Indeed, I am unaware of a single sentence that has been identified in the literature as having an Instrument as subject where the actual sentence containing that subject requires for its truth that the subject be used as an instrument.

Many sentences are unclassifiable by the original use of thematic roles if the title 'Instrument' is taken literally. These sentences look like those with Agent subjects, but there is no agency involved. Here are some examples:

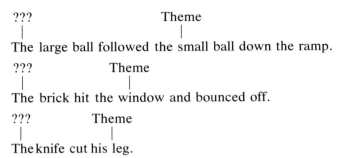

```
???                          Theme
 |                             |
The large ball followed the small ball down the ramp.
???                  Theme
 |                     |
The brick hit the window and bounced off.
???            Theme
 |               |
The knife cut his leg.
```

In all of these cases the subject *could* be the instrument used by an agent in the event in question, but it need not have been. The traditional proposal to identify an independent thematic role in these cases is correct, but, because it is optional whether the thing fulfilling the role is an instrument, 'Instrument' is a poor name. Instruments provide only one kind of example of things fulfilling the role. A better title might be 'Performer', if this is not understood as implying agency. I shall retain the term 'Instrument' out of deference to the literature, assuming that it includes all of the traditional cases plus the problem cases listed above.

5.4.2 NPs with Multiple Thematic Roles

The theory I have endorsed allows for each event to have at most one agent, at most one experiencer, at most one theme, and at most one performer. But this leaves it open whether an NP may simultaneously occupy more than one thematic role. I do not have in mind here examples such as 'Sam sees himself', in which Sam stands in both relations to the event. In the underlying form of 'Sam sees himself' we will have distinct occurrences of variables, one occupying the Experiencer position, and one occupying the Theme position. The question I raise now is whether the same *position* in the underlying form might be classified, say, as both Agent and Theme. I begin with some data that suggests that this often occurs.

There seem to be some systematic connections between many prepositions of motion and location. 'Onto' seems related in some way to 'on', 'into' to 'in', 'to' to 'at', and so on. These relations hold of the Motion senses of the former prepositions, and relate them to the Locative senses of the latter. The relations are illustrated by the following inferences:

If Sam hits the 8-ball *into* the pocket, then the 8-ball ends up *in* the pocket.

If Mary will chase the cat *onto* the lawn, then the cat will be *on* the lawn.

Using 'onto' and 'on' as a paradigm, my proposal is this: Any event that is onto something results in a state of being on that thing. The Themes of the event and the state are the same.

More precisely:

Onto(e,y) & Theme(e,x) & Cul(e,t) →

(∃s)[On(s,y) & Theme(s,x) & Hold(s,t)].

This postulate, which is independent of any choice of verb, yields all of the following inferences when applied to the logical forms of the sentences:

Mary will throw the ball onto the roof →
The ball will be on the roof

John will push the piano onto the rug →
The piano will be on the rug

Samantha kicked the frisbee onto the sidewalk →
The frisbee was on the sidewalk.

The same postulate applies to several other pairs of related motion and location prepositions, relating

'into' and 'in'
'to' and 'at'[8]
'out of' and 'outside of'
'away from' and 'away from'
'under' and 'under'
'behind' and 'behind'
'off' and 'off'

The "motion" use of the first preposition is intended, and the "location" use of the second.

The postulates yield inferences such as

Mary will push the cow into the barn →
The cow will be in the barn

John will fly the model airplane to the top of the hill →
The model airplane will be at the top of the hill

Samantha let the fly out of the bottle →
The fly was outside of the bottle

Samantha pulled the sticker off the bottle →
The sticker was off the bottle

Kim kicks the book under the sofa →
The book is under the sofa

Cathy chased the cat behind the barn →
The cat was behind the barn

(In the past tense examples, one must ignore the implication suggested by reading the antecedent and consequent in order, that the state that is reported held when the event began.)

This approach focuses attention on a host of similar inferences *not* accounted for in the theory as formulated so far, since the NP is not (so far) classified as a Theme:

Bill will run behind the house →
Bill will be behind the house

Mary will drive to the airport →
Mary will be at the airport

It would be wrong to expand the meaning postulate to thematic relations other than Theme, since this would yield incorrect inferences. For example, we might try to account for the two examples just cited by replacing Theme in the postulate by Agent, but that would yield false inferences such as:

Mary threw the book under the sofa →
Mary was under the sofa.

I propose that in certain cases an NP can have more than one thematic role. In particular, in many cases Agents and Performers can also be Themes. A simple rule effects this proposal:

Every verb takes a Theme.[9]

The subject of every intransitive verb thereby becomes a Theme, in addition to whatever role it already has, since the subject will be the only NP available for this role. The meaning postulate now yields many further inferences:

Mary ran into the store →
Mary was in the store

Sam will swim to Catalina →
Sam will be at Catalina

Kareem hops quickly onto the bus →
Kareem will be on the bus

Fido crawled under the house →
Fido was under the house,

and so on. Since the principles in question apply to the motion senses of the prepositions cited, they do not apply to a sentence such as 'Kathy looked under the sofa'.

This extension of Theme to the subjects of intransitives brings my use of the notion closer to the traditional uses. One general rule of thumb for "Theme" in the literature is that anything that is in motion in an event is a Theme, and also anything that is required to be at rest in an event of staying or remaining is a Theme. This makes the subjects of 'run', 'swim' and 'hop' all be Themes. It also makes the subject of 'stay' be a Theme, which is not relevant to my analysis of prepositions but which seems unobjectionable.

The notion of Theme may be one that comes naturally to human language learners, since we seem to have an intuitive understanding of it: we instinctively generalize to it from a small sample of paradigms. Classifying 'John' in 'John walks' as a Theme is simply an obvious truth for this intuitive understanding.

Many of the intransitive verbs of Modern English evolved from Old English forms that permitted syntactically overt Themes, subject to the provision that that Theme is a pronoun agreeing with the subject. For example, in Old English one could say either "He went home" or "He went him home".[10] But the semantic import of the Theme need not be lost just because the more complex form dropped out of the language.

Occasionally I use the term 'Agent-Theme' for any NP that is both Agent and Theme, and 'Instrument-Theme' for any NP that is both Instrument and Theme. In 'Agatha pushed the book under the sofa' the Agent and Theme are distinct, whereas 'Agatha crawled under the sofa' now has a single Agent-Theme, and 'The cup rolled under the sofa' has a single Instrument-Theme (Performer-Theme). The first sentence entails that the book ends up under the sofa; the second and third entail respectively that Agatha and the cup do.

A number of further details might be pursued. Not only can we infer from the cup's rolling onto the rug that it ended up on the rug but we may also infer that it was not on the rug just prior to its rolling on.

The principle at work here is something like

Onto(e,y) & Theme(e,x) & Cul(e) →
There is a time preceding the culmination of e such that for every time t that is between that time and the culmination of e there is no state s such that On(s,y) & Theme(s,x) & Hold(s,t).[11]

The relations between certain adverbs of motion and of location, such as 'home' in 'Fred went home' and 'home' in 'Fred is home' might also be explored. The postulate for prepositions can be stated for adverbs as well, yielding such inferences as

If Mary comes here, then she will be here.
If Sam dives deep, then he will be deep.
If Sharon goes away, then she will be away.

Relations between certain verbs and prepositions might also be explored. The relation between the verb 'cross' and the preposition 'across' provide a key example for Gruber (1976), who holds that they overlap in meaning. A relation between them can be encapsulated in the postulate

Across(e,x) ≡ Crossing(e) & Theme(e,x).

This postulate makes it redundant to add the preposition 'across' to 'cross', as in 'She crossed across the stream'. Gruber's theory (not described here) is intended to explain such data. Regarding the preposition, we ought also to be able to validate the inference

If Mary swam across the channel, then she crossed the channel.

The postulate does this as well, by classifying the swimming across as a crossing. However, it is rare to find a verb and a preposition etymologically related in this way, and the non-etymological cases are generally not plausible.[12]

This section has addressed a variety of semantical issues within the semantical framework of underlying events, combined with a thematic role theory. The semantical precision of the framework permits careful tests for such hypotheses, and the details make certain hypotheses simple and natural to express. Many other theories cannot capture these generalizations about motion and place prepositions and adverbs,[13] but obviously I have barely scratched the surface.[14]

5.5   Objections to the Use of Thematic Roles

5.5.1   Roles Have No Use in Syntax

The main discussion of thematic roles in recent work in linguistics has centered on their utility in theories of syntax, the majority view being that they are dispensable, and that the best theory of "autonomous" syntax does not appeal to them. However, the theory I am developing is a theory of semantics, and thematic roles in this theory have semantic import. The principles that link thematic roles with NPs in English sentences are meant to apply to any theory of syntax that can identify notions such as "subject" of a simple active sentence; they do not take sides on how this is to be done. A well-developed theory of syntax could extend the present "core" theory to a wide range of sentences I have not addressed, but the syntactic theory itself need not use thematic roles. So even if thematic roles are not appealed to in syntax, they might be useful in semantics, perhaps as in the theory under discussion.

5.5.2   Multiple Agents

The theory presumes that each event has at most one agent, at most one theme, and so on. Most apparent counterexamples to this have the Agent or Theme as a group. In 'The girls carried the piano upstairs', or 'Mary and Bob carried the piano upstairs', the Agent is a group: the group of girls in the first case, and the group consisting of Mary and Bob in the second. Fillmore (1968) discusses potential counterexamples to the principle that each sentence contain only one NP per thematic role. 'Bill robbed the bank with Mary' appears to have a reading in which Mary and Bill are equally seen as bank-robbers, and (perhaps) in which only one robbery is in question. This may be an example of what Fillmore calls a 'comitative' function, where the clause 'with Mary' indicates something like "displaced conjunction." That is, we might see the sentence (on the reading in question, assuming that it exists) as simply a variant of

Bill and Mary robbed the bank.

And this in turn could easily be seen as a sentence with a group NP as its subject.

Another reading contains the 'with' of accompaniment. Accompaniment is less than comitativity. For example

Bill walked home with Mary.

has an accompaniment reading not requiring that Mary walked too—
she might have been in a wheelchair, or on a bicycle. This reading
raises no issue of multiple agenthood.

5.5.3 Buying and Selling

Buying and selling offer good illustrations of examples that intertwine
issues about roles with issues of the identity of events. Consider:

Kim bought a tricycle from Sheehan.
Sheehan sold a tricycle to Kim.

The tricycle appears to be a Theme of both events, the buying and the
selling. Kim is the Agent of the buying, and Sheehan is the Agent of
the selling.[15] Some would insist that the buying and the selling are one
and the same event, differently described. This makes Kim the Agent
of the selling, and Sheehan the Agent of the buying, which entails that
Kim sold a tricycle to Kim, and Sheehan bought a tricycle from
Sheehan. Something is wrong.

The right answer is that the buying and the selling, while intimately
related, are not the same event. A full defense of this nonidentity
requires a global look at a number of issues, that I deal with only later.
But I can briefly defend my view without any essential reference to
roles. One possibility is that Kim bought the tricycle with his
MasterCard, though Sheehan did not sell it with Kim's MasterCard.
Likewise, Sheehan may have sold it with a hard sales pitch, though
Kim did not buy it with a hard sales pitch. And Kim might have bought
it quietly, without Sheehan's having sold it quietly (if, say, Kim's
purchase was handled by a middleman, with Sheehan shouting over
the phone). In all of these cases, the nonidentity of the events is forced
by the account of modifiers in the theory of underlying events, quite
apart from treating the subjects as Agents. In order to accommodate
all of our intuitions we may have to appeal to a notion of "transaction,"
or "situation," as an entity encompassing two or more events. Perhaps
each buying *transaction* is a selling *transaction*. But this does not
identify buyings and sellings.

5.5.4 Abstruments

David Dowty (personal communication) has raised an objection to my
principle about Themes, based on consideration of the following
sentences:

1 I emptied the tank.
2 I emptied the tank into the sink.
3 I emptied the tank of water.
4 I emptied water from the tank.
5 I emptied the water from the tank into the sink.
6 *I emptied the tank of water into the sink.

Sentences (3) and (6) are both ambiguous. The readings in question are *not* those in which the direct object of the verb 'empty' is 'tank of water', but in which 'tank' is the direct object and 'of water' plays some other role. Its role is supposedly indicated by the fact that (3) and (4) are meant to be (almost) synonymous, and that (5) and (6) would be practically equivalent if (6) were grammatical. Dowty argues that (6) is ungrammatical, and that this is a problem for the theory under discussion, since according to that theory (6) should make perfectly good sense.[16] Sentence (6) is obviously awkward, though one can attribute to it a fairly clear meaning. I return to this issue later, but first let us see how the theory of underlying events applies to these sentences.

The verb 'empty' in (3) is not the same as the verb 'empty' in (4); they are homonyms. One meaning is at play in sentences (4) and (5), and the other sentences all contain another. Sentences (4) and (5) both contain the same verb, and have straightforward treatments.

$(\exists e)[\text{Emptying}(e) \ \& \ \text{Theme}(e, \text{water}) \ \& \ \text{From}(e, \text{tank})]$

$(\exists e)[\text{Emptying}(e) \ \& \ \text{Theme}(e, \text{water}) \ \& \ \text{From}(e, \text{tank}) \ \& \ \text{Into}(e, \text{sink})]$

In these formulas my earlier discussion of adverbials of motion applies, and the sentences imply that the Theme (= the water) ends up away from the tank, and, in case (5), in the sink.

At first glance, sentence (2) seems an embarrassment. Since 'the tank' is the direct object, and since (2) contains the motion adverbial 'into the sink', the tank appears to be the Theme of the emptying, and so the tank should end up in the sink. But (2) does not say that the tank ends up in the sink; its contents do. So some other analysis seems to be required. In fact, sentences (1) through (3) and (6) are all "causative" constructions. These are discussed in chapter 6, but the basics are easy to explain. The form of sentence (1), for example, is complex:

1' I emptied the tank = I did something that caused the tank to become empty.

Here the verb 'empty' is analyzed in terms of an adjective ('empty') that applies to the tank. The logical form of (1) involves two events: the thing I did that caused the tank to become empty, and the becoming empty. The latter event is uniquely related to the final state of the tank: the tank ends up being empty. The whole analysis has the following complexity:

1′   For some event e:
         I am the agent of e
     For some event e′:
         The tank is the theme of e′
     For some state s:
         s is a being-empty
         the tank is the theme of s
     Further:
         e causes e′
         e′ is the becoming of s.

Then why doesn't

2   I emptied the tank into the sink

entail that the tank ends up in the sink? In (2), as in (1), there are two underlying events that might be "modified" by 'into the sink'. One is the caused event, the becoming empty of the tank. Since this is not a motion, it would be anomalous to predicate 'into the sink' of it. The other possibility is the causing event. Its character is completely undetermined by the logical form, except that I am identified as its agent. So nothing prevents applying 'into the sink' to it. It is also a plausible candidate, since the only way to empty a tank into a sink is to move its contents into the sink. That is, we know that this is what the sentence says, so, reasoning backwards, this tells us something about the nature of the causing event. In short, of the two underlying events to be characterized by 'into the sink', the second is ruled out by its meaning, and the first is plausible. An unproblematic form for (2) is then

2′   For some event e:
         I am the agent of e
         e is into the sink
     For some event e′:
         The tank is the theme of e′

For some state s:
    s is a being-empty
    the tank is the theme of s
Further:
    e causes e'
    e' is the becoming of s.

This form requires something to end up in the sink (namely, the unspecified theme of the causing event); it does not say what, not even that the something is the tank.

In each of the two remaining sentences containing the phrase 'of water', I see two different ways to analyze them. For

3   I emptied the tank of water,

'of water' can be seen as characterizing the final state of emptiness of the tank. The sentence says that I did something that made the tank end up empty-of-water. It does not say that I made it end up empty; perhaps I emptied it of water by filling it with mercury until the water all overflowed, so that it ended up empty of water but full of mercury. We capture this idea by modifying the final state in question; its form is a slight embellishment of that of (1):

3'   For some event e:
    I am the agent of e
  For some event e':
    The tank is the theme of e'
  For some state s:
    s is a *being-empty-of-water*
    the tank is the theme of s
  Further:
    e causes e'
    e' is the becoming of s.

This may require further analysis of the state-predicate 'being empty of water', but that analysis is not part of my present task.

Alternatively, (3) can be seen as telling us that I emptied the tank by doing something involving water. If we see the 'of' in 'of water' as identifying the Theme of the underlying causing event, then the analysis is

3"   For some event e:
    I am the agent of e
    The water is the theme of e

For some event e′:
    The tank is the theme of e′
For some state s:
    s is a being-empty
    the tank is the theme of s
Further:
    e causes e′
    e′ is the becoming of s.

This analysis is less plausible because it requires that the tank end up empty, without specifying what respect of empty. 'Empty' all by itself seems to mean by default 'completely empty', or at least 'completely empty of the sorts of thing that are normally contained'. Yet (3) clearly means that the tank ends up empty *of water,* not "completely empty."

A combined analysis in which 'of' forces the water to play a dual role would be

3   For some event e:
    I am the agent of e
    The water is the theme of e
  For some event e′:
    The tank is the theme of e′
  For some state s:
    s is a being-empty-of-water
    the tank is the theme of s
  Further:
    e causes e′
    e′ is the becoming of s.

I think that the first analysis is the right one and that the second and third are strained, but it is helpful to see them as possible options.

The problem sentence (6) now emerges as a combination of the constructions in (2) and (3). On the first method of analyzing (3), the analysis of (6) is

6′ For some event e:
    I am the agent of e
    e is into the sink
  For some event e′:
    The tank is the theme of e′
  For some state s:
    s is a being-empty-of-water
    the tank is the theme of s

Further:

    e causes e'

    e' is the becoming of s.

This fails to entail that the water ends up in the sink, a defect if the sentence is grammatical. The second analysis is

6″ For some event e:

    I am the agent of e

    e is into the sink

    The water is the theme of e

  For some event e':

    The tank is the theme of e'

  For some state s:

    s is a being-empty

    the tank is the theme of s

  Further:

    e causes e'

    e' is the becoming of s.

This entails that the water ends up in the sink, but it also entails (perhaps inappropriately) that the tank end up "empty" (as opposed to "empty of water").

  The "combined" analysis is:

6 For some event e:

    I am the agent of e

    e is into the sink

    The water is the theme of e

  For some event e':

    The tank is the theme of e'

  For some state s:

    s is a being-empty-of-water

    the tank is the theme of s

  Further:

    e causes e'

    e' is the becoming of s.

But even though the symbolization seems to get everything right, how can the theory be right if it attributes a clear meaning to sentence (6), which is (arguably) not fully grammatical?

  The problem with sentence (6) has nothing to do with either underlying events or with thematic roles. It can be solved by reflecting on the different kinds of function that 'water' is asked to play in the various analyses. In the construction 'empty the tank of water', 'water' occurs as a bare mass term, and its use in the analysis is in the adjectival construction 'empty of water'. If we replace this use of 'water' with an ordinary NP such as 'some water', this yields anomaly; what does it mean to "empty a tank of some water" or for a tank to be "empty of some water"? We can try to make sense of this, but it is unnatural. I suggest that (6) is unnatural because the construction

Empty the tank of X into the sink.

Demands an unquantified mass term for the "X" position, whereas 'into the sink' requires a Theme that can move. But the use of the unquantified mass term that goes with 'empty' cannot be the same as the one that can be a Theme of a motion. In terms of the logical forms laid out above, the blanks in

_____ is the Theme of e & e is into the sink

and

s is a being-empty-of-_____

cannot consistently be filled with the same kind of term. The former demands something that denotes an object or a particular quantity of stuff, whereas the latter demands something that denotes a *kind* of stuff. (6) is odd because we make sense of it only by using 'water' in two different ways. This is made clear by the way in which we describe the consequences of the sentence's being true. We say that the tank ends up "empty of *water,*" and the "*the water* ends up in the sink." In the first case we use the bare term 'water', and in the second we use 'the water'; replacing either of these by the other is odd, and forces an unnatural reading.

Something like this also seems to apply to several other examples that Dowty has gathered under the title "abstrument":

Rain leeched the soil of nutrients.
He unbridled himself of his fears.
The land was depopulated of its aboriginal inhabitants.
The waves washed the beach of seaweed.

Some of these contain (almost) bare plurals instead of mass terms, but bare plurals and mass terms are known to behave similarly, and the general point is the same. We cannot say, for example, "Rain leeched the soil of nutrients into the stream," because 'of' demands a word that refers to a kind of thing, whereas 'into the stream' demands an event with a theme that moves. In context, of course, one can force a reading in which 'of' takes a particular quantity of stuff, a quantity that can move. For example, one can force a reading on

Rain leeched the soil of the salt I put there yesterday,
and even

Rain leeched the soil of the salt into the stream.

The theory of underlying events can analyze these forced readings; I do not see this as a defect. Why the readings are *forced* is not unique to the theory under investigation.

5.6 Passive Sentences

The treatment of passive sentences has already been hinted at. A verb in the passive form has no effect on the translation of the verb itself— it still stands for the same property of events as in the active form. The presence and order of its arguments in the surface syntax of the sentence are, however, affected. In particular, for a passive sentence using an ordinary (single-object) transitive verb, the Theme becomes the subject. Whatever would normally have been the subject of the corresponding active sentence is optionally present, marked with the preposition 'by'.[17]

The distribution of thematic roles in simple sentences is a consequence of a three-stage process:

1. The Verb determines which thematic roles may be present in the sentence. 'Stab' may combine with an Agent and a Theme, 'walk' combines with an Agent-Theme, 'fall' with a Theme, and so on.
2. A set of principles determines which roles may occur in which positions in active surface sentences. These principles were illustrated in section 1 above.[18]
3. A set of principles determines which roles may occur in which positions in passive surface sentences. These principles may be stated so that they are parasitic on the rules for active sentences, as illustrated above, or they may be stated independently.

Special principles may also be needed for causative sentences (discussed in chapter 6), and additional principles will be needed for perception sentences, such as 'The bucket was seen by Mary to fall onto the pavement'.

The logical forms underlying simple sentences of English are always logically equivalent in their active and corresponding passive forms. For example,

Harriet loves Harvey.

and

Harvey is loved by Harriet.

have equivalent logical forms; each is equivalent to

(∃e)[Loving(e) & Exp(e,Harriet) & Theme(e,Harvey)].

The differences between the sentences themselves are entirely due to whether the verb is in its active or passive form, which NP ends up being subject, whether there is a direct object, and so on. These are all matters of syntax, not of logical form. Failures of equivalence between actives and passives are due to other phenomena. For example, it is well known that quantifier scopes tend to follow the order of quantifier NPs at the surface, and so the most natural readings of the following "corresponding" active and passive sentences differ:

Every boy dates some girl.
Some girl is dated by every boy.

But this is due entirely to the order of the quantifiers; the forms they are quantifying into are synonymous:

For every boy x: For some girl y: (∃e)[Dating(e) & Agent(e,x) & Theme(e,y)]

For some girl y: For every boy x: (∃e)[Dating(e) & Agent(e,x) & Theme(e,y)]

Corresponding actives and passives also have different VPs. In logical form this provides different structures for other elements in the sentence to operate on. I have avoided mention of logical forms of VPs in order to avoid complicating the text, but they are relevant to this issue. (See chapter 13 for details). Clearly, however, the difference between the active and the passive VPs is due to the VP formation rule, but the ingredients of the VPs of corresponding active and passive sentences are the same.[19] In the simplest cases, actives and passives containing the same NPs in corresponding places are logically equivalent.

5.7   The Utility of Thematic Relations

There are two fundamental but interdependent issues regarding thematic roles:

Issue 1. Should we appeal to thematic roles at all in a theory of semantics based on underlying events?   Instead of symbolizing 'Brutus stabbed Caesar violently' as:

(∃e)[Stabbing(e) & Agent(e,Brutus) & Theme(e,Caesar) & Violent(e)],

we might eliminate the complications of the thematic roles 'Agent' and 'Theme', writing

(∃e)[Stabbing(e,Brutus,Caesar) & Violent(e)],

where 'Stabbing(e,y,z)' means 'e is a stabbing by y of z'. What does the extra complexity of the additional conjuncts buy us? What is the evidence for it?

Issue 2. Are thematic roles univocal across verbs?   Suppose we have settled issue 1; we have established the utility of the logical forms in question. This does not automatically resolve the further issue of whether the thematic roles appealed to in the symbolism are univocal across verbs. Is there a relation of agenthood, for example, that is the *same* relation for both stabbing and kissing? For stabbing and running? The logical forms might be justifiable even if agenthood were relative to the type of event in question. Interestingly, this issue turns out to interact with the metaphysical issue of the identity conditions for events.

I call Issue 1 'The Utility of Thematic Relations' and Issue 2 'The Cross-Verbal Identity of Thematic Relations'. I discuss Issue 1 in this section, and Issue 2 in the next.[20] For both discussions, I presuppose the underlying event analysis, and I also presuppose that verb modifiers are properly construed in logical form as conjuncts containing predicates of the underlying event.

5.7.1   Articulation of the Options

Davidson's original 1967 paper did not employ thematic relations. Their use is a quite independent idea. Panini discussed them, Fillmore (1968) and others discussed them in the 1960s, and Castañeda (1967) suggested them as an addition to Davidson's theory. Davidson origi-

nally proposed a simpler account, one in which the verb contributes
a multiplace predicate to logical form, with a place for the event, and
an additional place for each of the NPs I have been treating as having
thematic roles. A simple illustration of the difference is given by these
alternative symbolizations of 'Brutus stabbed Caesar with the knife'.

Davidson's Original Proposal:

(∃e)[Stabbing(e,Brutus,Caesar) & With(e,knife)].

Using Thematic Relations:

(∃e)[Stabbing(e) & Agent(e,Brutus) & Theme(e,Caesar) &
With(e,knife)].

In each of these analyses the modifier remains a separate conjunct. In
the latter analysis the thematic roles appear as separate relational
conjuncts, whereas in the former they disappear into the meaning of
the verb. I refer to the latter option as the "independent conjunct"
analysis and the former as the "incorporation analysis," since on this
approach whatever meaning is contributed by the thematic role is
incorporated into the verb itself.[21]

There is no obvious reason why this logical difference should correspond to the difference between NPs that are traditionally thought
to be candidates for occupying thematic roles and other NPs. The real
question concerns which NP places, if any, are to be treated by the
incorporation approach, and which, by the independent conjunct
analysis.

5.7.2 Syntactic Marks of Thematic Roles

Thematic role NPs are not easily distinguished from others by their
surface marks. Languages generally identify traditional thematic roles
by word order, by differences in spellings, by inflections, or by the
use of prepositions. In Modern English the subject of a simple sentence
comes first, and this position helps identify its thematic role. Indeed,
the only way to distinguish the role of 'Brutus' from that of 'Caesar'
in 'Brutus stabbed Caesar' is by word order. Modern English also uses
differences in spelling in some cases; this is illustrated by the differences in 'He saw him' and 'She saw her'. These differences are mostly
redundant in standard Modern English, but in unusual poetic constructions we still might find 'him the woman saw', where the accusative
case spelling of 'him' would be important. Modern English does not

use inflections. It does use prepositions in some cases for thematic relations, such as 'to' in the second sentence:

Mary gave John the book
Mary gave the book to John.

There is even more variation across languages. None of these surface marks will therefore be a good guide to distinguishing thematic roles from nonthematic prepositions. Nor will any of them provide a good guide as to which NP places are to be analyzed using the incorporation account and which, the independent conjunct account. Each of the four devices is used by some language or other to indicate its thematic roles. If we are to find an important difference, we must look deeper.[22]

5.7.3   The Logic of Modifiers

Since the differences between the approaches involves a difference in logical forms, we might expect that a difference in logical consequences would help us decide between them. The main difference between the two approaches lies in how they handle optional NPs. In the independent conjunct treatment, if an NP is missing from a sentence, its conjunct is simply omitted. In the incorporation approach, if an NP is omitted then its place is existentially bound. Using the sentence 'Brutus stabbed Caesar violently in the back', we can extend the pattern discussed earlier. In the following list, each sentence entails each of the others that are obtained from it by omitting an NP or a prepositional phrase:[23]

a   Brutus stabbed Caesar violently in the back.
b   Brutus stabbed Caesar violently.
c   Brutus stabbed Caesar in the back.
d   Brutus stabbed Caesar.
e   Brutus stabbed violently.
f   Brutus stabbed in the back.
g   Caesar was stabbed violently.
h   Caesar was stabbed in the back.
i   Brutus stabbed.
j   Caesar was stabbed.

In fact, both approaches get these data exactly right. The independent conjunct approach analyses the inference from c to j as one from

$$(\exists e)[\text{Stabbing}(e)\ \&\ \text{Agent}(e,\text{Brutus})\ \&\ \text{Theme}(\text{Caesar})\ \&\ \text{In}(e,\text{back})]$$

to

(∃e)[Stabbing(e) & Theme(Caesar)].

This involves dropping two conjuncts. The incorporation account analyses it instead as an inference from

(∃e)[Stabbing(e,Brutus,Caesar) & In(e,back)]

to

(∃e)[(∃x)Stabbing(e,x,Caesar)],

by dropping one conjunct and existentially quantifying the "Brutus" place.

These considerations indicate that the logic of modifiers does not select between the incorporation account and the independent conjunct account.

5.7.4 Semantic Optionality

Davidson 1985 offers a proposal directed at finding out when we should apply the incorporation account and when, the independent conjunct account. He proposes that we "incorporate" any NP place that is necessarily filled by something in its logical form, and that we treat all others as independent conjuncts:

. . . reduce the number of places of the underlying verbal predicate to the smallest number that will yield, with appropriate singular terms, a complete sentence. But do not think you have a complete sentence until you have uncovered enough structure to validate all inferences you consider due to logical form. (232–33)

Thus, suppose we decide that every stabbing must have an agent and must be done with something, but, reflecting on cases such as 'Brutus stabbed, but he missed', we think that stabbings may lack themes. Then we must incorporate the agent and instrument case into the verb but leave the theme as a separate conjunct

Brutus stabbed Caesar with the knife =
(∃e)[Stabbing(e,Brutus,knife) & Theme(e,Caesar)],

where 'Stabbing(e,x,y)' means that e is a stabbing by x with y. This is a quite different proposal, markedly different from any natural one proposed elsewhere in the literature; its distinction between what is and is not incorporated into the verb bears no natural relation to the traditional category of thematic roles versus non-roles.[24]

It is not clear whether this proposal is correct. But reflecting on its rationale allows us to see that certain applications of the incorporation analysis must be incorrect, and that certain applications of the independent conjunct analysis must be incomplete. For example, we can now see that the incorporation analysis cannot be systematically applied to all cases of agents and themes. For consider the resulting analyses of the sentences

Brutus stabbed Caesar in the back =
(∃e)[Stabbing(e,Brutus,Caesar) & In(e,back)]

and

Brutus stabbed =
(∃e)[(∃y)Stabbing(e,Brutus,y)].

These forms illustrate that the former sentence entails the latter, and not vice versa, and they interact correctly with a wide variety of other such examples. But the latter form is wrong, because it is true only if Brutus stabbed *something*. Yet, if Brutus stabbed and missed, there is nothing that he stabbed.

Likewise, if we uniformly apply the independent conjunct analysis to all cases, we get an analysis that is incomplete. Consider these analyses:

Brutus stabbed Caesar with the knife =
(∃e)[Stabbing(e) & Agent(e,Brutus) & Theme(Caesar) & With(e,the knife)]

and

Brutus stabbed Caesar =
(∃e)[Stabbing(e) & Agent(e,Brutus) & Theme(Caesar)].

Again, the relationships are right; the former entails the latter, and not vice versa. But the latter now fails to entail that Brutus stabbed Caesar *with something*. This is not incorrect, but it has left something out of account.

5.7.5 The Dream Machine

I am not sure what the right analyses should be, but I am inclined to defend the following: (1) Davidson's proposal is correct if properly construed, and (2) when properly construed, it shows that all thematic relations should be analyzed by the independent conjunct approach.

It is well-known that what is required by the meaning of a phrase may differ from what follows necessarily from it. For example, there is a difference in meaning between

Fred is a giraffe or he isn't

and

Mary is a gorilla or she isn't,

even though the sentences, being tautologies, are logically equivalent. My point is subtler, and harder to defend. People often wish to make statements having certain (obvious) necessary consequences, where these consequences are not intended to follow from those statements when they occur within certain embeddings. In particular, a statement S may be made in describing an unreal situation, and in the real world S may require the truth of S', but S' is not intended to apply to the unreal situation. In such a case, S' follows necessarily from S, but S' should not be built into the logical form of S.

The unreal situations I appeal to are dreams, and the examples come from our attempts to accurately describe some of our dreams that are not only unreal but that in various ways verge on incoherence. In trying to describe such a dream, I may say

In a dream last night, I was stabbed, although in fact nobody had stabbed me, and I wasn't stabbed with anything.

I do *not* mean this to be a report that, according to the dream, I *had* been stabbed by somebody, but that the stabbing had taken place earlier than the events in the dream, and so I did not actually experience (in the dream) the stabbing. Such a report raises no interesting issues at all. I mean this to be a report of an incoherent dream, one in which, say, I am bewildered by the fact that I have been stabbed but not by anyone or anything. Such testimony should *not* be analyzed as containing an explicit contradiction, as in

I was stabbed, but not by anybody =
(∃e)[e is a stabbing of me by somebody & e was not by anybody].

In my report I use an "agentless passive," a construction in which the agent role is unoccupied. Any analysis that attempts to analyze this example by existentially quantifying an agent role will be wrong; it will attribute to me what I do not intend. I have not said anything from which it should be inferred that in the dream I was stabbed by somebody. My dream may have been incoherent, but I am not, and what I am saying should not contain a self-contradictory logical form.

The independent conjunct account of thematic roles can handle such examples perfectly. The missing NPs are genuinely missing. The incompleteness of the account is not a defect, for what is missing is not part of the meaning of what is said. It may be true that in the real world you can't stab someone without stabbing him or her with something, and this may be a truth known to users of the language. This explains why we infer an instrument when told of a stabbing. That is,

(e)[Stabbing(e) → (∃x)With(e,x)]

is a known truth—perhaps even a necessary truth—about real stabbings. But this should not be automatically built into the logical forms of sentences containing the verb 'stab'.

I propose this without having a general criterion of how we apportion truths into those due to the meanings of words and those due to knowledge of the world. There may be some arbitrariness here, in which case the account I propose is only one of many. But it seems to work correctly, and I don't know of others that do as well.

In summary, I propose to qualify Davidson's test so that it is clearly understood as saying only that the incorporation analysis should be applied to all NP roles that are required to be filled by the meaning of the verb. This test leads us to conclude that the incorporation analysis should not be applied to any such roles at all, a judgment resulting from reflection on descriptions of unreal situations.[25]

5.8   Cross-Verbal Thematic Roles

In this section I take for granted that, in simple sentences, NP positions not marked by prepositions (that is, positions such as subject, direct object, indirect object) are categorizable in terms of thematic roles such as Agent, Benefactive, Theme, and so on. There are two ways in which this might be implemented in logical form. One way is to represent the roles by relational predicates that appear as separate conjuncts. An example is the by now familiar:

Brutus stabbed Caesar =
(∃e)[Stabbing(e) & Agent(e,Brutus) & Theme(e,Caesar)].

Another way is in terms of the incorporation analysis *coupled with a system of classification by roles*. That is, we might retain the analysis

Brutus stabbed Caesar =
(∃e)[Stabbing(e,Brutus,Caesar)],

but add to it that the places occupied by names for Brutus and Caesar attribute to each of them a special relation to the event in question. The supplementary principle tells us that the second place of the stabbing relation identifies the Agent of a stabbing, and that the third place of the stabbing relation identifies its Theme:

$(\exists x)(\exists y)\text{Stabbing}(e,x,y) \rightarrow$

$[\text{Agent}(e,z) \equiv (\exists y)\text{Stabbing}(e,z,y)]$ &

$[\text{Theme}(e,z) \equiv (\exists x)\text{Stabbing}(e,x,z)].$

This policy attributes to 'Brutus stabbed Caesar' a different logical form than the one used in the independent conjunct analysis, but it still classifies the participants of the event in terms of their thematic relations to it.

There are two reasons for wanting to use thematic roles in one or the other of these ways. First, it offers a convenient (though perhaps dispensable) way to summarize the principles used to determine which NP places can end up as subject, direct object, and so on. If this is the *only* use of thematic roles, then they may be of little significance. On the other hand, the roles might also be seen as providing a cross-verbal comparison of relations between events and their participants. This is Issue 2 from the last section.

The point at issue is whether a relation, such as Agent, is the same relation when used with different verbs, or whether its significance changes with the verb. That is, having
analyzed the following sentences in these terms

Brutus stabbed Caesar =

$(\exists e)[\text{Stabbing}(e)$ & $\text{Agent}_S(e,\text{Brutus})$ & $\text{Theme}_S(e,\text{Caesar})].$

Brutus kissed Caesar =

$(\exists e)[\text{Kissing}(e)$ & $\text{Agent}_K(e,\text{Brutus})$ & $\text{Theme}_K(e,\text{Caesar})].$

can we assume that Agent_S stands for the same relation as Agent_K, and that Theme_S stands for the same relation as Theme_K? All of the previous exposition has been carried out as if these relations were the same, but it is worth considering what the theory would be like if we assume they are different.[26] I call the option according to which the roles can differ when used with different verbs the "Relative Role" option; I call the other the "Regular Role" option.

5.8.1 Cases in which No Evidence is to be Found

In many applications the two approaches are equivalent. Here are two such cases to consider. The first involves comparison of sentences in which the same verb is used. The group of sentences used in the last section will do as an illustration

a   Brutus stabbed Caesar violently in the back.
b   Brutus stabbed Caesar violently.
c   Brutus stabbed Caesar in the back.
d   Brutus stabbed Caesar.
e   Brutus stabbed violently.
f   Brutus stabbed in the back.
g   Caesar was stabbed violently.
h   Caesar was stabbed in the back.
i   Brutus stabbed.
j   Caesar was stabbed.

Each sentence in this list entails any other that is obtained from it by deleting NPs (and their associated prepositions, if any, and possibly by rearranging words). The theory of Regular Roles predicts this. But so does the theory of Relative Roles. This is because the same verb is used in every sentence, and so the relativity of role has no effect in this case. The roles can vary with the verb, but if the verb does not vary, neither do they. So both options are equivalent here.

A second case that leads us nowhere is the comparison of most unrelated simple sentences containing different verbs. An example is

Brutus stabbed Caesar =
$(\exists e)[\text{Stabbing}(e) \& \text{Agent}_S(e, \text{Brutus}) \& \text{Theme}_S(e, \text{Caesar})]$.

Brutus kissed Caesar =
$(\exists e)[\text{Kissing}(e) \& \text{Agent}_K(e, \text{Brutus}) \& \text{Theme}_K(e, \text{Caesar})]$.

These two sentences are logically independent, but this has nothing to do with whether the roles are the same or different in the two cases. The sentences have to be independent since 'Stabbing(e)' and 'Kissing(e)' are independent. We could establish a connection between the sentences only if there were a connection between kissing and stabbing, if, say, they picked out the same event.

5.8.2   Identity Conditions for Events

One thing that *is* at stake between the two options is the identity conditions for events. Suppose that these two sentences are true:

Mary wrote the check.
Mary paid the bill.

In a normal case in which the bill that Mary paid was supplied to her by the phone company, the following would *not* be true:

Mary wrote the bill.

In this case the Regular Role option makes a prediction that the Relative Role option does not. It predicts that the check writing is not identical with the bill paying. If they were the same, then on either option we should have the following:

($\exists$e)[Writing(e) & Agent$_W$(e,Mary) & Theme$_W$(e,check) & Paying(e) & Agent$_P$(e,Mary) & Theme$_P$(e,bill)].

But this, by reshuffling and omission of conjuncts, yields

($\exists$e)[Writing(e) & Agent$_W$(e,Mary) & Theme$_P$(e,bill)].

On the Regular Role analysis the subscripts are irrelevant, and this is the logical form underlying 'Mary wrote the bill', which should *not* follow from the two earlier sentences. So on the Regular Role analysis we must reject the possibility that the check writing and the bill paying are identical. Perhaps Mary paid the bill *by* writing the check, but this 'by'-relation does not connote identity of events.

On the Relative Role analysis, the nonidentity of the events is not predicted. The last form above contains subscripts that are not irrelevant. Since they differ, it is a well-formed piece of logical symbolism that is not the logical form of any sentence of English. It is certainly not the logical form assigned to 'Mary wrote the bill', since it contains a subscript 'P' where a subscript 'W' is required. It uses a role appropriate to the verb 'pay' instead of a role appropriate to 'write'.

We have found a difference between the analyses, but what does it tell us about them? If we were sure that the events were the same, it would refute the Regular Role analysis. If we were sure they were different it would be evidence (though not conclusive evidence) for the Regular Role analysis, since that analysis would be making an interesting and correct prediction that the Relative Role analysis fails to make. It is difficult to address this issue in a definitive way. Here are two considerations:

'By'-Phrases   We might try arguing that we have independent means of showing that the bill paying is different from the check writing. After all, Mary paid the bill *by* writing the check, she did not write the check *by* paying the bill. But they would be equivalent if the bill paying and the check writing were identical. Unfortunately, this argument is a little too cavalier. The form of the argument is

Mary paid the bill by writing the check.
The bill paying = the check writing.
∴ Mary wrote the check by paying the bill.

The argument involves, among other things, interchanging phrases in a 'by'-context when the things interchanged resemble descriptions of the same event. But it is not clear that 'by' governs descriptions of events in these contexts. This use of 'by' is a difficult one to analyze. It does not seem to be an ordinary preposition, taking ordinary NPs as objects. For example, we do not say things like:

*Mary paid the bill by the writing of the check.

If we did, the above reasoning might hold. But if we do not, we are left with the other idiom, 'by writing the check', and it is not clear what its logical form might be.

The reasoning would clearly be bad if 'by' created nonextensional contexts. But it is hard to find evidence for or against this. Suppose, for example, that Mary delighted the populace by killing the dictator. Suppose also that the dictator happened to be the butcher. Does it follow then that she delighted the populace by killing the butcher? I suspect that it does follow, and that this is indirect evidence that 'by' does not create nonextensional contexts. But the data are not clear, and even assuming that the inference is good we have not established the interchangeability of 'by writing the check' and 'by paying the bill', since further assumptions are needed about what the logical form is. I suspect that 'by' stands for a relation between two events, the one in the main clause and the one in its "object," and that the argument above proves that the bill paying is not the check writing, but I do not see how to establish this in a convincing way.

Modifiers I suspect that we can get better evidence for the nonidentity of the events in question by appeal to more ordinary modifiers. In particular, the following is true:

Mary paid the bill with a check,

and it is false that

Mary wrote the check with a check.

But if the bill paying is identical with the check writing, then the truth of the first sentence yields the truth of the second on either analysis— since modifiers are regular on either account. So we may be able to conclude that the check writing is not identical with the bill paying. If so, the Regular Roles analysis is saved from counterexample, and it may even be preferable for yielding a correct result (the nonidentity of the two events) from simple examples.

The issue is more complex than this in many ways. For example, 'pay the bill' may be a causative construction, which I discuss in the next chapter. And the discussion above uses phrases like 'the writing of the check' in crucial ways that explicitly refer to events. I discuss them in chapter 7. I return to the issue of identity and nonidentity of events in chapter 8. My discussion here does not yield a conclusive choice between Relative Roles and Regular Roles. I take for granted the Regular Role account throughout most of this book (excepting chapter 8), though I think that little depends on it.

Chapter 6
Causatives and Inchoatives

6.1 Introduction

Certain English word pairs or triples relate their words both logically and etymologically in interesting ways. A standard pattern of transitive verb—intransitive verb—adjective is illustrated in

Transitive Verb	Mary closes the door.
Intransitive Verb	The door closes.
Adjective	The door is closed.
Transitive Verb	Mary melts the wax.
Intransitive Verb	The wax melts.
Adjective	The wax is molten.

Some other triples of this form are

Trans.	Intrans.	Adjective	Sample Transitive Use
fell	fall	fallen	"fell the tree"
cool	cool	cool	"cool the soup"
break	break	broken	"break the window"
burn	burn	burnt	"burn the wood"
close	close	closed	"close the door"
harden	harden	hard	"harden the metal"
awaken	awaken	awake	"awaken the child"
fill	fill	full	"fill the tank"
melt	melt	molten	"melt the wax"
alert	—	alert	"alert the burglar"
solidify	solidify	solid	"solidify the emulsion"
brighten	brighten	bright	"brighten the color"
redden	redden	red	"redden the solution"
lighten	lighten?	light	"lighten the load"
randomize	—	random	"randomize the digits"
dirty	—	dirty	"dirty the rug"

empty	empty?	empty	"empty the ashtray"
fatten	—	fat	"fatten the cattle"
wet	—	wet	"wet the towel"
set	sit	—	"set the ax (on the rug)"
seat	sit	seated	"seat the couple"
run	run	—	"run the machine"
walk	walk	—	"walk the dog"
sink	sink	sunken	"sink the Bismarck"
fly	fly	—	"fly the kite"

(Dashes indicate absence of the form in question; question marks indicate doubt. This is merely a sample; there are hundreds of such cases in the language.)

The transitive verbs in these triples are usually called "causatives" because the transitive form of the verb has roughly the meaning of 'cause to V', where "V" is the intransitive form. To break the window is to cause the window to break; to cool the soup is to cause the soup to cool; to close the door is to cause the door to close, and so on.

Whatever the meaning of 'cause', we know that the transitive form entails the intransitive: if Mary closes the door then the door closes, if she fells the tree then the tree falls. It is also important in analyzing the logic of these examples that the intransitive alone not imply any form of the transitive. If the door closes, that does not entail that anyone or anything closes it; if the soup cools, then we may not infer that anyone or anything cools it, and so on.

When the intransitive forms are related to an adjective, they are called "inchoatives." An inchoative verb has the meaning of 'become Adj', where 'Adj' is the related adjective. For the door to close is for it to become closed, in the adjectival sense of 'closed'; for the clay to harden is for it to become hard; for the wax to melt is for it to become molten. Some care is needed in distinguishing the adjectival forms, since many of them are identical with the past participle forms of the verbs. In the case of 'open' there is a clear difference, and there is no danger of confusing

an open door   (a door that is not closed)

with

an opened door   (a door that has been opened).

But with 'closed', both forms are spelled alike:

a closed door,

and so the construction is ambiguous; in its adjectival reading it pertains to a door that is not now open, and in its past participle form it pertains to a door that has previously been closed. The former reading would apply to a door that was created in a closed position and never moved; the latter would be false of such a door. It is important to keep these two straight. An inchoative intransitive verb means 'become X' where 'X' is the adjective, not the past participle.

In order to get the logic right, we must remember that the adjective form need not imply any version of either verb form; an open door might be a door that has never opened, and never been opened by anyone or anything. But the truth of the intransitive form entails the truth of the adjectival form at the same or a later date: if the door closes at t, then at t (or right after) the door must be closed, and if the wax melts, then at that time (or just after) the wax must be molten.

This chapter deals with the proper analysis of causatives and inchoatives in terms of events and states.

6.2   Causatives in the Generative Semantics Tradition

One account of causatives and inchoatives stems from the early Generative Semantics tradition, especially from the work of Lakoff and McCawley.[1] This account would attribute to the sentence 'Mary closes the door' a "deep structure" something like

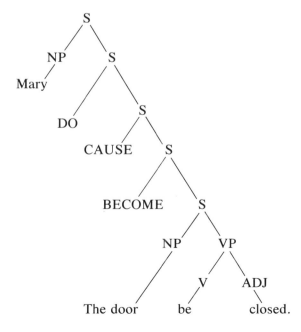

In Generative Semantics this deep structure was actually treated as a form from which the *syntax* of the sentence 'Mary closed the door' should be derived; the semantics of the sentence was also supposed to be pictured in the deep structure displayed. There were many objections to this account on syntactic grounds, and the general framework has been rejected by most linguists for syntactic reasons. But the semantical analysis implicit in the proposal can be considered independently of the framework within which it was first proposed; it is that 'Mary closes the door' somehow has these ingredients:

Mary DO CAUSE BECOME the door be closed.

In a sense the theory of underlying events already has one of these additional ingredients: the role of the DO may be captured by the deep case relation of Agent. That is, if 'Mary' ends up in logical form in the context 'Agent(e,Mary)' then the semantical import of the DO may have been taken care of. This leaves the other ingredients to consider.

David Dowty (1979) gives an analysis of causative and inchoative structures within the symbolism of Montague Grammar. Simplifying his notation somewhat, his form for 'Mary closes the door' is

$(\exists P)[(P(Mary))CAUSE(BECOME(The\ door\ is\ closed))]$,

where CAUSE stands for a relation between the two propositions

P(Mary)   and   BECOME(The door is closed),

and where BECOME maps the proposition that the door is closed to another proposition: the proposition that the door becomes closed. The whole analysis is supposed to be read as

Mary does something that causes the door to become closed.

The proposed reading of Dowty's analysis seems to me on the right track, and his particular proposal is the best way of capturing this intuitive reading in the framework he had at his disposal. But the analysis should be improved upon. For one thing, nothing in the proposed analysis itself captures the idea that Mary *did something,* as opposed to, say, that Mary *had a property.* Further, the CAUSE in Dowty's analysis does not link what Mary did with the becoming closed of the door; rather, it links the proposition that she did it with the becoming closed of the door. Likewise, the idea that what is caused is a proposition, as required in the symbolization, instead of an event, seems counterintuitive.[2]

According to Dowty's analysis, the notions DO, CAUSE, and BE-COME all take scope over whole sentences. If this were true it would be evidence for a bisentential analysis of causatives and against a bievent analysis. But there is little evidence for these notions having scope; they do not create opacity, and they do not interact with other scope bearing items such as quantifiers. There is no evidence that 'Mary breaks every window' is ambiguous between

For every window w, (∃P)[(P(Mary))CAUSE(w breaks)]

and

(∃P)[(P(Mary))CAUSE(For every window, w, w breaks)].[3]

6.3   An Analysis of Causatives in Terms of Events

I take over the idea behind the proposed analysis from the Generative Semanticists and Dowty. The guiding idea is that

Mary flew the kite

means

Mary did something that caused a flying of the kite.

Within the underlying events framework, this form contains quantifications over two events: what Mary did, and what the kite did. The general form of analysis is as follows: If TV is a causative transitive verb derived from an intransitive verb IV, then the translation of 'x TV y' is

(∃e)[Agent(x,e) & Cul(e) & (∃e′)[IVing(e′) & Cul(e′) & X(e′,y) & CAUSE(e,e′)]],

where 'X' is the thematic relation specified by the intransitive verb IV as its normal subject.

The translation of 'Mary fly the kite' will then be

(∃e)[Agent(e,Mary) & Cul(e) & (∃e′)[Flying(e′) & Cul(e′) & Theme(e′,kite) & CAUSE(e,e′)]],

where 'Flying(e′)' means 'e′ is a flying'. This 'flying' is formed from the intransitive verb 'fly', not from the transitive verb 'fly', so it refers to the kind of thing the kite does, not to the kind of thing Mary does in flying it.

This analysis yields the right logical relations between the transitive and intransitive forms; the logical form given above entails the logical form of the sentence 'The kite flies':

(∃e′)[Flying(e′) & Cul(e′) & Theme(e′,kite)].

(And this, in turn, does not entail that anyone flies the kite.)

'Walk the dog' is different from 'fly the kite' in terms of its thematic relations. In causatives, the syntactical direct object of the causative transitive verb corresponds to the syntactical surface subject of the underlying intransitive. This means that the dog will be an Agent-Theme in 'walk the dog', but the kite will be the Theme in 'fly the kite'. This is an automatic consequence of the analysis and is essential if the transitive form is to entail the intransitive form.

The rule above needs to be supplemented to allow for modifiers in the sentence. Syntactically, causative transitive verbs seem to allow the same modifiers in their sentences as other transitive verbs. But in logical form these modifiers may go with either of the underlying events, within certain general guidelines. Consider the argument

Agatha is over the lake.
So, Agatha is flying her kite over the lake.

The conclusion seems ambiguous: the argument is valid on one reading and invalid on the other. The proposed explanation is that, on the interpretation that validates the argument, the modifier 'over the lake' applies to the causing event, to what Agatha is doing. On the other interpretation it applies to the caused event, to what the kite is doing.

One rule of thumb is that instrumentals always seem to go with the causing event; 'Samantha walked the chimpanzee with a cane' cannot mean that the chimpanzee walked with a cane. Also, adverbials of direction and motion always modify the caused event, not the causing one.

Since a causative sentence contains reference to two events, the question arises of how the complex form is related to time. Does such a sentence become true when the causing event occurs or when the caused event occurs? Or is there some third alternative? Most speakers treat causatives in such a way that for a past tense sentence to be true, both events must culminate in the past, and for a future tense sentence to be true, both must culminate in the future. So a past tense causative is not true until the caused event culminates, and a future tense causative is no longer true after the causing event culminates. Present tense causatives are almost impossible to use reportively unless the causing and caused events are very close together in time. Further, if the causative contains a temporal adverbial specifying an interval of time, the sentence is not true unless both events culminate in the interval, no matter the tense. 'Yesterday, Mary exploded the bomb' is not true unless both what Mary did to explode the bomb, and the exploding itself, occurred yesterday.

Actually, the "data" are less clear in these cases than I have indicated. Some speakers simply identify the culmination time of the causative with that of the causing event, and others identify it with the caused event, and still others sense an ambiguity between these two options. Any of these policies can be adapted into the framework; I accept the commonest interpretation.[4]

6.3.1 Variants

Within the Generative Semantics framework a popular view was that some triads of words with unrelated spellings also have the semantics of causatives and inchoatives. The most famous case is

kill   die   dead

It was proposed that 'die' is to be analyzed as 'become dead', and 'kill' is to be analyzed as 'cause to become dead'. The lack of similarity of 'kill' to 'die' and 'dead' is misleading, since this triad originates from another that contained related spelling. Old English had a causative pair related as in "kill-die," but it was not etymologically related to 'dead', but to 'kill'. The spelling was

cwell—kill
cwel—die

The latter term 'cwel' was eventually replaced by the Scandinavian term 'die', thus destroying the etymological connection between our terms for dying and causing to die, but preserving that meaning.[5]

As Dowty points out, the idea that 'kill'-'die'-'dead' might form a causative-inchoative triad gets additional support from the fact that there seems to be no English causative of the form 'deaden' with the meaning of 'cause to become dead', in spite of the fact that adjectives form causative transitives quite freely in a regular manner. There is a general principle, called "blocking," which holds that regular patterns of word-formation in English are blocked if there already exists in the language a common word with the meaning of the word that would be generated by the pattern. Thus, since 'kill', already in the language, means 'cause to become dead', this "blocks" the formation of 'deaden' with that meaning.[6]

It is difficult to find any other examples of "apparent" causatives or inchoatives in English, that is, of examples with dissimilar surface forms.[7]

6.4 Objections to the Analysis of Causatives

The idea behind the above analysis has been around for a long time, and there are a number of objections to it in the literature that depend on its origin within the particular details of the framework of Generative Semantics. Instead of discussing them, I focus on what I take to be common to all such analyses—the idea that to break a window is to cause it to break, to close a door is to cause it to close, and so on. There are five objections to such analyses. The first is that 'cause' is the wrong term to use in the analysis. The second is that the analysis gets the times of the events wrong. The third is that tenses and temporal modifiers work incorrectly. The fourth is that 'by'-phrases work incorrectly. And the fifth is that some verbs of causative form are not causatives at all.

Objection 1: 'CAUSE' cannot mean 'cause'; indirect causation and control. If 'CAUSE' means the same as the English word 'cause' then there are apparent counterexamples to the analysis, because the English word 'cause' applies in cases of "indirect causation," whereas causatives do not seem to work in this way. Suppose I hire someone to intimidate a shop-owner, and that person throws a brick through the shop-owner's window. Then I seem to have caused the breaking of the window, but I did not break it. This particular objection is not overly persuasive, because in the case described it is not obvious that I did cause the breaking—perhaps I just motivated somebody else to do it. The causing gets more plausible in the other cases. If I hold a person's arms and force him to gesture in such a way that a brick from his hand goes through the window, then it is clearer that I caused the window to break. But now we may be able to say that I broke the window (by making the person's arms move in such a way that . . .). Reactions to examples of these sorts tend to fall into two classes:

Reaction 1: "The counterexamples all fail, since the causatives are indeed synonymous with their paraphrases with 'cause'."

In defense of this reaction, I suggest that finding some way to understand 'break the window' that on *some* occasion differs from *some* way of understanding 'cause the window to break' presents no difficulty for the analysis. After all, we are dealing with vague terms, and there is leeway in their interpretation. It is easy to construct situations in which we vacillate over whether the agent broke the window; yet we do not want to conclude that 'break the window' is not synonymous with 'break the window'. The question is whether, for any applicable use of 'break the window' there is a corresponding use of 'cause the window to break' that works the same. If so, the paraphrase is a good one, and an analysis that depends on it, getting all the other details right, may be correct.

Reaction 2: "The defense of the proposal sketched in (1) is not plausible. There are clear cases in which causative constructions and their paraphrases with 'cause' diverge, because the paraphrases truly apply to situations in which the causal path is indirect, while causatives truly describe only situations in which the causal path is direct."

This appears to be the most popular reaction to examples of the sort discussed. Dowty (1979, 98) says, "It is now widely assumed that there are at least two kinds of causation evidenced systematically in natural languages, direct (or *manipulative*) causation and indirect (or *directive*) causation." The implication is that the former is the meaning that is needed for CAUSE in analyzing causatives, and that the English word 'cause' encompasses both kinds. The consequence is that CAUSE does indeed differ in meaning from 'cause', since the former means something like 'directly cause and control'. Both 'CAUSE' and 'cause' are generally thought to stand in need of further analysis, but I shall not attempt it here.

I remain neutral between these two "reactions," using 'CAUSE' without commitment as to whether it is synonymous with the ordinary English word 'cause'. Fortunately, the exact analysis of the notion is not needed to account for the major logical characteristic of causatives—that, for example, if Mary cools the soup then the soup cools. That inference is guaranteed by the forms of the sentences; it does not depend on the content of the term 'CAUSE' at all.

Objection 2: 'CAUSE' cannot mean 'cause'; lack of interchangeability. This attack comes from examples such as the following from Barbara Partee, quoted in Dowty 1979:

1a A change in molecular structure caused the window to break.

1b A change in molecular structure broke the window.

2a The low air pressure caused the water to boil.

2b The low air pressure boiled the water.

3a   The angle at which the door was mounted caused it to open
     whenever it wasn't latched.

3b   The angle at which the door was mounted opened it whenever it
     wasn't latched.

Partee notes (correctly, I think) that some people will feel that the (a)
and (b) examples are accurate paraphrases of one another. But more
will find them divergent, thinking that the (b) examples are typically
false when the (a) examples are true.

   None of these examples is directly relevant to the present analysis,
since they all involve nonagentive subjects. I believe that these sentences have quite different logical forms from the ones discussed
above. When we say that Mary broke the window, and then that the
explosion broke the window, we are saying quite different things. Mary
breaks the window by *doing something* that causes the window to
break, whereas the explosion itself breaks the window—it isn't something that the explosion *does* that breaks the window. The constructions in which an event itself appears as subject with a causative verb
will be analyzed in chapter 7.

   Examples (2) and (3) seem to show that the English 'cause' applies
to situations in which a *state* is a causal factor in a causing situation,
whereas causatives are (probably) not correctly used in such situations. If so, then 'CAUSE' has a narrower range than 'cause', but this
does not speak to the question of whether these notions coincide in
cases where events are concerned.

Objection 3: Tenses work incorrectly. Jerry Fodor (1970) gives "Three
Reasons for Not Deriving 'Kill' from 'Cause to Die'." Two apply to
standard causatives, and so Fodor also argues against deriving 'Floyd
melted the glass' from 'Floyd caused the glass to melt'.[8] Although the
theory sketched above does not "derive" the former sentence from
the latter (syntactically), it links them closely in meaning, and it is
worth considering whether Fodor's arguments raise difficulties for it.

   Fodor's first argument is that although one can say,

17   Floyd caused the glass to melt on Sunday by heating it on
     Saturday,

the following "derivation" from it is ungrammatical:

18   *Floyd melted the glass on Sunday by heating it on Saturday.

One of the simplest ways to incorporate this idea into a framework with underlying events is to suppose that adjectives pick out kinds of states. The door's becoming closed is the coming-to-be of a state of the door's being closed. I use 'BECOME' to stand for this relation between an event and its "target" state. Then 'x closes' is analyzed as follows:

'x closes' = ($\exists$e)[Cul(e) & Theme(e,x) & ($\exists$s)[Being-closed(s) & Theme(s,x) & Hold(s) & BECOME(e,s)]].

A few additional facts hold of the BECOME relation. One is that the Theme of its event is the same as the Theme of its target state:

BECOME(e,s) $\rightarrow$ [Theme(e,x) $\equiv$ Theme(s,x)].

With this assumption, either of the Themes in the analysis given above could be dropped. A second assumption about becoming is that the target state of a becoming does not hold prior to the becoming itself. Introducing times into the notation (temporarily) to clarify this point, the assumption is[11]

BECOME(e,s) & Cul(e,t) $\rightarrow$
Hold(s,t) & $\neg$ ($\exists$t')[t'<t & Hold(s,t')].

With these assumptions, the analysis could be simplified to

'x closes' = ($\exists$e)[Cul(e) & Theme(e,x) & ($\exists$s)[Being-closed(s) & BECOME(e,s)]].

Alternatively, the assumptions could be built into the analysis:

'x closes' = ($\exists$e)[Cul(e) & Theme(e,x) & ($\exists$s)[Being-closed(s) & Theme(s,x) & Hold(s) & $\neg$PAST(Hold(s)) & BECOME(e,s)]].

With this version, it is not even clear that BECOME is needed anymore. This bears thinking about.

The best version of the theory may not hold that adjectives pick out kinds of states but that they are simple predicates of individuals. In such a version BECOME should probably be a predicate operator, mapping a predicate of individuals to a predicate of events. BE-COME(Red) would pick out those events that result in things becoming red. The analysis of Inchoatives on this version would look like

'x closes' = ($\exists$e)[Cul(e) & Theme(e,x) & BECOME(Closed)(e)].

One additional variant is that in the case of certain inchoatives such as 'redden', the theme does not become red but instead becomes redder. The theme *may or may not* start out being red. This variant is consistent with the analysis given so far; it merely requires the further assumption that the state that the theme comes to be in is redder than any state it was in previously. Something like the following is required:[12]

BECOME(e,s) & Cul(e,t) → Hold(s,t) & (s')(t')[t' is just before t & Hold(s',t') → Redder(e,e')].

6.7   Causative-Inchoatives

Causative-Inchoatives are transitive verbs that are derived from a related adjective with the "cause to become ADJ" meaning. There may or may not be an inchoative intransitive verb "between" the adjective and the transitive verb. We have

fell, fall, fallen

but

randomize, -----, random.

In either case we can express the meaning of the transitive verb by combining the analyses of the causative and the inchoative discussed above:

x closes the door =

(∃e)[Cul(e) & Agent(e,x) & (∃e')[Cul(e') & Theme(e',door) & CAUSE(e,e') & (∃s)[Being-closed(s) & Theme(s,door) & Hold(s) & BECOME(e',s)]]].

As with individual causatives and inchoatives, the extra underlying events and states are subject to modification by modifiers in the sentence.[13]

6.8   Modifiers of Events and Modifiers of States

By the time we have three underlying eventualities in sentences it is no surprise that there is a variety of things for modifiers to modify. All my remarks about modifiers in causatives hold for causative-inchoatives as well, but the presence of underlying states offers new possibilities.[14] In particular, the states may be modified. This is clearly indicated in the following example that mixes the 'with' of "adornment" with the instrumental 'with':

We loaded the wagon with hay with pitchforks.

'With pitchforks' modifies the cause, and 'with hay' modifies the caused state. (The sentence entails that the wagon ends up in the state: loaded with hay. It does not end up in the state: loaded with pitch-forks.[15]) This shows that both are sometimes modified. In case the modifier is simple, the typical indication of state modification as opposed to event modification is the appearance of the modifier as an adjective instead of an adverb. An example is 'x closed the door tight', in which 'tight' indicates the type of final state in question. These adjectives appear as additional conjuncts on the state variables:

x closes the door tight =

$(\exists e)[Cul(e) \ \& \ Agent(e,x) \ \& \ (\exists e')[Cul(e') \ \& \ Theme(e',door) \ \&$
$CAUSE(e,e') \ \& \ (\exists s)[Being\text{-}closed(s) \ \& \ Theme(s,door) \ \& \ Hold(s) \ \&$
$BECOME(e',s) \ \& \ Being\text{-}tight(s)]]].$

In paraphrase,

x CAUSES the door to BECOME tightly closed (or "closed tight").

Other examples are 'chop the onions fine', 'fatten the pigs good and round', 'sink them deep under the sea', 'burn it black'.[16]

As noted above, instrumentals modify the causing event, not the caused state. If you alert a burglar with a floodlamp, you do something with a floodlamp that causes the burglar to become alert. The burglar does not end up in the state: alert with a floodlamp.

It is a measure of the "productivity" of the causative-inchoative process that underlying adjectives bring their modifiers with them to the causative-inchoative constructions. We have seen how 'tight' in 'tightly closed' surfaces in the above example.[17] 'Partway' does this as well. Just as we can refer to a door as 'partway closed' we can say 'x closed the door partway'. The difference is that 'partway' modifies the adjective 'closed' in a different way than does 'tightly'. 'Partway' is a "non-standard" modifier of modifiers; if something is partway closed, it does not follow that that thing is closed, as it does if it is tightly closed. 'Partway' is syntactically very special; it occurs in contexts in which other adjectives may not:

Partway up the ladder, she got stuck.
*Quick(ly) up the ladder, she got stuck.
*Quiet(ly) . . .
*At noon . . .
*With a knife . . .
*In the back . . .

Modifiers of this sort have been much studied in the literature, and the consensus seems to be that they are best modeled as predicate operators. Thus 'partway closed' is formed by applying the functor 'partway' to 'closed', yielding 'partway(closed)'. This seems correct to me and also independent of the question of whether 'closed' is a predicate of states or of individuals. The treatment of 'x closes the door partway' is

x closes the door partway =

(∃e)[Cul(e) & Agent(e,x) & (∃e′)[Cul(e′) & Theme(e′,door) & CAUSE(e,e′) & (∃s)[Being-partway(closed)(s) & Theme(s,door) & Hold(s) & BECOME(e′,s)]]].

This entails that the door ends up partway closed; it does not entail that it ends up closed. Other examples are 'wet the cloth thoroughly', 'break it completely', and 'fill it mostly with cream'.

In addition to ordinary causative-inchoatives, a special and interesting kind of construction in English is illustrated in the following examples (again, I rely on Dowty 1979):

Agatha hammered the metal flat.
Sam pulled the rope taut.
Mary ran herself silly.

Although similar in surface form to 'x closed the door tight' they do not contain causative verbs, and so they require another analysis. They are unlike ordinary causative-inchoatives in having an extra adjective stuck on the end, but they are like causative-inchoatives in having meanings involving causing and becoming. I call them "resultative tags." They are like causative-inchoatives in which we are given additional information: we are told *how* the agent caused the becoming. The difference between 'Agatha flattened the metal' and 'Agatha hammered the metal flat' is that the latter tells us how Agatha flattened the metal. These constructions may be analyzed like causative-inchoatives, with the additional information about the type of the causing event made explicit:

x hammered the metal flat =

(∃e)[Cul(e) & Agent(e,x) & Hammering(e) & Theme(e,metal) & (∃e′)[Cul(e′) & Theme(e′,metal) & CAUSE(e,e′) & (∃s)[Being-flat(s) & Theme(s,metal) & Hold(s) & BECOME(e′,s)]]].

Resultative tags are logically related to causatives that are based on the adjectival tag. It follows from the analysis given that if I hammer the metal flat then I flatten the metal, and if I shoot him dead then I kill him. These inferences seem right. Other modifiers also carry over from one to the other; if I quietly shoot him dead with a revolver then I quietly kill him with a revolver.[18]

There is another possible application of the notion of resultative tag. In section 5.4.2, I proposed principles that let us infer 'The bike will be on the lawn' from 'Mary threw the bike onto the lawn'. The principle involved an inference from an "onto" event to an "on" state having the same theme. The same phenomenon might be predicted by viewing apparent motion adverbials as tag causatives involving locative adverbials. That is, we analyze

Mary pushed the bike onto the lawn

on a par with

Mary hammered the metal flat.

It gets a form meaning "Mary did some pushing that caused the bike to become on the lawn." I haven't explored evidence that might favor this account over the one given previously.

6.8.1 Becoming Uncrated

The transitive verb 'uncrate' has a quite ordinary analysis as a causative-inchoative. To uncrate something is to cause that thing to become uncrated. Here the adjective is 'uncrated', as in "No uncrated bicycles may be carried in the cargo hold." The implication that if you uncrate something it had to start out crated is accounted for by the same implication that if you open something it has to start out closed.[19] The significance of this is that no special logical form is needed for the transitive verb 'uncrate'; in particular, it need not be analyzed in terms of negation plus the positive adjective 'crated'.[20] The thing that is special about the causative-inchoative verb 'uncrate' is that it comes from a special adjective, 'uncrated', which is composed of a prefix 'un-' and the adjective 'crated'. Assuming that adjectives are predicates of states (see chapter 10), the meaning of the adjective 'uncrated' might be elucidated by

$(x)(t)[(\exists s)[\text{Theme}(s,x) \ \& \ \text{Hold}(s,t) \ \& \ \text{uncrated}(s)] \equiv$
$\neg(\exists s')[\text{Crated}(s') \ \& \ \text{Theme}(s',x) \ \& \ \text{Hold}(s',t)]].$

I.e., a thing is in an uncrated state if and only if it is not in a crated state. (This may need to be limited to physical objects that are appropriate for crating.) An uncrated bicycle need not be a bicycle that has ever been taken from a crate.[21]

6.9   An Alternative Version of the Theory

I do not fully discuss the nature of the Progressive, 'Mary is singing', until chapter 9. I mention it here because the main theory I propose there does not fit well with the analysis of causatives and inchoatives just developed. The favored theory of the Progressive is one in which 'Cul' is replaced in the translation of a verb by 'Hold'. For example, we replace

Mary leaves:
$(\exists e)[\text{Leaving}(e) \ \& \ \text{Agent}(e, \text{Mary}) \ \& \ \text{Cul}(e)]$

by

Mary is leaving:
$(\exists e)[\text{Leaving}(e) \ \& \ \text{Agent}(e, \text{Mary}) \ \& \ \text{Hold}(e)]$.[22]

This move insures that the fact that Mary *is leaving* does not entail that Mary actually leaves, either now or in the future: she might be interrupted. However, the account of causatives and inchoatives proposed above is in danger of producing a similar consequence that, if not clearly incorrect, is at least odd. Consider the analysis of the causative-inchoative 'x closes the door':

x closes the door =

$(\exists e)[\text{Cul}(e) \ \& \ \text{Agent}(e,x) \ \& \ (\exists e')[\text{Cul}(e') \ \& \ \text{Theme}(e',\text{door}) \ \&$
$\text{CAUSE}(e,e') \ \& \ (\exists s)[\text{Being-closed}(s) \ \& \ \text{Theme}(s,\text{door}) \ \& \ \text{Hold}(s) \ \&$
$\text{BECOME}(e',s)]]]$.

If we try to capture the meaning of 'x is closing the door' by changing 'Cul' to 'Hold', the result is

x is closing the door =

$(\exists e)[\text{Hold}(e) \ \& \ \text{Agent}(e,x) \ \& \ (\exists e')[\text{Hold}(e) \ \& \ \text{Theme}(e,\text{door}) \ \&$
$\text{CAUSE}(e,e') \ \& \ (\exists s)[\text{Being-closed}(s) \ \& \ \text{Theme}(s,\text{door}) \ \& \ \text{Hold}(s) \ \&$
$\text{BECOME}(e',s)]]]$.

This, then, does not entail that x ever closes the door, which is correct. But suppose that x is closing the door and is in fact interrupted. The analysis still entails something that may be equally objectionable: it entails that *there is* an event caused by what x is doing—presumably the door's closing—and *there is* a state of the door's being closed that holds. So even though x does not succeed in closing the door, the door ends up closed.

This requires a change in the analysis of the inchoative, independently of whether it requires a change in the analysis of the causative. Suppose we change the status of BECOME (renaming it 'BECOME#') so that it is now a predicate operator; in this role it maps predicates of states to predicates of events. For example, the complex predicate

BECOME#(closed)

will be a predicate true of an event if and only if that event is "a becoming closed." This permits simple inchoatives to have simple forms: they are treated just like other intransitive verbs, except that the predicate contributed by the verb is complex. The translation of 'The door closes' will be

(∃e)[BECOME#(closed)(e) & Cul(e) & Theme(e, the door)].

As with the earlier analysis of BECOME, a meaning postulate is now required, linking the event with the target state, if there is one:

BECOME#(closed)(e) & Theme(e,x) & Cul(e) → (∃s)[Being-closed(s) & Hold(s) & Theme(s,x) & ¬PREVIOUSLY(Hold(s))].

Or we could use the original BECOME and say

BECOME#(closed)(e) & Cul(e) → (∃s)[BECOME(e,s)].

It is less clear whether a similar change is required in the analysis of causatives. If Mary is closing the door, is the door closing? Certainly we usually say 'Mary is closing the door' in a situation in which the door is actually closing, and a similar generalization holds for other causatives as well. But there might also be situations in which Mary closes the door by the use of a device that is actuated prior to the door's starting to close. There would then be a period between the initial actuation of the device and the door's beginning to close, in which it might be true to say that Mary is closing the door but the door is not yet closing. If this is so, then another analysis of causatives is needed.

For this (possible) revision we could introduce CAUSE# as a predicate operator that maps predicates of events to predicates of events. 'Agatha flies the kite' is analyzed as

Agatha flies the kite =

(∃e)[CAUSE#(Flying)(e) & Cul(e) & Agent(e, Agatha) & Theme(e, the kite)].

As with BECOME#, this will require a meaning postulate to the effect that, if an event of the type CAUSE#(Flying) actually culminates, then it causes a culminated flying event whose theme is the theme of the original event:

CAUSE#(Flying)(e) & Cul(e) → (∃e′)[Flying(e′) & Cul(e′) & (x)[Theme(e,x)) ≡ Theme(e′,x)] & CAUSE(e,e′)].

As before, causative-inchoatives are analyzed by combining the analyses of causatives and inchoatives. Modifiers are allowed in the same places as before, though we shall need something like lambda abstracts to symbolize complex predicates. Since 'onto the truck' modifies the falling of the tree in 'Agatha felled the tree onto the truck', the analysis of the whole construction will be

(∃e)[CAUSE#(λe[BECOME#(Being-fallen)(e) & Onto(e,the truck)])(e) & Cul(e) & Agent(e,Agatha) & Theme(e,the tree)],

in which CAUSE# operates on the complex predicate 'fall onto the truck':

λe[BECOME#(Being-fallen)(e) & Onto(e,the truck)].

So far as I can see, these two modifications of the theory, coupled with the indicated meaning postulates, account for the same data as the unmodified theory in the case of nonprogressive sentences.

Chapter 7
Explicit Discourse about Events

English has a wide variety of locutions that are used to refer to and to quantify over events: 'Mary's singing', 'the destruction of the city', 'the accident that occurred last night', and so on. Some simple and detailed account of how these locutions are used, and their relationships to the events they appear to be used to talk about would be gratifying. It would be even neater if this account were to link these locutions with the simple sentences of English to which they appear to be related. I have in mind relationships such as those illustrated by the following pairs (phrases referring to events are italicized):

The destruction of the city . . . ; the city was destroyed.

Mary saw Brutus stab Caesar; Mary saw *the stabbing*.

Amundsen's flight over the north pole took place in May, 1926; Amundsen flew over the north pole in May, 1926.

Mary's singing broke the glass; Mary broke the glass.

The explosion broke the window; Mary broke the window.

God's waving his hands caused the world to come into existence; God caused the world to come into existence.

In fact, a small number of principles yield a surprisingly simple and intuitively plausible explanation of these various relationships within the context of the theoretical account developed in previous chapters. No new primitives are needed; they are already present in the theory.

7.1 Basic Principles

We refer explicitly to events in much the same ways in which we refer to other sorts of entities—primarily by the use of NPs. Since we rarely dub particular events (as opposed to "courses of events," such as wars) with proper names, the NPs we use are primarily of the form Determiner + Common Noun Phrase. These NPs consist of a Determiner followed by a common noun modified by adjectives, restrictive relative clauses, and prepositional phrases, as in

Every stabbing
The destruction
An immoral killing
A loud singing
The immoral stabbing of Caesar by Brutus
The loud singing by the choir that hurt Cynthia's ears

along with a construction that will require special comment:

Brutus's immoral stabbing of Caesar.

The Determiners of these constructions are not special in any way; they work exactly as in NPs dealing with individuals, such as

Every cow
The plantation
A prehensile tail
An illegible mark
The large tail on the bull that swished back and forth

The portion of the logical form the Determiner contributes is the same in all these cases, so that, for example, the overall logical forms of

Every brown cow . . .

and

Every loud singing . . .

are, respectively

$(x)(x$ is a brown cow $\rightarrow$ . . . x . . .)

and

$(e)(e$ is a loud singing $\rightarrow$ . . . e . . .).

This reduces the topic of the semantics of these structures to two questions. How do we characterize events by means of the common noun phrases in the antecedents in these examples? And what do we say about events in the consequents? I discuss the former in this section and the next, and the latter in sections 7.3–7.6.

7.1.1 Common Nouns That Pick Out Events

The constituents of common noun phrases that characterize events include

Head common nouns: *singing*
                        destruction

Adjectives that modify the noun: *loud* singing

Prepositional phrases: singing *in the park*
                         stabbing *of Caesar by Brutus*

Relative clauses: singing *that hurt Cynthia's ears*

The common nouns that pick out events are of two general types. First, in English we systematically form *nounlike gerunds* from event verbs: 'singing' from 'sing', 'stabbing' from 'stab', 'killing' from 'kill'. As in the examples, such gerunds are often used as common nouns that are true of events; I call them '*event* gerunds'. (Gerunds also have another use, as "*propositional* gerunds," which I discuss below.) Second, English also has a wide variety of nouns derived from verbs in other ways: 'destruction' from 'destroy', 'production' from 'produce', 'arrival' from 'arrive', 'jump' (as a noun) from 'jump' (as a verb).[1] These are often called 'derived nominals'.[2] Some derived nominals have uses in which they do not pick out events; 'invention' has a variety of uses, including one in which it is true of the product of an inventing; likewise for 'production'. I use the term "*verbal event nouns*" to encompass both nominal gerunds and derived nominals in their uses as common nouns for events. Alone among common nouns that pick out events, verbal event nouns bear special relationships to other constructions in language—to the verbs from which they are derived, and to certain prepositional phrases that modify them.

I suggest that the meaning of a verbal event noun contributes to logical form *exactly the same* predicate of events as the verb from which it is derived. The formula 'Singing(e)' in the underlying logical form of 'Mary sings' is exactly the same as the formula 'Singing(e)' in the underlying form of 'Every singing . . .'. The rationale for this proposal lies in the abundance of correct consequences that flow from it within the context of the underlying event theory of language.

There are other common nouns of events. 'Accident' is related to the adjective 'accidental', and to the adverb 'accidentally'. I assume that all three of these contribute exactly the same predicates of events to their respective logical forms. Generic terms, such as 'thing', can pick out any sort of entity whatsoever, and so these can apply to events in constructions such as 'One thing that startles Cynthia . . .'. Since these constructions work the same for all kinds of entities, no special treatment is needed for their use in event talk.

7.1.2 Adjectives of Events

Adjectives that modify event nouns work the same as adjectives in other uses in language. Most of them contribute predicates that are true of the kind of thing being discussed. Most adjectives of events therefore yield predicates that are true of events. 'Loud' in 'a loud singing' is true of events that are loud. Many of these adjectives are closely related to adverbs that are derived from the adjective by adding 'ly' to the end; examples are 'quickly' from 'quick', and 'gently' from 'gentle'.[3] I propose that when an adjective has a corresponding 'ly' adverb, then the adjective and adverb contribute exactly the same predicate of events to logical form. As with event gerundives, the rationale for this proposal lies in its consequences within the theory. For example, these proposals help me account later for the near equivalence between 'Brutus's *violent* stabbing of Caesar occurred in the Senate' and 'Brutus stabbed Caesar *violently* in the Senate'.

Some uses of adjectives do not yield predicates of events. The adjective 'alleged' is not a predicate of people in

The alleged assassin escaped,

nor is it a predicate of events in

The alleged murder took place after dark.

Adjectives of this sort have been much studied in the literature, and their use in connection with events raises no new issues.[4]

7.1.3 Prepositional Phrases

I further suggest that prepositional phrases modifying event nouns contribute to logical form exactly the same predicates of events as when they modify verbs. 'With the knife' and 'in the Senate' contribute the same predicates in

A stabbing with a knife in the Senate . . .

as in

Brutus stabbed Caesar with a knife in the Senate.

As with passive sentences, 'by' often indicates the NP that would be the subject of the sentence that is related to the gerundive nominal, so that 'by Brutus' in

A stabbing by Brutus

indicates the Agent relation to Brutus of the stabbing. And 'of' is often used to indicate the Theme of the event, as in

A stabbing of Caesar.[5]

7.1.4 Relative Clauses

In English a relative clause beginning with 'which', 'who', or 'that' is just like a sentence except that it is missing one of its NPs. The relative clause in 'The book that Mary wanted him to have' has the form 'Mary wanted him to have NP', except that the NP is null. In logical form the relative clause functions as a predicate—as a lambda abstract that is produced by abstracting on a free variable that occupies the place of the "missing" NP. The logical form of the relative clause 'that Mary wanted him to have' is

λx[Mary wanted him to have x].[6]

This technique carries over without modification to event talk. In 'The loud singing that hurt Cynthia's ears' the clause 'that hurt Cynthia's ears' has the form

λe[e hurt Cynthia's ears].[7]

7.1.5 Putting it All Together

How do we combine these predicates, which the constituents of eventive common noun phrases contribute to logical forms, to produce a single predicate of events? The answer is that they are conjoined with one another.[8] So the logical form associated with

A loud singing by the choir that hurt Cynthia's ears . . . ,

whose gross form is

$(\exists e)(e$ is a loud singing by the choir that hurt Cynthia's ears &
. . . e . . .),

has the detailed form[9]

$(\exists e)(e$ is loud & e is a singing & e is by the choir & e hurt Cynthia's ears & . . . e . . .).

7.2 Nominal and Verbal Gerundives

Two interestingly different kinds of gerundive constructions in English
are sometimes called *verbal* and *nominal* gerundives. The *verbal* forms
are very tightly constrained to resemble the sentences from which they
derive. An example is

Mary's having sung the song sweetly,

which clearly bears a close relationship to

Mary has sung the song sweetly.

Verbal gerundives retain the full word order of English sentences; a
sentence may be converted into this form only by putting the subject
into the genitive and converting the initial verb into a gerund. In
addition, the sentence loses its tense in the transition to the gerundive
form.

The *nominal* gerund is so-called because it has the grammatical
structure of a noun phrase. An example is

Mary's sweet singing of the song,

which resembles in structure

Mary's neat book on the wombat.

The key mark of these constructions is the 'of' following the verb that
introduces what would be the direct object in a sentence. In nominal
gerundives, adverbs disappear and are replaced by adjectives, and
certain verbal elements may not be present; thus the following are not
grammatical:

*Mary's singing of the song sweetly
*Mary's having sung of the song.[10]

Verbal and nominal gerundives are quite distinct and mutually incompatible, except that in their simplest versions their structures coincide.
There is not enough complexity in

Mary's singing in the shower

to tell whether we have a nominal or a verbal gerundive. But because
of the clarity of the distinction in more complex cases, these simple
forms are usually thought of as ambiguous between verbal and
nominal.

What are their semantics? I agree with the traditional view that they
have two quite different uses, a "propositional" use, and an "eventive"

one. (Wik 1973 calls these "factive" versus "active".) The propositional use is illustrated by

Mary's singing the song sweetly amazed us.
I just couldn't believe her singing so sweetly!

and the eventive use is illustrated by

Mary's awkward singing of the first song took place in the dining room.

The propositional use is virtually synonymous with the use of the corresponding that-clause, adding tense from context:

Mary's singing the song sweetly amazed us =
That Mary sang the song sweetly amazed us.

I just couldn't believe her singing so sweetly! =
I just couldn't believe that she sang so sweetly!

Opacity is typical of the propositional use. If Mary's insulting the king was hard to believe, it does not follow that Mary's insulting the butcher was hard to believe, even if the king, unbeknownst to the believers, *is* the butcher. But in the eventive use there is no opacity. If Mary's insulting of the king took place in the Senate, then her insulting of the butcher must have taken place there too if the king is the butcher.

What is the relation between the two syntactic forms, the verbal and nominal gerundives, and the two semantic uses, propositional and eventive? Unfortunately, the relation is not neat. As Zeno Vendler (1967) points out, the question of whether we are dealing with a propositional or an eventive use of the gerundive has a great deal more to do with the context in which it occurs (Vendler's "container") than with the syntactic form of the gerundive itself. Although the verbal gerundive is almost always usable in contexts in which a propositional reading is natural, and the nominal gerundive is always usable in contexts in which an eventive reading is natural, the forms mix quite freely in many contexts. It would be neater for the theorist if there were a simple relation between the syntactic forms and their uses.

Derived nominals such as 'destruction' or 'arrival' can almost always replace nominal gerundives in nominal gerundive constructions when the derived nominals have readings synonymous with the nominal gerunds. Whenever I speak of nominal gerundives I intend to include constructions that are exactly like nominal gerundives except that the gerund is replaced by a derived nominal form. Even these derived forms permit propositional uses in addition to their eventive uses; we can say, for example, 'The destruction of the city surprised and saddened us', meaning 'That the city was destroyed surprised and saddened us'. Ramsey (1960) noted this fact:

The truth is that a phrase like 'the death of Caesar' can be used in two different ways; ordinarily, we use it as the description of an event, and we could say that 'the death of Caesar' and 'the murder of Caesar' were two different descriptions of the same event. But we can also use 'the death of Caesar' in a context like 'He was aware of the death of Caesar' meaning 'He was aware that Caesar had died'; here (and this is the sort of case which occurs in the discussion of cognition) we cannot regard 'the death of Caesar' as the description of an event; it if were, the whole proposition would be 'There is an event E of a certain sort such that he is aware of E', and would be still true if we substituted another description of the same event, e.g. 'the murder of Caesar'. (p. 241)[11]

Many of the constructions discussed in the preceding section have propositional as well as eventive uses—e.g., 'Each jump by the elephant amazed the audience'.

My focus on the eventive use of nominal gerundives ignores all propositional uses as well as eventive uses of verbal gerundives. I do so for three reasons. First, propositional uses of verbal gerundives are to be analyzed in much the same ways as are the that-clauses to which they are simply related. There is an enormous literature on the semantics of that-clauses. Second, propositional uses of nominal gerundives present a fascinating field of study not at all well developed, but also not my central concern. Finally, eventive uses of verbal gerundives can easily be projected from that of the corresponding nominal gerunds.[12]

This leaves an account of eventive uses of nominal gerundives to be developed. We can view nominal gerundives used eventively as special cases of the constructions discussed in section 7.1, except for the examples containing a possessive subject. For them, we need only add the provision that

Mary's sweet singing of the song

means the same as

The sweet singing of the song by Mary.[13]

We are now ready to turn to the issue of what it is we say *about* events when they are explicitly under discussion. Section 7.3 discusses

intransitive event verbs: 'The stabbing *occurred* in the Senate'. Section
7.4 examines event causatives: 'The explosion *broke* the window'.
Section 7.5 discusses event perceptions: 'Mary *saw* the explosion'.
And section 7.6 concludes the chapter with a discussion of transitive
event verbs with ordinary objects: 'The explosion *caused* the breaking
of the window'.

7.3   Intransitive Event Verbs: 'Occur', 'Happen', 'Take Place'

Some intransitive verbs take events as subjects and require no special
treatment at all. The sorts of logical forms previously given for other
verbs apply to them as well. To say that the singing lasted for three
days is on a par with saying that the king ruled for three days.

A few intransitive verbs are used in special ways with event NPs;
they include 'occur', 'happen', and 'take place'. There are several
reasons to treat these verbs differently than the verbs that occur with
NPs for individuals. One reason is that although these verbs freely
form propositional gerundives, they do not form natural event gerundives. For example, the following sentences with propositional gerundives are fairly natural:

The stabbing's occurring in the Senate amazed us.

The occurring of the stabbing in the Senate amazed us.

But these containing event gerundives are terrible:

The occurring of the destruction of the city lasted three days.

The singing's occurring {in the Senate} hurt my ears.

And this eventive is awkward, at least:

The occurring of the explosion caused the breaking of the glass.

Propositional gerundives are formed by an automatic process that
applies to any verb whatsoever, including 'occur', which is certainly
a verb. But some types of verbs, including 'occur', have a special
relation to events, and this constrains the formation of event nominals
containing them. On my account, words like 'occur' do not form event
gerunds at all, because they have different logical forms than normal
verbs such as 'stab' and 'walk'. Our (weak) tendency to treat them as
forming gerundives that appear to refer to events is explained by our
tendency to generalize syntactic forms. 'Occur' is a verb, after all,
and verbs produce those forms, so 'occur' sounds as if it should
naturally form event NPs. The forms in question make good sense

when read propositionally, but they have no clear meaning if read eventively. Those that seem to be meaningful eventively are successful only because the gerund itself is redundant. 'The occurring of the explosion broke the window', if meaningful at all, just means 'The explosion broke the window'.

Reichenbach (1947) discusses two additional reasons for treating these verbs as having special logical forms. The first has to do with what he calls "thing-splitting versus event-splitting." His idea is that facts can be analyzed alternatively as telling us something about a thing, or as telling us something about an event—and the two forms are equivalent. A natural illustration is

A flight by Amundsen over the north pole occurred ≡
Amundsen flew over the north pole.

Although the use of 'occur' without anything following it seems stylistically awkward, the first sentence makes sense and is equivalent to the second; this equivalence needs explanation. It is also clear that this is something special about 'occur'. We get the same equivalence with 'happen' and 'take place', but it is hard to think of other intransitive verbs that even make sense here, let alone ones that yield the equivalence.

I call Reichenbach's second generalization "transference"; modifiers following the verb 'occur' transfer to the event itself:

A flight by Amundsen occurred over the north pole in a light aircraft in May 1926 ≡

A flight by Amundsen over the north pole occurred in a light aircraft in May 1926 ≡

A flight by Amundsen over the north pole in a light aircraft occurred in May 1926 ≡

A flight by Amundsen over the north pole in a light aircraft in May 1926 occurred.

These are remarkable patterns and need some explanation. I suggest that 'occur' (and 'happen' and 'take place') are special in having no content of their own; they merely assert the culmination of an event identified by other means. Modifiers that follow them, on the English pattern of other verbs, are not really theirs but belong instead to the event that they are "predicated of."

The syntactic pattern of these intransitive verbs is that they combine with event variables as their subjects, and they may be followed by a string of event modifiers. The (untensed) atomic formulas formed with their use are syntactically of the form

e occur M_1 . . . M_n,

where M_1, . . . ,M_n are event modifiers, such as 'loud', 'with a knife', . . . The logical form of such a structure is much simpler than that which underlies other sentences; there is already an explicit event variable in the subject, there is no additional underlying quantification over events, and 'occur' contributes only the culmination. The logical form is

$Cul(e)$ & $\overset{\circ}{M_1}(e)$ & . . . & $\overset{\circ}{M_n}(e)$.[14]

For example, the tenseless 'e occur in 1926' has the logical form

$Cul(e)$ & $In(e,1926)$.

All of Reichenbach's principles now follow from this treatment. An equivalence that comes from both principles working jointly is

A flight by Amundsen over the north pole occurred in 1926 $\equiv$
Amundsen flew over the north pole in 1926.

The first sentence has a form that results from combining the logical form associated with the subject

A flight by Amundsen over the north pole . . . =
$(\exists e)[Flight(e)$ & $Agent(e,A)$ & $Over(e,\text{the N.P.})$ & . . . e . . .]

with that associated with the predicate

occur in 1926 = $Cul(e)$ & $In(e,1926)$.

Thus the whole form associated with 'A flight by Amundsen over the north pole occurred in 1926' is

$(\exists e)[Flight(e)$ & $Agent(e,A)$ & $Over(e,\text{the N.P.})$ & $Cul(e)$ & $In(e,1926)]$.

This is equivalent to the logical form associated with 'Amundsen flew over the north pole in 1926' by previous rules:

$(\exists e)[Flight(e)$ & $Agent(e,A)$ & $Cul(e)$ & $Over(e,\text{the N.P.})$ & $In(e,1926)]$.[15]

Quite apart from Reichenbach's equivalences, verbs like 'occur' combine with other sorts of NPs, and the account given here produces correct forms with them as well. The sentence

Every flight by Amundsen over the north pole occurred in 1926

has the gross form

(e)[e is a flight by Amundsen over the north pole → e occurred in 1926]

which, upon refinement, yields

(e)[Flight(e) & Agent(e,A) & Over(e,the N.P.) → Cul(e) & In(e,1926)].[16]

This account also explains why it is anomalous to say 'Mary occurred'. The sentence is either ill-formed in the symbolism (because 'Mary' cannot be substituted for an event variable), or, if well-formed, says that Mary culminates, which is something only an event can do.

Although the account does not allow us even to generate the awkward

The occurring of the explosion caused the breaking of the glass,

(because this contains 'occurring' used as an event nominal), the idea behind the account meshes with our feeling that this construction is not particularly bad. 'Occurring' is used here in a very restricted context in which 'The occurring of the explosion' can simply be viewed as synonymous with 'the explosion' all by itself; 'occur' does no further work in the sentence.

I assume that 'take place' and 'happen' are synonyms of 'occur', with the one difference that prepositional phrases with 'to' are used with 'happen' to indicate some notion of "being acted upon," perhaps "being the Theme of an event in which something else is the Agent or Performer." Thus 'A stabbing happened to Mary' would entail that Mary was stabbed, whereas 'A singing happened to Mary' would entail something impossible—that Mary was sung. 'A walking happened to Mary' would entail something that has no simple expression in English—that she was the theme of a walking, with some other agent. These terms have many stylistic idiosyncrasies not captured by the simple treatment given here.

7.4   Event Causatives

In treating causative constructions such as 'Mary broke the window' we appealed to an extra underlying event—the thing Mary did that resulted in the window's breaking. It is no surprise, then, that explicit event NPs can be the subjects of causatives too; in addition to 'Mary broke the window', we have 'The explosion broke the window'. These new forms are related to the constructions just discussed and to the causative constructions discussed in the previous chapter.

The logical form assigned to 'Mary broke the window' is that there is an event of which Mary is the agent and that causes a breaking of the window. Without tense, this is

(∃e)[Agent(e,M) & Cul(e) & (∃e′)[Breaking(e′) & Cul(e′) & Theme(e′,the window) & CAUSE(e,e′)]].

But what about 'The explosion broke the window'? We certainly do not want to say that the explosion is the agent of some further event that caused the breaking of the window; the explosion did this by itself. That is, in comparing the forms associated with the two constructions

x broke w
e broke w

we should find the latter one to be simpler. 'e broke the window' should be

Cul(e) & (∃e′)[Breaking(e′) & Cul(e′) & Theme(e′,the window) & CAUSE(e,e′)].

This has as an immediate consequence that, if Mary's singing broke the glass, then Mary broke the glass. (To avoid the complexities of definite descriptions I use 'A singing by Mary broke the glass'.) By combining the form associated with 'A singing by Mary'

A singing by Mary:
(∃e)[Singing(e) & Agent(e,M) & . . . e . . .]

with

e broke the glass:
Cul(e) & (∃e′)[Breaking(e′) & Cul(e′) & Theme(e′,the glass) & CAUSE(e,e′)],

we get the logical form of 'A singing by Mary broke the glass'

(∃e)[Singing(e) & Agent(e,M) & Cul(e) & (∃e′)[Breaking(e′) & Cul(e′) & Theme(e′,the glass) & CAUSE(e,e′)]].

But the symbolization of 'Mary broke the glass', using the technique from earlier chapters, is just

(∃e)[Agent(e,M) & Cul(e) & (∃e′)[Breaking(e′) & Cul(e′) & Theme(e′,the glass) & CAUSE(e,e′)]].

And the latter follows from the former, since they are identical except for the presence of a conjunct in the former that is missing from the latter. They both say that Mary did something that caused the window to break; the difference is that 'A singing by Mary broke the glass' tells what it was she did to break the glass, and 'Mary broke the glass' does not.

7.5   Event Perceptions

Previously, I gave accounts of both

Mary saw Brutus

and

Mary saw Brutus stab Caesar.

But what about

Mary saw the stabbing of Caesar by Brutus?

If Mary saw Brutus stab Caesar, then she saw the stabbing, and vice versa. This is easily accommodated by attributing to the construction

x see e

the form

$(\exists e')[\text{Seeing}(e') \ \& \ \text{Cul}(e') \ \& \ \text{Experiencer}(e',x) \ \& \ \text{Theme}(e',e)]$.

It then follows that these are automatically equivalent:

Mary saw Brutus stab Caesar $\equiv$ Mary saw a stabbing of Caesar by Brutus.

7.6   Transitive Event Verbs

In addition to verbs that take events as their subjects, some verbs take them as their direct objects. The most famous of these is the English word 'cause', an unusual word in English, and one with a special semantics. 'Cause' seems to have a meaning much like that of a causative verb. In particular, we can have both

Mary caused the breaking of the window

and

The explosion caused the breaking of the window.

Furthermore, we have the familiar pattern that if Mary's singing caused the breaking of the window then Mary caused the breaking of the window—because for Mary to cause the breaking of the window is simply for her to do something that causes the breaking of the window. As earlier, the more eventlike we get in the subject and object positions, the less we pack into the analysis of the verb. The form associated with the event-causation sentence is

e cause e′ = Cul(e) & cause(e,e′).[17]

And the form associated with individual-causation sentences is

x cause e′ = (∃e)[Agent(e,x) & Cul(e) & cause(e,e′)].

Thus, 'Mary's singing caused the breaking of the glass' has the form

cause(Mary's singing, the breaking of the glass).

On the other hand, 'Mary caused the breaking of the glass' has the form

(∃e)[Agent(e,Mary) & Cul(e) & cause(e, the breaking of the glass)].

When 'Mary's singing' is expanded in the former, it is seen to entail the latter.

These forms use the English word 'cause', not the underlying predicate 'CAUSE' used in the analysis of causatives. The relationship between

Mary caused a breaking of the window

and

Mary broke the window

is a matter of much debate. The logical forms for these two sentences differ only in that one contains 'cause' where the other contains 'CAUSE'; the question of their equivalence is thus a matter of how the English word 'cause' is related to the notion of causation used in the analysis of causatives. (See section 6.4.) Similar remarks apply to

The explosion caused a breaking of the window

and

The explosion broke the window.

A consequence of the analysis sketched here is that *the English word 'cause' cannot be modified by a verb modifier.* We do not have English sentences such as

*The explosion caused the breaking of the window gently/slowly/ with a rock/ . . .

And although we have

Mary cleverly caused the breaking of the window,

this construction forces the Sentence Modifier (or Subject-oriented) reading of 'cleverly'. In other cases, modifiers that are present belong with the subject or object, as in

The explosion caused the breaking of the window *at noon*
Mary caused the breaking of the window *with a knife*

In the latter sentence, 'with a knife' applies to the underlying event of which Mary is the agent. Likewise, the following two sentences are on a par in attributing slowness to the melting (= intransitive verb 'melt') of the glass:

The flame slowly melted the glass.

The flame slowly caused the melting of the glass.

PART II
Reflections and Refinements

Chapter 8
Metaphysical Issues

In this chapter I discuss a variety of issues from the philosophical literature on events as those issues impact my study. After summarizing the nature of events and states according to the theory under investigation, I touch on reductionistic accounts of events and questions of event identity. That discussion leads to a consideration (and rejection) of two hypotheses to the effect that all event verbs are causatives.

8.1 The Nature of Events and States

I began this investigation by making minimal assumptions about the nature of events and states, assuming that such information is more the result of investigation than a prerequisite for it. Although I have so far presented the theory only in broad outline, it clearly requires events and states of certain sorts. First of all, they are individual, as opposed to generic. There may be such a thing as generic stabbing, but the theory requires that we distinguish Brutus's stabbing of Caesar from my stabbing of my finger, for the former was violent, and the latter was not. Similarly for states; though we may speak of *the* state of being asleep, the theory does not require such a thing. The theory needs John's state of being asleep to be different from Mary's, for his was on the lawnchair, and hers was in the study. This follows from the application of the theory to the sentences 'John was asleep on the lawnchair', and 'Mary was asleep, but not on the lawnchair'. (States are discussed in chapter 10.)

Most events and states are concrete entities, not abstract ones. First, they are located in space. Since Brutus stabbed Caesar in the marketplace, the theory tells us that there was a stabbing, by Brutus, of

Caesar, and the stabbing itself was in the marketplace. Further, events are perceivable. If Mary saw Brutus stab Caesar, then, according to the theory, it was the stabbing that she saw. This should not be surprising; after all, we *do* say, "She saw the stabbing." The present theory tells us that we can take this at face value, taking a certain event to be the object of perception, where this is the very same thing that is quantified over in simple event sentences. Similar remarks apply to states as well: if Mary saw John naked, then his being naked ("his nakedness") is a state, and that is what she saw. (I anticipate discussion in chapter 10.) I do not cite these results as evidence for the theory, or even as philosophically desirable consequences. The evidence for the theory lies in its ability to explain a wide range of data better than other existing theories. The existence and nature of events and states are by-products, in the same way that the symmetry of space and time are by-products of investigations in physics.

I have had as a major goal the production of a theory that has instrumental value, as well as one that is likely to be true. These are two different goals; I adopt them both. One requirement for an instrumentally useful theory is that it be understandable by us at this moment in time. I have tried to accomplish this in part by minimizing the appeal to primitive theoretical vocabulary that I use essentially in the theory. I assume understanding of the logical notions used in the formulation of the ordinary predicate calculus with identity.[1] As for terms such as 'Running' when used as a predicate, I have assumed them to be perfectly ordinary English terms, and so already familiar to us. If I say 'Her running lasted three hours' I use 'running' as a term true of runnings; this is the meaning utilized in the predicate 'Running' that appears in the logical forms. It is debatable whether I can claim the same advantage for symbolizations of state sentences. I propose, for example, that the logical form of

Agatha is clever

is

$(\exists s)[s$ is a being-clever & Theme$(s,$Agatha$)]$.

Here I spell out the predicate as 'is a being-clever' in order to make clear that I intend a predicate that is true of states of cleverness. Instead I could perhaps write 's is a state of cleverness', which looks more like ordinary English. Ordinary or not, I assume that we understand the terminology.

I assume also that a variety of other predicates applied to events and states are terms of ordinary English. For example, in symbolizing 'Agatha sang loudly' I write

(∃e)[Singing(e) & Agent(e,Agatha) & Loud(e)].

Here I assume that 'Loud' is the English word 'loud' as it is used in constructions like 'Her singing was loud'. This assumption is plausible in the case of adjectives that have related '-ly' adverbs, but it is less certain in the case of modifiers that are prepositional phrases. For example, it is unclear whether it is good English to say 'The stabbing was with a knife'.

The principal technical terms I use are that of an event's *culminating* at a given time and that of a state's *holding* at a given time. I do not see how to avoid such terminology altogether. I also assume that it makes sense to talk of one moment of time as being *before* or *after* another; this seems safe to me, quite apart from philosophical qualms about whether there are any such things as moments of time.

So for the most part the terminology I use in the theory is familiar; this is important for the theory to be understandable. It is quite another matter whether the theory is *a priori* plausible. I have had as my goal to develop a theory that will be understood upon first reading, not one that will be believed upon first reading. If you end up believing the theory it should be as a result of surveying the evidence for it, not because it appears initially plausible. (It is clear from even a brief survey of the philosophical literature on events that many will find the theory implausible prior to considering the evidence.)

In this chapter I limit myself to the question of how the issues that arise in the philosophical literature concerning events bear on the theory under discussion. Before doing so, I wish to address in a global way the question of whether the discussion of such issues is even relevant. I think that it is, but this needs explanation. I use the term 'event', and others contributing to the philosophical literature also use that term. But why should I assume that we are all using the word in the same way? If we are not doing so, then is it possible that we are addressing different topics?

I think that this is sometimes the case and sometimes not. That we may be talking about different things is highly relevant, I think, to comparing my discussion with talk of "events" in modern physics and with any talk of "events" in connection with probability theory and inductive logic. Physical events as they are construed in contemporary physics may be a quite different sort of thing than I discuss here. I shall not pursue the question, as I am uncertain about its outcome. My impression is that the events of quantum theory, for example, are not the same sort of thing as, say, a stabbing of Caesar by Brutus, though they may be interestingly related. It is even clearer that the "events" of probability theory and inductive logic are distinct from the ones I discuss. Crudely put, the "events" of probability theory are propositions, not events. If the president is the tallest spy, then the event of the president's singing is the same event as the event of the tallest spy's singing, as 'event' is used in this theory. But the probability of the president's singing may differ considerably from the probability of the tallest spy's singing, if it is not certain (probability = 1) that the president is the tallest spy. (Recall that truth is a quite different matter from having probability = 1.) Any confusion of the one kind of "event" with the other arises from not distinguishing (what I called in chapter 7) the "propositional reading" from the "event reading" of phrases such as 'the president's singing'.

My discussion will be relevant to a fair amount of discussion of "events" in the philosophical literature. The key point to be decided is whether the word 'event' is being used there in the same or different sense as I use it here. The crucial way to decide this question is to see whether each of our discussions takes for granted that phrases such as 'Agatha's loud singing' pick out events, and whether the event picked out is automatically the same event as 'The president's loud singing' if Agatha is the president. If so, we are probably discussing the same thing; if not we may be discussing unrelated issues using the same terminology. In some cases it will be difficult to decide.

The philosophical literature on events is enormous, and a critical survey of it deserves at least a book of its own. Fortunately, while I was finishing this manuscript Jonathan Bennett's book *Events and Their Names* (1988) was published; it surveys the literature and draws many of the same conclusions I probably should draw. I refer the reader to this work for a general consideration of the terrain; I shall appeal to it in various places when it is relevant.

8.2 Reductionistic Accounts of Events and States

Many philosophers approach any discussion of events expecting first and foremost to see how the author intends to "reduce" events to something more basic. I have not addressed this concern at all; this section explains what I do not cover and why.

When one speaks of reducing entities of one kind to entities of another kind, what is really at issue is reducing a theory of entities of one kind to a theory of entities of the other kind. For reduction is a relation between theories, not between entities. Many different theories deal with events, focussing on many different aspects of them. My primary focus in this section is whether it is possible to reduce the theory I present to another that either eliminates events entirely or "constructs" them out of other things.

During the last century two different kinds of "reduction" have interested philosophers. I call them "definitional" reduction and "ontological" reduction, though these terms are only heuristic.

8.2.1 Definitional Reduction

By "definitional" reduction I understand the following. We suppose that we have available two theories, each containing its own vocabulary and principles. A definitional reduction is a set of definitions that define the nonlogical vocabulary of the reduced theory in terms of that of the reducing theory. By means of these definitions, principles of the reduced theory are then logically entailed by the principles of the reducing theory. The two most famous examples of this are the (attempted) reduction of arithmetic to logic by Frege, and the (actual) reduction of the classical thermodynamics of gases to the statistical mechanics of molecules in physics. In the former reduction, arithmetical vocabulary such as '2', '+', '<' is defined in terms of logical notions, such as 'extension', 'entails', and so on, and the laws of arithmetic are then derivable from laws of logic applied to the definitions.[2] In the latter reduction, notions such as 'temperature' and 'pressure' are defined using terms such as 'average kinetic energy', and then the classical gas laws (such as that the ratio of temperature to pressure is constant when volume remains unchanged) are seen to follow from principles of statistics together with classical laws of physics applied to molecules.

I confess that I do not know how to give a definitional reduction of the theory of events to some previously known domain of knowledge, using only terminology already present in that domain. I therefore have little to contribute here. If I were to attempt a definitional reduction, I might begin by looking at Montague's (1974) notion that events are properties of moments of time, embedded in a framework of a theory of language such as he gives in various essays. However, I haven't seen how to carry out the task. For anyone who wishes to try, I suggest that a potential stumbling block might be the treatment of perception statements, such as 'Mary heard Agatha sing', which Montague does not address. The task is a fascinating one that I have pursued with little success.

8.2.2 Ontological Reduction

In this century, philosophers have become interested in a different kind of reduction. I call it "ontological" because its most typical motivation is either to avoid commitment to there being entities of a certain sort or to show that entities of that sort are not "basic." An ontological reduction differs from a definitional one only in that the vocabulary of the reducing theory required for the reduction may not already exist; if it does not already exist, we invent completely new primitive terms for the reducing theory and we establish the definitions using them. This technique is typically employed when we already have a good understanding of the theory that is being reduced, so that we can suppose the definitions are readable backwards; we provide the meanings of the new primitive terms of the reducing theory in terms of our understanding of the terms of the reduced theory.

Ontological reduction has two different goals, and they have very different consequences when successful. I call the first "eliminative ontological reduction": its goal is to "eliminate" entities of a certain kind, i.e., to defend the claim that there are no such entities. I call the second "ontological construction," since it presupposes that there are entities of the reduced kind; it wants only to establish that some other kind of entity is more basic.

8.2.3 Eliminative Ontological Reduction

Eliminative ontological reduction is designed to show that there are no entities of a certain kind, or, at least, that apparent talk about them need not commit us to the view that there are any such entities. This imposes the requirement that the reducing theory may not quantify over entities of the suspect sort. An example of such a reduction is Ryle's (1931) attempt to explain away the apparent need to refer to fictional entities, such as Mr. Pickwick, that do not exist. He recognizes that claims such as 'Mr. Pickwick is a fictional entity' are true, and he attempts to show how we can accept this without commitment to fictional entities. His proposal goes something like this:

'Mr. Pickwick is a fictional entity' means that some author used the name 'Mr. Pickwick' in such and such a way.

The analysis is designed to rid us of commitment to fictional entities, explaining the things we say that apparently commit us to them in terms of things we may say that do not. The problem in the displayed account, of course, is the terminology 'such and such a way'. The proposer of such accounts often does not feel it important to explain what the "way" in question is, preferring instead to establish only the *theoretical possibility* of filling in the information. Once this theoretical possibility is granted, we are to see that commitment to fictional entities is theoretically avoidable.[3] Our feeling perfectly at home using phrases such as 'Mr. Pickwick is a fictional entity' is supposed to give us sufficient understanding of the missing theoretical terminology that, if spelled out, would specify the "such and such a way." The point of the "reduction" is to show that we may consistently maintain that there are no fictional entities while also letting us grant that Mr. Pickwick is a fictional entity.

I am unaware of how eliminative ontological reduction could be carried out for my account of events and states. Here is a stumbling block for any such attempt. If a witness says, "I saw three stabbings during the riot," this statement may be true. Any eliminative reduction will have to "analyze" it in such a way that the analysis does not commit us to stabbings. I have already alluded to difficulties with certain natural ways of providing such an account. For example, it will not work to analyze 'I saw three stabbings' as 'Three times I saw someone stabbed' because the stabbings might have been simultaneous, and also because the phrase 'see someone stabbed' remains unanalyzed. I am dubious about any possibility of eliminative reduction of events.

8.2.4 Ontological Construction
A second goal of ontological reduction is showing that, although there are entities of a certain kind, they are not "basic," and they may be "constructed" out of other entities. For this type of reduction, the reducing theory may quantify over nonbasic entities, but they must all be "constructable" out of basic ones. This enterprise may be pursued for a wide variety of purposes. One is the purely abstract one of wanting to establish an ontological hierarchy, with each thing having its own place in the hierarchy. Another is to use the construction of

the reduced entities to clarify a claim about the "identity conditions" of entities of that kind.

Suppose we want to establish that, although there are ordinary physical objects such as people, airplanes, trees, and the like, these things are not basic. Atoms and molecules are basic. Nonbasic things are *sets* of basic things. For example, I am actually the set of molecules that make up my body, my automobile is the set of molecules comprising it, and so on. Thus ordinary things are "reduced to" or "constructed out of" basic things.

This raises a problem. On the most popular version of this account, sets are abstract entities, and so they cannot be perceived. Now suppose that Mary sees a truck. Since a truck is a set, she apparently sees a set, which is impossible. Doesn't this refute the theory? No, it merely requires more details. An additional part of the reduction needs to define notions such as "seeing" in theoretical terms. That is, we need definitions of terms such as 'see', which apparently relate perceivable objects, in terms of relations between sets of molecules. Suppose we define 'x sees y' in the following way:

x sees y $=_{df}$ the set of molecules to which x is reduced sees$_2$ the set of molecules to which y is reduced.

'Sees', a relation between perceivable things, is thereby reduced to 'sees$_2$', a relation between sets, which solves the problem noted above. However, we have now introduced a new term 'sees$_2$' without definition or explanation. Our choice of terminology may conceal the sleight-of-hand: except for the subscript, 'sees$_2$' looks like a term we understand. But the spelling is only heuristic; it really is a new term, and it needs explanation. However, here is where the reduction comes cheap. Given that we understand the term being defined, namely 'sees', we can figure out the meaning of the new term, 'sees$_2$', by reading the definition backwards.[4] Epistemologically, the reducing theory is explained (partly) in terms of the reduced theory. This may seem odd, but it will seem less odd when the motivation of the enterprise is kept in mind. This type of reduction is not intended to expand our knowledge, as definitional reduction is sometimes supposed to do; its motivation is solely to make a theoretical point about ontological relations. As such, the backwards epistemology is not a defect; it is an acceptable theoretical technique.[5] One might wonder about its motivation, but if the motivation is not epistemological, the epistemological priority of the reduced theory over the reducing theory is no impediment.

There are many different ways to provide an ontological construction of events that would preserve the appeal to events while classifying them as nonbasic, constructed entities. Techniques for doing this sort of thing are widely employed in current philosophical theory, and many proposals in the literature already suggest how to construct events out of propositions, properties, ordered n-tuples of such things, and the like. (See Montague 1974, Taylor 1985, and Bennett 1988.[6]) To do the job in detail, of course, can be very complicated and difficult, and this may explain why attempts in the literature are often rather programmatic. I have not pursued such construction because there are so many ways of carrying it out, and because it is unclear what it accomplishes, but I have no arguments against its possibility or objections to its pursuit.

8.3   Event Identity: Coarse-Grained and Fine-Grained Accounts

In this section I wish to specify what my account does and does not say about the identity of events and to compare it with other positions in the literature. The point is not to defend the theory on these matters, but only to understand its consequences.

I make no attempt here to provide "criteria of identity" for events; I agree with Bennett 1988 that a request for criteria of identity is typically a conflation of many questions, with no clear notion of success possible. I also agree with his assessment that proposed criteria of identity in the literature rarely have the consequences their proponents desire. When I speak of "event identity" I allude to any issue of the form, "Is A = B?", where 'A' and 'B' denote events. I have no general theory about such questions, but the theory of underlying events has consequences for certain of them.

8.3.1   Coarse-Grained and Fine-Grained Accounts
It is common to contrast "coarse-grained" with "fine-grained" views of event identity. The former are often associated with Davidson and the latter with Kim, though it is arguable whether either view is required by the theories these writers endorse. (See Bennett 1988.) The contrast can be illustrated by the following examples

Davidsonian Claims

Suppose that I signal by raising my hand. Then my signaling is identical with my hand raising.

Suppose that I come home, flip a light-switch connected to a floodlight, and thereby alert a burglar. Then the flipping of the switch is identical with the alerting of the burglar.

Kimian Claims[7]

Suppose that I illegally kill someone, and thereby murder her. Then my murdering her is different from my killing her.

Suppose that I sing loudly. Then my singing is distinct from my singing loudly.

In addition to the Davidsonian and Kimian traditions, another (sometimes associated with Quine) identifies events if and only if they "occupy" the same spatiotemporal regions. Some examples:

Quinean Claims

If I fall off a cliff, my falling off the cliff is identical with my body's falling off the cliff.

If a sphere rotates and simultaneously heats up, the rotating of the sphere is identical with its heating up.

Davidson, Kim, and Quine all have theories about the identity of events, and their theories may or may not yield the above examples as consequences. For discussion of the theories and their consequences, I again refer the reader to the literature (e.g., to Bennett 1988). I will discuss instead what the theory of underlying events says about examples like the ones cited.

In discussing examples it is essential to keep in mind that the theory of underlying events utilizes the same predicates to symbolize verbs as to symbolize eventive gerunds. If Brutus stabs Caesar, then the phrase 'the stabbing of Caesar', in its event reading, refers to the same entity that makes true the sentence 'Brutus stabbed Caesar' (by being the thing that verifies the underlying existential quantification over stabbings). Without this assumption, none of the following reasoning holds up. But if Caesar is stabbed more than once, it is unclear which stabbing (if any) is referred to by 'the stabbing of Caesar'. For simplicity, I assume that the context of discussion is one in which a single event is under discussion. In discussing 'Brutus stabbed Caesar' I assume that Brutus stabbed Caesar only once in the situation under discussion.

8.3.2   How the Theory Sometimes Forces Identity of Events

The theory of underlying events requires that various kinds of substantive identity claims about events be true. Any loud singing provides an example of one such claim that is automatically yielded by the theory. If I sing loudly, then my singing is identical with my loud singing, as a consequence of the logical forms

My singing: (The e)[Singing(e) & Agent(e,me)]

My loud singing: (The e)[Singing(e) & Agent(e,me) & Loud(e)]

If both of these refer, then they must refer to the same thing (by ordinary principles of predicate logic). So the theory takes sides here against the most extreme examples in the Kimian tradition. Similar points apply to all cases in which the two event descriptions differ only with respect to the presence or absence of verb modifiers.

Passives provide another source of examples. On the underlying event account, passives and the corresponding actives have logically equivalent forms, at least in simple cases.[8] For example, the theory says that the two following descriptions refer to the same event, in spite of their difference in form:

Caesar's being stabbed by Brutus
Brutus's stabbing of Caesar.

This goes together with the view that one and the same event verifies both of

Caesar was stabbed by Brutus

and

Brutus stabbed Caesar.

The theory also yields true identity claims that arise from the theory in conjunction with identity of event participants. Suppose that the king is the butcher. Then these must be the same event:

The stabbing of the king.
The stabbing of the butcher.

The "Quinean" example above may or may not be of this sort. In particular, if it is true that I am identical with my own body, then my falling off the cliff is identical with my body's falling off the cliff. It will also be true that my stabbing the king is identical with my body's doing so. On the other hand, if I am not identical with my body, then these events are different, since their participants are different. Both sides of the issue are disconcerting, but no more so than both sides of the self/body issue in general; the theory of events contributes no new puzzles here.

In other cases the theory is strictly neutral, but additional evidence suggests that certain event identities are true in the light of the theory. Suppose that I murder Caesar. Are the descriptions

My killing of Caesar
My murdering of Caesar

descriptions of the same event? I suspect that they are. The reason lies in an auxiliary hypothesis that is not yielded by the theory but is consistent with it:

Every murder is a killing.

Why should this hypothesis be true? It is clearly *not* true if murder is taken in the technical sense of 'homicide', since a homicide may be an act in which I am responsible for someone else's killing the victim. But take it in the ordinary sense in which you cannot murder someone without killing him or her yourself. This still does not yield the identity of murderings and killings according to the underlying event theory. But the additional hypothesis appears to be a reasonable one, because it explains in a plain way the following mass of data:

If x murders y with a knife, then x kills y with a knife.
If x murders y in the hallway, then x kills y in the hallway.
If x murders y violently, then x kills y violently. . . .

I suggest that the above pattern holds for any verb modifier applied to 'murder' and 'kill'. If so, then these data are explained by the additional hypothesis that every murder is a killing. The theory does not entail the additional hypothesis, but it encourages it by providing a framework within which that additional hypothesis explains the mass of data. (If I am wrong about the data, then the theory can be used in conjunction with the counterexample to show that some murders are not killings.) Some readers may have expected that the theory would automatically entail answers to questions of this sort, without appeal to additional data or reasoning. I initially had that hope, but I now suspect that it is futile.

8.3.3 How the Theory Sometimes Forces Difference of Events

The theory sometimes contradicts event identity claims. When a verb-modifier appears truly in one source sentence and falsely in another, the events cannot be identical. If I both brush my teeth and sing, but if I brush my teeth loudly without singing loudly, then the theory entails that the singing is not the same event as the tooth-brushing. So much is to be expected. The more interesting cases are ones that are in dispute in the literature. One can use examples of this sort to take sides against certain Quinean examples. Suppose, for example, that during a certain period a sphere both rotates and heats up. The theory distinguishes the rotation from the heating up, since, e.g., the rotation was rapid when the heating up was slow, or Mary heard the rotation without hearing the heating up, and so on. (At the very least, the rotation was at X radians per second, when the heating up was not, and the heating up was from 10 degrees to 20 degrees, while the rotation was not.) Of course, a defender of the theory can bite the bullet and defend the identity by denying the apparent data. Someone might insist that Mary did hear the heating up; she had to hear it because she heard the rotation, and the rotation *is* the heating up. The theory of underlying events does not provide proof against such insistence.

In other cases the theory forces difference of events because of a difference in the participants. Suppose that Mary plays the sonata by playing her clarinet; then the clarinet playing and the sonata playing are not the same. For the former has the clarinet as its theme, and the latter has the sonata as its theme.[9] (This should not be odd, since the former is a process and the latter is not a process.) In addition, she might also have played the sonata slowly while playing her clarinet quickly, or vice versa; also she played the sonata with her clarinet yet she did not play her clarinet with the clarinet. Yet the (whole) clarinet playing and the sonata playing apparently occupied the same place and time.

Another case in which the participants matter is this: suppose that "in a single action" I hit the 8-ball into the corner pocket and hit the 9-ball into the side pocket. (This example is due to Wallace 1966.) Then the two hittings are not the same. For if they were, they would have the same participants, and I would then have hit the 8-ball into the *side* pocket and the 9-ball into the *corner* pocket. That is, if the hittings are identical, then this would be true:

(∃e)[Hitting(e) & Theme(e,8-ball) & Into(e,corner) & Theme(e,9-ball) & Into(e,side)].

But reshuffling conjuncts and eliminating some of them entails

(∃e)[Hitting(e) & Theme(e,8-ball) & Into(e,side)],

which is the logical form for 'hit the 8-ball into the side pocket'. I haven't featured reasoning of this sort involving participants, since it depends on how participants are related to events, and this is one of the least clearly established parts of the theory. But it is usually dispensable in the case of event identity, for we can easily use other reasoning to undercut the notion that events done "in the same action" must be identical. Just suppose that in one and the same action I hit the 8-ball into the corner pocket violently, and hit the 9-ball into the side pocket gently. Then the former hitting is violent and the latter one gentle, so they are different.

Another case in which the theory forces a difference of events is the signaling case, sometimes taken to be a persuasive case for event identity. Suppose we have agreed that I shall signal that I am the secret agent by saying that I have come to pick up the garbage. Then, if I say that I have come to pick up the garbage, in certain circumstances, *nothing further is required* for me to have thereby signaled that I am the agent. That nothing further is required motivates the view that the saying *is* the signaling. Nothing further is required because I have *already* signaled. But how could this be the case, unless the saying *is* the signaling?

The argument is not conclusive. Just because I do B *by* doing A does not show that A and B are the same event. And indeed, there is ample reason to distinguish them. The signaling, for example, is secret, yet the saying is not. (By openly saying that I come for the garbage I secretly signal that I am the agent.) Furthermore, the signaling need not have been clumsy, even if the saying was. (Perhaps the agreed-on signal is to say *clumsily* that I came for the garbage.) Other cases work equally well. Taylor (1985) cites Wiggins' example: if I signal by walking uphill, I do not signal uphill. Or if I signal by walking sideways/onto the grass/in a zig-zag pattern I do not thereby signal sideways/onto the grass/in a zig-zag pattern.

I am exploring the consequences of the theory of underlying events, not defending it. Some philosophers will find the consequences abhorrent and will reject the theory for that reason. But the defense of the theory lies in its explanatory abilities, not in its conformity to *a priori* intuition. On the other hand, as Taylor 1985 points out, it is not difficult to coin a notion of *kinship,* where two events are *akin* if they are identical according to your favorite theory. We then say that two events are "the same" if and only if they are akin in this sense. Since we often use "the same" to stand for some salient sense of similarity short of identity, this notion may save the *a priori* intuitions without contradicting the theory.

8.3.4 Cases Left Unresolved

The theory automatically leaves unresolved all claims about the modal essences of events. Since it is formulated in nonmodal terms, it is consistent with any self-consistent view about modal essentialism. (See Parsons 1969 for logical details.) I do not see this as a defect since I find that I lack the intuitions on which arguments about the essences of events depend, and I see talk about such essences as strictly independent of the linguistic data.

Finally, I have tried to avoid discussing examples that involve causative-inchoative verbs, such as that of flipping the switch and alerting the burglar. To alert the burglar is to cause the burglar to become alert, and so there are two events: the causing, and the becoming alert. I postpone discussing these until sections 8.5 and 8.6.

8.4 Arguments from the Philosophical Literature

Various arguments concerning events in the philosophical literature might be used to falsify the theory given here.

Objections Based on Construing Propositional Gerundives as Event Gerundives   In chapter 7 I distinguished two readings of phrases like 'Mary's singing', one sense using the phrase to refer to an event, the other using it to refer to a fact or proposition: that Mary sang. The former use occurs in 'Mary's singing was so loud it hurt my ears', and the latter in 'Mary's singing was hard to believe; we thought she would never recover her voice'. If these readings are not kept separate then it is easy to provide putative counterexamples to the theory. For exposition and examples, see Bennett 1988 chapter 1 and throughout.

Objections Based on Construing Non-Verb Modifiers as Verb Modifiers
Counterexamples to the theory are easily found if modifiers that are
not verb modifiers are construed as verb modifiers, especially when
the two sorts are homonyms. For example, there is a reading of
'rudely' for which the following inference is *not* a good one:

Rudely, she answered with her mouth full
∴ Rudely, she answered.

But if 'rudely' is construed as a verb modifier, the inference should
be a good one. The answer, of course, is that the inference is good
when 'rudely' is interpreted as a verb modifier, and bad when it is not.
(The fronted position of the modifier in the argument displayed above
pushes us toward the reading in which it is not a verb modifier.)

There are so many cases of this sort that it would be futile to try to
discuss them all, so I merely leave the reader with the warning to
watch for them. (I discuss types of modifiers in chapter 4, sections 4.1
and 4.5.)

Objections Based on the Notion of Cause   Seemingly plausible objections can be formulated using the notion of causality. The following
objection is due to Goldman (1970):

John's answering the phone ≠ John's answering the phone rudely

because

John's answering the phone was caused by its ringing

John's answering the phone rudely was caused by his fight with his
wife.

There is no equivocation on 'rudely' here; the point can be made while
resolutely sticking to its use as a verb modifier. The solution is that
such uses of causal talk force us to construe the gerunds as propositional instead of as referring to events. The examples become much
less persuasive when the clauses are reworded in a way that suggests
the event construal:

John's answering of the phone was caused by its ringing

John's rude answering of the phone was caused by his fight with his
wife.

This tendency of certain kinds of causal talk to replace "event causation" with "fact causation" is discussed in detail in Bennett 1988.
Although I am uneasy with many of the *analyses* of causation Bennett

examines, he makes it clear how causal talk does not threaten the underlying event theory.

Objections Based on the Time at which Events Occur   Various puzzles concerning when events happen are bound to impact any theory of events in some way. The standard example is Thomson 1971. Suppose that x shoots y but that y dies a year later. When did x kill y? And when did the killing occur? If it occurred when y died, then how can it be identical with the shooting, which occurred much earlier?

Since the theory that I am examining treats 'kill' as a causative verb, the sentence 'x kills y' has a complex underlying form that contains quantification over two events:

$$(\exists e)[\text{Agent}(e,x) \ \& \ (\exists e')[\text{Dying}(e') \ \& \ \text{Theme}(e',y) \ \& \ \text{CAUSE}(e,e')].$$

The two events we thus obtain are the shooting and the dying. Because I think that 'x will kill y' is true when said before the shooting, and not after, and that 'x killed y' is true when said after the dying, and not before, I am left with the period between the shooting and the dying in which neither the future nor the past tense sentence is true. This can be captured by the theory as formulated in chapter 11, where tenses are considered in detail.

It is another matter to say when "the killing" occurred. There seem to be three choices. One is to insist that 'the killing' refers to the causing event, in this case to the shooting. This means that the killing occurred before y died, which sounds a bit odd, but perhaps only a bit. The second is to insist that 'the killing' refers to the caused event, which entails that the shooting preceded the killing by a year. Again, this seems odd, but not conclusively so. The third, and easiest, choice is to suppose that 'the killing' is ambiguous; it may refer to either of the events. This explains both the naturalness and the oddity of the other two choices.

8.5   Defenses of the Coarse-Grained Version Involving Postulation of Underlying Basic Actions

Wallace (1966) and Lombard (1985) separately defend a view that would make all transitive verbs be causatives, in attempting to save Davidson's coarse-grained identity conditions for actions. Such an analysis is implicit in other views in the literature. This approach has two versions. One distinguishes actions from events, saving the course-grained view of actions by fiat; it also isolates the theory of action from any data from language. The other makes all event verbs be causative-inchoative in the sense discussed in chapter 6. I discuss the former in this section, and the latter in the following section.

According to Lombard 1985, logical forms of action sentences quantify over actions, event, and states. Such a sentence says that the agent performs a certain action, that the action causes a certain event, and that the event terminates in a certain state. As an example, the sentence

Brutus stabbed Caesar

tells us that Brutus performed some action, which caused an event, which terminated in Caesar's being stabbed:[10]

For some action a: Brutus is the agent of a,
For some event e: a causes e,
For some state s: s terminates e, and s is a being-stabbed of Caesar.

This is supposed to save the coarse-grained theory of action individuation as follows. Suppose that x A's y and that x B's z, and that x A's y M-ly but x does not B y M-ly. On the underlying event theory, we conclude that x's A-ing is not the same event as x's B-ing. On Lombard's theory, however, we can still claim that x performs the very same action in both cases. My argument shows only that the events are not the same; it does not show that the actions are not the same. For example, if I flip a switch and thereby alert a prowler, I may be able to show that two different events are involved, since I used a floodlight to alert the burglar but not to flip the switch. But on Lombard's account this leaves the *actions* untouched; it is still possible for me to have performed exactly one action with two consequences.

There are two natural ways to evaluate this proposal when comparing it with the simpler theory of underlying events. The first interpretation begins by producing a logically equivalent version of Lombard's account that resembles the underlying event account and then compares the two. I use 'x stabbed y' as a sample sentence form

Lombard

$(\exists e)[(\exists a)(x$ is the agent of a & a causes e) &
$(\exists s)(s$ is a being-stabbed of y & s terminates e)].

Underlying Event

(∃e)[Agent(e,x) &
(e is a stabbing & Theme(e,y))].

Each analysis is an existentially quantified conjunction, and there is a clear correspondence between the parts. Ignoring differences in the second conjunct, one can view Lombard's

(∃a)(x is the agent of a & a causes e)

as an *analysis* of the underling event term

Agent(e,x).

That is, this theory analyses the relation of Agency between an *event* and its agent; it holds that x is the Agent of an event if and only if x is the agent of an action that (directly) causes that event.

So far as I can see, this proposal is immune from attack on the basis of linguistic evidence, since it merely adds structure to a primitive of the underlying event theory. If the latter is correct, then the former cannot be faulted on formal grounds. For the same reason, however, we cannot hope to find linguistic evidence for it—it transcends the linguistic data. The additional structure in the account is motivated not by linguistic considerations but by considerations from action theory, where any objections are to be found.[11] Because it posits entities (actions) outside the purview of the underlying event approach, the two accounts do not compete with each other.

8.6 Defenses of the Coarse-Grained Version Based on a Universal Causative Analysis

Dowty (1979) discusses the idea that *all* accomplishment event verbs are causative-inchoatives. This includes the proposal that 'x hit y' means that x causes y to become to be in a certain state. It is a mere linguistic accident that there is no adjective in English for the resultant state of being hit, and that there is no intransitive verb that is true of y just in case y is becoming to be in this state. English just happens to lack such terms in its vocabulary.

This idea coheres with a different interpretation of Lombard's proposal. On this version, we interpret his 'x is the agent of a' as synonymous with my 'Agent(a,x)', and we view actions as certain events. This makes his proposal practically identical with the analysis of causative-inchoatives in chapter 6.[12] We can therefore view Lombard's proposal as formulated entirely within the theory of underlying events; it expands that theory by adding the claim that all event verbs are causative-inchoatives.

Issue 1. Is the Coarse-Grained View Consistent with the Underlying Event View?   There are two issues here. The first is whether Lombard's account, *if correct,* lets us preserve a coarse-grained theory of event identity. I do not see how invoking causative-inchoatives can make the theory of underlying events consistent with a coarse-grained account of events. Using Lombard's example, which I think *is* a causative-inchoative, assume that I flip a switch connected to a flood-light, and thereby alert a burglar. Lombard wishes to preserve the coarse-grained account by identifying the flipping of the switch with the alerting of the burglar. But which events are referred to by 'the flipping of the switch' and 'the alerting of the burglar'? Since in a causative there are two underlying events, do the cited nominals refer to the causing events (which Lombard would call actions) or to the caused events (the becoming flipped and the becoming alert)? I am not certain which they naturally refer to, but the causing events are clearly the ones at issue. All parties agree that the switch's becoming flipped is a different event from the burglar's becoming alert. The controversy is whether my flipping is the same as my alerting. I shall assume that these causing events are the referents of the nominals in the following discussion.

The argument against their identity is simple: I alerted the burglar with the floodlight, and I flipped the switch but not with the floodlight, so the alerting is distinct from the flipping. This follows from the analysis

$(\exists e_1)$[I am the agent of e_1 & e_1 is with the floodlight & $(\exists e_2)$[e_2 is a becoming-alert of the burglar]]

$(\exists e_1)$[I am the agent of e_1 & $\neg(e_1$ is with the floodlight) & $(\exists e_2)$[e_2 is a becoming-flipped of the switch]].

By predicate logic, these are inconsistent if the e_1's are the same in each case.

This argument has an apparent loophole. If there are two underlying events to modify, why does 'with the floodlight' go with the causing event rather than with the caused event? The answer is that instrumental 'with' always modifies the causing event in a causative. Suppose that I break a window with a rock. This has the causative analysis

($\exists e_1$)[I am the agent of e_1 & ($\exists e_2$)[e_2 is a breaking by the window & e_n is with the rock]].

Now suppose that e_n is actually e_2. Then this follows:

($\exists e_2$)[e_2 is a breaking by the window & e_2 is with the rock].

But this is the analysis of

The window broke with the rock,

which is false if not a category mistake. (A similar point can be illustrated directly in connection with 'I flipped the switch with my finger'; if the 'with'-clause modifies the caused event, then it follows that the switch flipped with the finger. The point cannot be illustrated with 'alert' simply because it has no intransitive version. But the analogue of the intransitive is available: if I alerted the burglar with the floodlight and if the 'with' clause modifies the caused event then it follows incorrectly that the burglar became alert with the floodlight.) I conclude that the above argument shows that the causative analysis is not consistent with identifying the causing events in the switch flipping and burglar alerting.[13]

Issue 2. Are all event verbs causative-inchoative?   I doubt that all event verbs are causative-inchoative.[14] My main argument is the claim that certain verbs, such as 'stab', 'hit', 'kiss', have no states of the sort needed for the analysis. As Davidson (1985) points out in another connection, it is hard to see what state is caused to come to be by a hitting, other than the state of having been hit. This is unlike, say, the state of being closed that results from a closing, which is a state that a thing may be in quite independently of whether it was ever closed by anyone or anything. In a normal causative-inchoative, the kind of state used in the analysis is such that a state of that kind can obtain even without the truth of the causative-inchoative. There is a kind of state K such that

Necessarily, if x V's y then y becomes in a state of kind K,

but it is false that

Necessarily, if y is in a state of kind K, then something V'd y.

In the case of hitting, the state of *having been hit* passes the first half of the test but fails the second half, and it is hard to find another candidate. This does not prove the proposal false, but no evidence for it is visible.

These objections may simply be based on our limited perspective of being speakers of a language that lacks simple terms for the events and states we are seeking. In fact, nothing in the theory I am developing commits one to the view that not all event verbs are causative-inchoative. If all verbs *are* causative-inchoative, however, we need the following proviso: that the extra events and states posited to underlie verbs that are not "apparent" causative-inchoatives are not available for modification by adverbs, adjectives, or prepositional phrases. They are completely hidden from view.

Chapter 9

The Progressive in English: Events, States, and Processes[1]

This chapter has two goals. The first is to formulate an adequate account of the semantics of the progressive in English: the semantics of 'Agatha is making a cake', as opposed to 'Agatha makes a cake'. Several proposals in the literature have difficulty with the so-called imperfective paradox: that 'Mary is building a house' might be true even if she is permanently interrupted in her building, so that 'Mary has built a house' is never true. I propose an account of the progressive in terms of underlying events. For event sentences the nonprogressive form of the verb requires that its underlying event culminate, whereas the progressive version requires only that the underlying event be going on (it need only "hold"). This account is immune to the imperfective paradox. I consider some objections to the analysis and discuss other proposals by David Dowty, Leonard Åqvist, and Michael Bennett.

The second goal of the chapter, taken up in the final section, is to refine the notion of a "process" so as to account for the infamous "category switch" problem: how it is that modification of a verb like 'run' by an adverbial like 'to the store' can turn a Process phrase ('run') into an Event phrase ('run to the store').

9.1 History of the Problem: The "Imperfective Paradox"

The progressive form of a verb is formed by preceding the verb with 'be' and following it with the suffix '-ing'. 'Be leaving', for example, is the progressive form of 'leave'. One of the longstanding questions in linguistics has been how the meaning of a sentence using the progressive is related to the meaning of the corresponding nonprogressive; for example, how the meaning of

1   Mary is leaving

is related to that of

2   Mary leaves.

   An early proposal given by Dana Scott and Richard Montague (1974, 125) is that a simple sentence in the progressive is true at a given time t if and only if the corresponding nonprogressive sentence is true at every moment throughout some open interval about t. Thus 'John is walking' is true at time t just in case there is an open interval of time surrounding t such that 'John walks' is true at each moment in that interval. This analysis is now known to be inadequate. It leads to what Dowty (1979, 133 ff.) calls the "imperfective paradox." Consider the sentence

3   Mary has left.

This sentence will be true at a time t just in case the corresponding present tense sentence is true at some earlier time. The imperfective paradox is this. The Scott/Montague analysis tells us that sentence (1) entails sentence (3): if Mary is leaving then Mary has left. For if (1) is true at t then there is an open interval of times around t—and thus containing points of time prior to t—such that (2) is true at every point in the interval. So (2) is true at some time or times before t, which makes (3) true at t. But this seems wrong in the case in question, and the wrongness is even more blatant in other cases. The analysis implies that if Samantha is (right now) building a house, then she has already built a house.

   This situation is paradoxical, of course, only if one has persuasive reasons to believe the analysis that leads to it. Most researchers have concluded that the analysis merely needs to be corrected. But this has not proved to be an easy task. Michael Bennett and Barbara Partee (1978) were led to make a radical proposal that is now widely accepted: we should no longer analyze sentences in terms of their being true at instants of time, as has been the custom in tense logic; instead, sentences should be viewed as being true with respect to intervals of time. This idea offers a much more flexible framework for tense logic, and Bennett and Partee hoped it would provide a way of solving the imperfective paradox. Let us call a unit interval of time—that is, an interval containing just one instant—a "moment" of time. Then they propose:

A simple progressive sentence is true at an interval of time I if and only if I is a moment of time, and there is an interval I' which contains I such that the nonprogressive form of the sentence is true at I'. (p. 13)

For example, 'John is building a house' might be true at high noon today because there is an interval of time (say, starting two years ago and terminating three years from now) at which the sentence 'John builds a house' is true. This avoids the original form of the imperfective paradox because the progressive sentence does not require for its truth at moment I that there be any totally past interval at which the nonprogressive sentence is true. Unfortunately, the proposal falls prey to fancied-up versions of the paradox. For example, suppose that

4   Mary is building a house

is true at high noon today. Then, according to the analysis, there is an interval surrounding noon today at which the sentence

5   Mary builds a house

is true. But then there will be some moment later than every instant in that interval, and at that moment the sentence

6   Mary has built a house

will be true. In crude terms, if Mary is now building a house, then it will be true at some time in the future that Mary has built a house. But she may never finish. If Mary were to be struck down by lightning with the house only half complete, we should then say that she was building a house when she was struck down, but we should never say that she had built a house.

A quite different approach due to David Dowty is that a progressive sentence should be true at a given time just in case the corresponding nonprogressive sentence is true in all inertia worlds, where an "inertia world" is a possible world that is exactly like the actual world up to the time in question "and in which the future course of events after this time develops in ways most compatible with the past course of events" (Dowty 1979, 148). The idea is that the progressive sentence is true just in case the nonprogressive version would have been true in any situation like this one that proceeded "normally."

This proposal seems very natural, but there are difficulties with it, the principal one being that "inertia world" is defined so as to strongly suggest that the actual world itself is one of the inertia worlds. Prima facie, things sometimes appear to proceed in ways "most compatible with the past course of events." But if there is ever a single case in which this happens, the actual world becomes an inertia world for that time, and the analysis then requires that no progressive sentence be true at that time unless its nonprogressive version actually becomes true then or later—which revives the imperfective paradox for that moment in time. Clearly some subtle refinement in the notion of inertia world is needed if this proposal is to work correctly. Whether this can be provided is at present an open question.[2]

Difficulties with the imperfective paradox that have impinged upon previous accounts of the progressive suggest that we consider some completely different approach.

9.2 An Analysis of the Progressive Using Events

One natural idea for analyzing the progressive is that the analysis should appeal to intent or some other mental activity, since if Mary is sitting still taking a break, there sometimes seems little else, apart from her intent, to distinguish situations in which she is still building a house from situations in which she has abandoned that activity. But intent cannot be made part of a general analysis of the progressive, on pain of falsifying examples such as

The river is undercutting the bank.

The analysis must not require that intent be irrelevant, but neither must it require its presence.

The inertia worlds approach focuses on the idea of what would be the case (described in nonprogressive terms) if present activities were to go on uninterrupted. I suggest that the present activities are the whole story.[3] My proposal for treating progressive sentences rests on my earlier point that a verb such as 'cross' is true of all crossings independently of whether they culminate. If John crosses the street and reaches the other side, then he is the subject of a crossing that culminates; if he gets partway across and is then struck down by a truck he is, for a while, the subject of a crossing that does not culminate. In a nonprogressive event sentence, the sentence requires for its truth that the eventuality picked out by the verb culminate; a progressive event sentence requires only that the eventuality "go on" for a while. The rule for dealing with the progressive form of the verb can then be

If 'A' is an event verb, then 'be A-ing' is to be treated semantically as a state verb; otherwise, 'be A-ing' is to be treated the same as 'A'.[4]

Semantically, changing an event verb to the progressive form requires that it be treated as a state verb; the sentence in question thus requires for its truth that the event in question *hold,* not that it *culminate.* Event sentences in the progressive therefore translate differently than those not in the progressive. The nonprogressive sentence

Agatha crossed the street

will, by our former rules, receive the translation

$(\exists t)[t < \text{now } \& \ (\exists e)[\text{crossing}(e) \ \& \ \text{Subject}(e,\text{Agatha}) \ \& \ \text{Object}(e,\text{the street}) \ \& \ \text{Cul}(e,t)]]$.

We use Cul in the translation because 'cross' is an ordinary event verb. The sentence

Agatha was crossing the street

is treated in exactly the same way, except that 'is crossing' is classified as a stative verb form. We therefore choose Hold instead of Cul, and the resulting translation is

$(\exists t)[t < \text{now } \& \ (\exists e)[\text{crossing}(e) \ \& \ \text{Subject}(e,\text{Agatha}) \ \& \ \text{Object}(e,\text{the street}) \ \& \ \text{Hold}(e,t)]]$.

This might be true even though the corresponding version with 'Cul' is never true.

The proposed analysis is immune to "paradoxes" of the imperfective kind, since saying of an event that it holds at a given time does not imply that it culminates at that or any other time. This analysis also preserves all the advantages of the underlying event approach articulated in chapter 2.[5] This proposal gets the logical relationships right, has a plausible intuitive motivation, and is incorporated into a robust semantical framework for the semantics of English—one capable of addressing a wide variety of interesting phenomena.

A variant of this proposal might be better for some purposes. It might be equally plausible that, for every event that is ever in progress, there is a uniquely associated state, the "In-Progress" state of the event, which holds as long as the event is in progress. If we replace 'Hold(e,t)' in the analysis above by 'Hold(In-prog(e),t)', where 'In-prog(e)' denotes the state uniquely associated with e, this gives an alternative account, one that conforms to the idea that only states, never events, can properly be said to "hold." Some will see this as a decided advantage. This account also meshes better with the historical origins of the progressive, discussed in chapter 12. For the issues discussed in this chapter, the two accounts are equivalent; I explore the former one because it is simpler.[6]

9.3   Absent Processes and Unfinished Objects

Two serious objections to my analysis of the progressive are that there sometimes seems to be no independently specifiable present process that makes the progressive true, and that the theory commits us to "unfinished" objects.

9.3.1   Specifiability
The first objection has been raised on a number of occasions by David Dowty. The theory given above supposes that an event verb picks out a kind of event, independently of whether an event of that kind has culminated. If the progressive is true, then there must actually be an event *of the kind in question* that is going on. But this is puzzling in certain cases. Consider an example of Dowty's:

John is making me a millionaire.

This sentence, if true, could be made true by a wide variety of activities, none of which has any regular relationship with my becoming a millionaire. In the case of 'cross' we know exactly what kind of event to look for to see whether Agatha is now crossing the street, but in the case of John's making me a millionaire we have little idea what kind of event to look for—except that it must be one that, were things to go in certain ways, would result in my becoming a millionaire.

Dowty is right to find examples of this sort puzzling. However, the source of the puzzle does not lie with the progressive, but rather with the special character of his example, which is a case of the "causative-inchoative" construction in English that was discussed in chapter 6. A causative-inchoative is a construction whose truth involves the notion of causality plus that of a final state. 'John opens the door', means something like:

John opens the door =
John does something that causes the door to become open.

If such a sentence is true, then there must be

something John does to cause the door to open,
something that the door does: it opens, and
a final state of the door: it must end up open.

The first of these may, but need not, be a type of event that regularly ends up with a door's being open. Traditionally, John's opening of the door has been analyzed in terms of his doing something that causes an opening of the door, and an opening of the door has been analyzed in terms of the coming to be of a state of being open. In this example, we have English words for all parts of the process: a transitive verb (spelled 'open') for what John does, an intransitive verb (spelled 'open') for what the door does, and an adjective (again spelled 'open') that describes the final state of the verb. In other such triads the spelling changes by a regular pattern: Mary *fells* the tree; the tree *falls,* and it ends up *fallen.*

I believe that Dowty's problem arises inevitably for any causative-inchoative verb. The progressive sentence 'John is opening the door' requires for its truth that a certain event hold. Which event is this? It is an event that is "causing an opening." This is a fairly abstract description of a kind of event, which is what bothers Dowty, but it is accurate. Its roundabout nature is not forced on us by the proposed analysis of the progressive, but by the causative-inchoative nature of the verb in question. It will be difficult in many cases to decide whether a given event is indeed causing another event of the appropriate sort. But this is the nature of the situation. The same is true of "making me a millionaire." John is doing that now if he is engaged in an activity of *some* kind that is now causing me to become a millionaire, independently of whether I eventually become one.

It is indeed difficult, in the case of causative-inchoatives, to describe the caus*ing* event picked out by the verb so that the description is independent of the verb but also make clear the verb's connection with what is being caused. This is a fact about causative-inchoatives, but it is not incompatible in any way with the proposed account of the progressive, and so it is not an objection to it.

9.3.2   Unfinished Objects
The second major objection has to do with the objects of verbs in the progressive. According to the analysis, if x is A-ing a B, then there is a B that x is A-ing. So long as we avoid intentional verbs (such as 'imagine'), this pattern seems correct in most cases. Somehow we need to explain why, if Mary is pushing a cart, then there is a cart that she is pushing, and if Harry is slicing a cantaloupe, then there is a cantaloupe that he is slicing. (In general, these examples tell against the progressive's being a kind of intensional operator.) But "verbs of

creation" raise a special and interesting objection. If Mary is building a house, then her building event has an object that is a house, and so there is a house that she is building. Now suppose that Mary is struck down by lightning with the house only one-fourth finished. The objector takes me to the location and demands, "Where is the house? All I see is a foundation and portions of some wall-framing!" My answer is that we are looking at the house—it is merely an incomplete or unfinished one. This will no doubt raise some eyebrows, but, given the linguistic conventions of English, the object before us is properly described as a "house."

In northern California one can visit Jack London State Park and see the house that Jack London was building when he died. At least this is what the tourist guides say. It isn't much of a house—only a foundation and parts of some walls. But native speakers of English call it a house. What evidence could there be that they are wrong? Ordinary language seems to be governed here by something like Plato's theory of forms: material things that "aspire after" ideals are named after those ideals, in spite of their failure to live up to the ideal itself. In short, people describe unfinished houses as "houses," and my analysis assumes that this is correct usage.

The problem is not ontological—everyone agrees that the thing in question exists. The issue is whether it is a house. I take this to be primarily a question of the proper use of words—whether an unfinished house is properly called "a house."

This gives rise to various worries. How much of a house needs to be built before it is correctly describable as a house? Suppose that Mary had only drawn up the plans; would this be enough for there to be a house she is building? My answer again lies in English usage. If we were willing to say that Mary was building a house, and to maintain this in the face of ordinary sorts of criticism, then that would be enough. In the case where Mary had planned to build a house but the construction had not yet begun, the accurate description is that Mary is still in the planning stages, that she is not yet building a house. In that case, the analysis does not require there to be a house, finished or unfinished, since 'planning to A' does not imply 'A', no matter how 'A' is analyzed.

Still, a suspicion remains that some cleverly chosen example might drive this theory into ontological excesses. But it will not be easy to find one. First, no problems for the analysis can be based on intentional verbs. Granted, 'Mary is imagining a unicorn' should not entail that there is a unicorn, and it is not at all clear how such constructions should be analyzed. But this problem is not unique to the progressive, since for verbs like 'imagine' the very same problem arises for the nonprogressive 'Mary imagined a unicorn'.[7]

For similar reasons no problem for the present analysis can arise from infinitival expressions such as 'plan to', 'try to', 'start to', 'be going to', 'want to', and so on. Certainly, it should not follow from 'Mary is planning to build a house' that there is a house (that she is planning to build). But this is because of the opacity of 'plan to'; it equally must not follow from 'Mary planned to build a house' that there was a house that she planned to build. Any problem due to these infinitival constructions is not a special problem for the progressive.[8]

Finally, a "futurate" use of the present tense should not mislead us.

"What are you doing this morning?"
Answer: "I'm making a cake."

This may announce the intention of making a cake long before the ingredients are even purchased. Some people would hold such a sentence true if the plan to make a cake is sincere, even though "the cake" never gets made. Again, the problem is not special to the progressive. Suppose the answer had been

First I clean the bedroom, then I make a cake, then . . .

The phenomenon is the same, but the progressive is missing.

Suppose that the cake-making endeavor has started. Won't there be a time at which it is true to say that I am making a cake even though there is not yet any cake? Before you measure out the first ingredient it is not yet true to say that you are making a cake (you are only preparing to make a cake), but once the first ingredient is measured out it is then true that you are making the cake. At that time the question "*Where* is the cake?" has no answer. Then, doesn't this show the analysis to be false? There may very well be a problem here, but it is a general problem about the ontological presuppositions of the things we are inclined to say, and it is not peculiar to the progressive. Of the following claims

Sam put the cake into the oven.
After he blended and mixed it, he put it in the oven,

the first seems to commit us to there being a cake before it was baked, and the second seems to commit us to there being a cake even at the point of blending. Neither of these involves the progressive. We ordinarily assume that there are such things as cakes even during the early stages of their creation, and even perhaps before they have well-defined spatial locations. If this assumption were false, then claims such as

He put the cake in the oven

would be, strictly speaking, false. But this would merely reveal a discrepancy between our ordinary assumptions and the truth; it would not cast doubt on the analysis of the progressive.

We seem to use the progressive in two sorts of cases: when the process in question has clearly begun, and when we are preparing to begin that process. We may sometimes say "I'm making a cake" when we have not yet started to make the cake but when we are making preparations, such as getting out the bowls. I see this as a form of the "futurate" use of the progressive, used in a situation in which the literal present tense version is false. It is often difficult to locate a clear borderline between the preparatory conditions and the process itself, and this will raise uncertainty over any analysis of the progressive. But it should not tell against any particular analysis over the others.

9.3.3 Inertia Worlds Again

Some readers may now be longing for a revitalized version of the inertia worlds approach as a way to avoid the issue of unfinished objects. The inertia worlds analysis construes the progressive morpheme as an operator having scope. If its scope is always over the verb alone, then it requires unfinished objects, just as does the analysis of the progressive I propose.[9] But its scope can instead be taken to extend over the object position as well, so that the form of

Mary is building a house

is

PROG$((\exists x)[x$ is a house & Mary builds x $])$.

This would be true on the inertia world account if Mary builds a house in every inertia world, even if in the actual world there is no house at all. However, the "objects" of progressive verbs cause problems for this approach too. Suppose that the notion of inertia world has been developed so that it works as intended, to include only worlds in which Mary's house building goes on to culmination. The inertia world theory thus says of Mary's aborted house building that this is true:

Mary was building a house

(since 'Mary builds a house' becomes true in every inertia world). It also says that this is never true:

Mary built a house,

since she never finishes in the actual world. This analysis escapes the imperfective paradox and does not require a house. But since in every inertia world a house gets finished, the theory says also that this sentence is true:

Mary is building a house that she will finish.

But no reading of this sentence would be true in the circumstances envisaged.

Any analysis that treats the progressive as an operator that operates on verb phrases or sentences will confront this problem. So long as quantified objects of progressive verbs (such as 'a house') are forced to come outside the scope of the progressive operator, then we get unfinished objects. But if they are allowed to come inside, the "finish" issue will have to be faced.

Since in practically all cases 'x is A-ing a B' entails 'there is a B that x is A-ing', and since the ontological and terminological issues raised by verbs of creation arise with the nonprogressive as well as the progressive, I conclude that the analysis in terms of underlying events works as well as any alternative.

9.3.4 Åqvist's Analyses
For those who are still uncomfortable with unfinished things, and equally troubled by the consequences of the inertia world analysis, here is an intermediate position. Leonard Åqvist (1977, 38) worries about sentences such as

Mary is drawing a circle.

The problem is, of course, that if she is interrupted then no circle gets completed. And many will insist that an incomplete circle is no circle at all; it is only an arc with uniform curvature. Åqvist agrees with me that there is a present object of the drawing activity, but he agrees with the critics that this object is not a circle. He says,

. . . it is perfectly possible for an agent a to be drawing an object b in such a way that it is becoming more and more the case that this object b is a circle without its therefore being the case either that b was a circle at some past time, or that b is ever going to be a circle in the future . . .

Åqvist's analysis of 'Mary is drawing a circle' is, roughly, that Mary is drawing something (an arc) in such a manner that it is becoming more and more the case that that thing is a circle. (Michael Bennett (1977, 504-05, 508) makes a similar proposal.)

Despite its obvious intuitive appeal, this proposal, has serious drawbacks. First, people do refer to unfinished houses as houses, and even—though more reluctantly—to unfinished circles as circles. Second, the verb 'draw' is a tricky one; you can draw a unicorn just as easily as you can draw a horse, and this has nothing at all to do with the progressive. But, most important, as Åqvist himself points out, this approach prohibits our having a uniform account of all progressives. For example, the sentence

Mary is pushing a cart

cannot be treated just like 'Mary is drawing a circle', for it is simply not true that the object she is pushing is becoming more and more a cart. This requires a different analysis, roughly to the effect that

It is being the case that there is a cart Mary pushes.

Åqvist also requires a third analysis for 'Mary is closing a door', namely. 'Mary is closing something in such a way that it is becoming more and more a closed door'. One wonders how many different analyses of the progressive are necessary. Åqvist seems to want to classify the analyses by verb types, but even this will not do. Compare

Mary is drawing a circle

with

Mary is drawing an arc.

The former is analyzed in terms of something's becoming more and more a circle, but this will not do for the latter since an arc does not become more and more an arc just by getting longer. Still, in the end a piecemeal approach may be the only kind with any hope of accuracy.

My worry is that this does not really advance the issue. For the case in which we have just measured out the first ingredient for "the cake," on Åqvist's analysis there is something that is becoming more and more a cake. But where is this thing? And what is it, if not our old friend, the unfinished cake?

9.4   Interval Semantics: Bennett's Refined Analysis

The proposal that sentences might be evaluated with respect to whether they are true at intervals of time instead of at points of time has now been adopted by a large number of researchers. The obvious advantage this idea offers is its flexibility. But increased flexibility is purchased at the price of testability. In ordinary tense logic we have a rough intuitive test for whether a sentence is true at a moment of time; we imagine the sentence uttered at that moment and we use our skill as native speakers to judge whether that utterance would be true then. In interval semantics we can do roughly the same for short intervals. We imagine an utterance of the sentence that occupies roughly that interval, and we judge whether the utterance would be true. But for long intervals no such test is possible. So proposals for the truth-values of sentences at large intervals of time cannot be directly tested in this manner.

The following proposal is paraphrased from Dowty 1979, 169:

'x moves' is true at interval I just in case x is located at one place at the beginning of I and at another place at the end of I.

Now consider an object x that is moving in an ellipse, and consider an interval I of length 387 years during which the object makes exactly seventeen revolutions, so that, at the end of I, x is at exactly the same place it occupied at the beginning of I. According to Dowty's analysis, the statement 'x moves' is false at interval I, even though x was in movement at every instant in I. Does this show that the analysis is incorrect? Certainly the object was moving *throughout* I, but was it moving *at* I? There is no way to tell, because the theoretical notion of "moving at an interval" has not been given any connection with the data, at least for large intervals. (How do you tell whether 'x moves' is true *at November?*) In the absence of further information, there is simply no way to test the proposal. We can test only the whole theory of which it is a part, to see what that tells us about the truth-values of utterances. The whole subarea of tense logic that utilizes intervals as opposed to instants faces the same consequence.

Most people who work with interval semantics do not treat such analyses as untestable, or as requiring indirect test. They talk as if one can show piecemeal that a given proposal is or is not correct. This requires an explanation, which I hazard below. My explanation is based on some remarks made by Michael Bennett (1981, 14–15) in the context of presenting his own analyses of the perfect and the progressive, which he attributes in part to Glen Helman. So far as I can see, Bennett's analyses escape all the objections discussed so far (even though they, like the underlying event approach, require unfinished objects). Here is a portion of the discussion:

We give (1) as the truth condition for 'Jones has left'.

(1) 'Jones has left' is true at interval of time I if and only if I is a moment of time, and there exists an interval of time I' (possibly a moment) such that I' is a closed interval, $I' < I$, and Jones is in the extension of 'leave' at I'. . . .

We give (2) as the truth condition for 'Jones is leaving'.

(2) 'Jones is leaving' is true at interval of time I if and only if I is a moment of time, and there exists an interval of time I' such that I' is an open interval, I is included in I', and Jones is in the extension of 'leave' at I'.

Condition (2) has the consequence that 'Jones is leaving' neither implies 'Jones has left' nor implies, in effect, 'Jones will have left', as there is no guarantee that Jones is in the extension of 'leave' with respect to a CLOSED interval.

Bennett avoids the imperfective paradox by distinguishing between open and closed intervals; the truth of a sentence in the progressive depends on someone's being in the extension of a verb at an open interval, and the truth of a simple sentence not in the progressive depends on someone's being in the extension of that verb at a closed interval. But even though we see that someone is in the extension of a verb at "an interval," how do we tell whether the interval before us is open or closed? Bennett acknowledges that the distinction is "subliminal," and earlier he says "Almost everyone initially finds the analysis to be mysterious—a 'logician's trick'."

But this is misleading. True, the analysis involves a logician's trick, and a rather nice one. But it does not depend on our ability to discriminate subliminally, and it is not really mysterious at all, for Bennett (1977 and 1981) explains quite clearly how the trick is done. One such explanation is contained in certain passages omitted from the quotations above (I have added some emphasis).

One intuition motivating this analysis [i.e., (1) above] is that if Jones is in the extension of 'leave' at an interval I, then *the event* of Jones's leaving is regarded as starting at the beginning of I, taking place during I, and finishing at the end of I. This reflects our intuition that the truth condition should involve some past INTERVAL of time during which Jones is leaving and eventually *completes this act*. The requirement that the past interval be closed reflects the intuition that the present perfect tense always *describes a performance;* the perfect aspect *indicates a completion* . . .

The requirement that **I'** be an open interval in condition (2) reflects the intuition that the present progressive always *describes an activity.* (Bennett 1981, 14–15)

A simple way of viewing the proposal is to see intervals as encoding eventualities:

Let us say that *activities* are represented by open intervals . . . and that *performances* are represented by closed intervals. (Bennett 1977, 505)

Bennett's "activities" appear to be the same as my events that do not culminate, and his "performances" seem to be the same as my events that actually culminate. If so, the distinction between open and closed intervals is simply a way of coding whether an eventuality culminates, without using any notions that are not definable by the resources of pure interval semantics. Suppose that we have pinned down the period of an eventuality precisely, except that we do not yet know whether this interval includes its end points. Instead of deciding this by more careful measurement, we stipulate that if the eventuality culminates then its subject is in the extension of the relevant verb at the closure of that interval, and if the eventuality does not culminate then the subject is in the extension of the verb at the interval minus its end points. Piecemeal testability of the semantics then rests on two matters: the assumption that simple sentences pick out eventualities, and the notion of *culminating* (Bennett's "completion").

This appeal to eventualities is not peculiar to Bennett. Writers who endorse interval semantics almost always find themselves explaining the application of their ideas by talking in terms of events, states and the like (see Dowty 1979, Tedeschi 1981). But whether this linking of eventualities with intervals makes for piecemeal testability of individual analyses depends on the particular theoretical framework in question.

Interval semantics does not normally refer to eventualities in the official formulation of the semantics. It does so only in the informal guidelines that come with the system, as when the primitive non-logical notions to be used are explained. Many people with ontological scruples prefer it this way, for they are wary of theories with excess ontological commitments. I do not share that view. But can a "pure" interval semantics be empirically adequate for the phenomena of ordinary speech without appeal to eventualities? For one thing, English explicitly refers to all sorts of eventualities, for example, in 'There were three accidents last night'. Such sentences are sometimes true, and it is difficult to see how this can be admitted without holding that there are eventualities. But then a "theoretical" avoidance of commitment to eventualities would seem academic.

Second, certain constructions involve adverbs of frequency that seem to require more than just intervals of time. Bennett (1977, 511) considers the problem sentence

Miles was wounded by a bullet twice yesterday.

The natural treatment of this sentence within interval semantics would be to propose something like

For two distinct intervals, I_1 and I_2, each contained in yesterday, Miles was in the extension of 'be wounded by a bullet' at both I_1 and I_2.

Unfortunately, such an analysis would entail that the woundings were not simultaneous, yet there is a natural reading of the sentence that does not say this. In response, Bennett proposes tentatively that we might say instead that there are two contemporaneous *occurrences* of the generic event *Miles being wounded by a bullet*. This brings in quantification over "occurrences," which look suspiciously like events. His other suggestion is to paraphrase the original sentence by

Miles was wounded by two bullets yesterday.

But this idea will not work for even simpler cases, such as

Miles was wounded twice yesterday,

where no bullets need be involved at all.

Finally, it is unclear whether the pure interval approach, devoid of eventualities, can address the rich array of phenomena mentioned in chapter 2 and *passim*.

9.5 Processes and the Progressive

One of the liveliest topics in the literature on the Aristotelian classification of linguistic items has to do with the so-called category switch brought about by certain cases of adverbial modification. A sentence such as

Mary ran

is supposed to be a paradigm example of a process sentence, since 'run', by itself, does not seem to imply any particular notion of culmination. Yet the sentence

Mary ran across the street

is an event sentence with a clear culmination. How is it that modification of 'run' by 'across the street' can turn a process into an event?

This passage from Vendler (1967, 100) illustrates the problem further

> If it is true that someone is running or pushing a cart now, then even if he stops in the next moment it will still be true that he did run or did push a cart. On the other hand, even if it is true that someone is drawing a circle or is running a mile now, if he stops in the next moment it may not be true that he did draw a circle or did run a mile. . . . Running a mile and drawing a circle have to be finished, while it does not make sense to talk of finishing running or pushing a cart. Thus we see that while running or pushing a cart has no set terminal point, running a mile and drawing a circle do have a "climax," which has to be reached if the action is what it is claimed to be.

The problem is that either running a mile or running to the store involves runnings, yet a running to the store is an event and a mere running seems to be a process. Uncertainty over whether a "mere" running can have a culmination is reflected in uncertainty over classification of the verb 'run' in the linguistic literature. Bach (1981, 67, 73) cites 'John *ran*' as a paradigm process sentence, but he later notes that we are forced to give an event interpretation to 'John ran yesterday'. Bennett and Partee (1978), in trying to classify 'play', are forced to say that it is ambiguous between an event verb and a process verb. (Similar considerations force the same conclusion for many verbs.) Ritchie (1979, 100) also finds that the process/event distinction does not classify properly.

What *is* the difference between a process and an event? An often-cited test for distinguishing them is that process sentences obey the principle

A is Xing only if A has Xed,

whereas event sentences obey something like the principle

A is Xing only if A has not Xed.

(This test is originally due to Kenny 1963. Bennett (1977, 498) makes a similar suggestion.) Yet the first principle is doubtful for processes such as walking, when one has just begun to walk, and the second is, as Bach (1981) notes, literally false. (If Mary is painting a house, she might have painted it many times before.)[10]

My account of the difference between processes and events is that a process is actually a series or amalgam of events. A walking process is a bunch of overlapping walking events—small ones, large ones, and so on. A so-called "process verb" is a verb having the property that when it is true of an event e it is typically true of many culminated "subevents" of e that have the same subjects and objects. A running is an event that typically consists of "shorter" events that are also runnings by the same person.[11] If Agatha runs to the store then she may do this by running four blocks along the way; the running-to-the-store is a running, and so is each of the block-runnings. We need only add that English usage requires that when we discuss an event that constitutes a process we usually have in mind a "maximal" event of its kind, so that if someone asks about "Agatha's running" we assume that the person is mentioning the whole run, not one of the parts. Typically a (maximal) running culminates when the subject intentionally stops running, or stops at a preplanned point, although a running, like a street crossing, may terminate before its culmination if something interferes. Unculminated runnings do not usually occupy our attention since they have "subrunnings" that do culminate, but they are important in avoiding the imperfective paradox.

The effect of this proposal is to broaden the scope of the earlier analysis without affecting its formulation. We just treat process verbs as a special kind of event verb, applying the theory as before. So 'Mary ran' will translate just as if it were an event verb:

$(\exists t)[t < now \ \& \ (\exists e)[running(e) \ \& \ Subject(e, Mary) \ \& \ Cul(e,t)]]$.

Since 'run' is construed as an event verb, its progressive form will not receive the same translation as its nonprogressive form; the progressive form will use 'Hold' where the nonprogressive uses 'Cul'.

What consequences will this have? One has to do with the principle that, if 'Mary is running' is true at a given time, then 'Mary has run' should be true at that time also. The logical forms associated with the sentences do not by themselves guarantee this. The result accrues instead from the principle that, if a process verb is true of an event, then it is also (typically) true of some (proper) subevents of that event, including some that culminate earlier than the one in question. If this were a universal principle, it could perhaps be elevated into a meaning postulate for the verbs in question. But there is some doubt about its applicability, say, to very small segments of walkings (see Dowty 1979).

   Some further consequences of this approach are that the sentence

Mary ran across the street

entails both

Mary ran,

and

Mary was running across the street.[12]

In contrast, the sentence

Mary was running across the street,

although it entails

Mary was running,

it fails to entail

Mary ran across the street,

and it thus avoids the imperfective paradox.[13]

   The much-discussed category switch that is a supposed consequence of modification of a process verb with an adverb of motion now receives a very simple explanation. 'Run' is a process verb—that is, in our new terminology, 'run' is an event verb that, when true of an event, is also typically true of other culminated subevents of that event having the same subject. But 'run to the store' is not a process phrase—it is an event phrase that is *not* usually true of culminated subevents of the events it is true of. The reason for this is that 'to the store', all by itself, is not usually true of any culminated subevents of the events it is true of. (For a "to the store" event to culminate, its Theme must reach the store.) And since the logical form of 'run to the store' conjoins the adverbial phrase with the verb, the so-called category change for the whole phrase is simply a result of ordinary predicate logic.[14] With the analysis of processes in terms of events the framework is simplified, and the category switch which is due to adverbial modification receives a simple explanation.

Chapter 10
States

10.1 Introduction

What kind of logical forms are we to attribute to *state* sentences,[1] those not seeming to report events or processes?[2] Certainly, we do not want to appeal to underlying *events* in

A Brutus is clever

B Brutus has a dog.

But why not underlying states? Why not attribute to these sentences forms such as

A′ (∃s)[s is a state of being clever & Subj(s,Brutus)]

B′ (∃s)[s is a having & Subj(s,Brutus) & Obj(s,a dog)]?

Is there evidence for such analyses, as there was in the case of event sentences? Or evidence against? Or what?

There is indeed evidence in favor of the underlying state approach for state sentences, but there is not as much of it, and it is not as easy to evaluate, as the evidence for the underlying event approach for event sentences.

I am tempted by the following picture, which I discuss in detail in the remainder of the chapter:

Verbs All verbs stand for kinds of events or kinds of states. 'Stab' picks out a kind of event, whereas 'have' picks out a kind of state. The logical forms of simple sentences with state verbs are exactly like those with event verbs, except that we use Hold instead of Cul. So, for example, the logical form of (B) above is

B″ (∃x)[x is a dog & (∃s)[s is a having & Subj(s,Brutus) & Obj(s,x)
    & Hold(s,now)]].

Adjectives Adjectives pick out kinds of states. An adjective occurring with a copula (as in 'was clever') yields the same kind of logical form as a state verb. The logical form of (A) above is

A″ (∃s)[s is a state of being clever & Subj(s,Brutus) &
    Hold(s,now)].

Locatives Locatives that occur with the copula stand for predicates of states. The logical form of

C   Brutus is under the tree

is

C″ (∃s)[Under(s,the tree) & Subj(s,Brutus) & Hold(s,now)].

These predicates are the very same as those that occur in the logical forms of other sentences, such as

Brutus sat under the tree.
Mary played the clarinet under the tree.[3]

For example,

(∃e)[Playing(e) & Agent(e,Mary) & Theme(e,clarinet) &
Under(e,tree) & Cul(e, before now)].

Nouns Nouns probably do *not* pick out events or states (except for "higher-order" nouns, such as 'killing' or 'accident'). Their logical forms are exactly as they are generally supposed to be in logic texts. For example,

D   Fido is a giraffe

has as its logical form

D″ Giraffe(Fido),

and

E   A giraffe ran

has as its form

E″ (∃x)[Giraffe(x) & x ran].[4]

It *is* possible to interpret nouns as standing for kinds of states, having logical forms resembling those of verbs. For example, it is possible to interpret 'Giraffe(x)' as being short for '(∃s)[s is a state of being a giraffe & Theme(s,x)]'. I know of no objection to this. But I also know of no evidence in its favor. If states are used in this way, then they are just excess baggage in a theory of language.

10.2 State Verbs

State verbs include transitive verbs such as 'have', 'love' 'believe', and intransitive verbs such as 'stand' and 'sit' when these are read statively. 'Sit' is a state verb when read with the meaning "be situated," although not when read as something a person does; in the latter usage it is a process verb. The stative reading is found in 'At 3:00 the statue stood in the corner (but by 4:00 it had been moved)'.

Two possible sources of evidence for an underlying state reading of sentences with state verbs are due, respectively, to the logic of modifiers, and to the occurrence of state sentences as objects of perception verbs.

Modifiers   State sentences do not contain most of the modifiers found in event sentences. We do not have sentences such as 'Brutus has a dog quietly' or 'Brutus is clever in the back with a knife'. Some state verbs take adverbs of manner, as in

Mary believes *fervently* that John loves her.

But we cannot discover much about the logic of modifiers when dealing with sentences containing only a single modifier. Since none of these verbs takes adverbials of motion or direction, we are left with little to work with. The best examples I can find are like the following:

The statue stood on its left leg on the grass.

If this is a state sentence, then we can duplicate the arguments of chapter 2 in favor of the underlying state analysis, and the logical form of the sentence would be

(∃s)[s is a standing & Subj(s,statue) & On(s,grass) & On(s,left leg)].

This accounts for the fact that the sentence entails each of the following:

The statue stood on the grass.
The statue stood on its left leg.
The statue stood.

Further, it accounts for the fact that the following two sentences

The statue stood on its left leg on the grass
The statue stood on its right leg on the sidewalk

do not jointly entail

The statue stood on its left leg on the sidewalk,

as they would if we were to analyze the adverbials as independent conjuncts applying to the statue instead of the state.

I have several reservations about this evidence. First, these constructions are all odd ones, as evidenced by the near anomaly of the bare 'The statue stood' when read statively. Second, to make the example work, we have to interpret a case in which the statue is standing on both legs as one in which it is standing on its left leg and also standing on its right leg. Yet each of these alone seems to carry an implication that the statue is *not* standing on both legs. Third, there is a strong tendency to read 'The statue stood on its left leg on the grass' as 'The statue stood on its left leg, which was on the grass' (that is, the leg was on the grass). The latter reading makes the example irrelevant, because it cannot then have the displayed form.

Some other examples may avoid most of these objections. Consider a TV set perched between a desk and a table that almost touch one another. Then the following might be true:

The TV sits on the desk by the lamp.
The TV sits on the table by the computer.

These should not entail that

The TV sits on the desk by the computer.[5]

These seem to be naturally interpretable as two sittings (two situatings), one on the desk and by the lamp, and another on the table and by the computer.

I have not been able to find better examples of state verbs occurring with multiple adverbials that might be state modifiers. The absence of such examples is not evidence against the underlying state analysis, but it is disappointing that we cannot do better.

Perception Constructions   Nonmental state verbs seem to occur as the objects of perception verbs. For example,

For three hours we watched it stand under the tree without moving. Finally we concluded it was the statue of the gorilla, and not the gorilla itself. Then it moved, and we discovered we were wrong.

All of the discussion in chapter 2 about event verbs seems to carry over to these examples—provided, of course, that 'stand' occurs with a stative meaning in these examples. Again, it is difficult to find other examples. Mental state verbs such as 'love' and 'believe' do not occur in these constructions, which is not surprising, since (intuitively) the putative states are unobservable. But perhaps not in principle. One can imagine a future development of neuropsychology in which people develop indirect ways to test for such states; then they might very well say "For two continuous hours we watched the patient hate her mother." If these make sense, and I think they do, then the occurrence of perception verbs provides weak and indirect but confirming evidence for an underlying state analysis of such contexts.

10.3   Adjectives

Adjectives form a puzzling class. In some languages they do not exist at all. In others, such as English, they form a fairly well-defined class, though it is sometimes difficult to guess from the meaning of a word whether it should be an adjective or a verb. Indeed, many adjectives of Modern English evolved from verbs of Old English with apparently the same meaning, as in

Old English: She hungers
Modern English: She is hungry

My hypothesis is that adjectives are the statives par excellence of English, and that there is a tendency of Modern English to express state meanings by adjectives instead of by verbs. This is why it is difficult to find clear examples of intransitive state verbs in Modern English; they tend to be reexpressed as adjectives. Transitive verbs convert less easily into adjectives, because of the need to preserve their objects, and so transitive state verbs tend to stay in the language.

Adjectives occur in two main ways: predicate occurrences with the copula, such as 'Cleo is clever', and attributive occurrences modifying nouns, such as 'the gorgeous giraffe'.

10.3.1   Copula Plus Adjective

Modifiers   Examples of adjectives in copula position[6] that take other state modifiers are difficult to find. There seem to be no adverbials of manner, direction, or motion that occur in the blank in 'Brutus is clever _____'. However, some few adjectives take multiple modifiers. I have in mind examples such as

The board is grooved with sharp furrows along its edge.

This appears to parallel earlier event examples, such as 'Brutus stabbed Caesar with a knife in the back'. If we attribute to it the form

($\exists$s)[s is a state of being grooved & Theme(s,board) & With(s,sharp furrows) & Along(s,edge) & Hold(s,now)],

then the logic turns out right. In particular, the sentence entails each of the following:

The board is grooved with sharp furrows.
The board is grooved along its edge.
The board is grooved.

And in conjunction with

The board is grooved with blunt furrows across its center,

it does *not* entail

The board is grooved with sharp furrows across its center.

Again, this is because the state of being grooved with sharp furrows is different from the state of being grooved with blunt furrows, even though the board is in both states.

   This type of example seems to be a special form; the sentence has the superficial look of an agentless passive. If so, it comes from an active *event* verb, 'groove'. So the example might be thought to be an event sentence in disguise. However, the relevant reading is not that of an agentless passive. The sentence

When Mary arrived, the door was closed

has two readings, indicated by these paraphrases:

When Mary arrived, the door was immediately closed in her face with a loud crashing noise.

When Mary arrived, the door wasn't open.

The former paraphrases the agentless passive form of an event sentence. The latter paraphrases a reading that is not an agentless passive, a reading in which there is no entailment that anyone *ever* closed the door (maybe it was built closed). This is the natural reading of the "grooved board" sentence. The form of the sentence on that reading genuinely seems to be copula+adjective; it is not an event sentence in disguise.

There are plenty of other examples of this sort:

The door is latched loosely with a thong.
The door is latched tightly with a bolt.

This pair does not entail

The door is latched loosely with a bolt,

and so the adverbial modifiers cannot apply directly to the door. Another is

The door is latched at the top with a thong.
The door is latched at the bottom with a bolt.[7]

Yet another seems to be

The toys are evenly distributed among the children.

In addition to cases of reiterated modification, there are examples in which single adverbs modify adjectives, where the logical form does not seem to be that of independent predicates of the subject. Examples are

The door is tightly closed.
The book is brightly colored.

In these cases it seems awkward to attribute the modifier directly to the individual in question. In the former sentence we cannot suppose that 'tightly' applies to the door, since then 'the door is tightly closed' coupled with 'the door is fastened' would entail 'the door is tightly fastened'. The underlying state form seems to make sense here. For example, if we attribute to the first sentence the form

($\exists$s)[s is a state of being closed & Theme(s,door) & Tight(s) & Hold(s,now)],

then this entails 'The door is closed', which it should. So the form is unproblematic, at least.[8]

Evidence Stemming from Perceptual Idioms   At first sight, there seem to be no parallels between event and state clauses as the objects of perceptual verbs. One can say

Mary saw Brutus stab Caesar

but it is not English to say

Mary saw John be under the tree

or

Mary saw John be naked.[9]

But there is perhaps another way for state clauses to become the objects of perceptual verbs. A popular idea is that the copula 'be' typically appears in sentences as a carrier of the *tense* of the sentence, so that the verb 'be' appears in

Agatha is clever

primarily "because" a verb is needed to carry the present tense.[10] But the clauses that form the objects for perceptual verbs are not tensed. This suggests that state sentences that ordinarily contain 'be' should be able to appear as the objects of perceptual verbs but lacking their copulas. And we do get constructions of exactly that form:

A   Mary saw John under the tree.

B   Mary saw John naked.

The semantics of these constructions needs explanation. (B) means something different from either

B'   Mary saw that John is (was) naked.

or

B"   Mary saw John & John was naked.

Clearly (B) and (B') are different; Mary may see John naked without seeing *that* he is naked. Likewise, if John is the prime minister, then (B) entails that Mary saw the prime minister naked, but (B') does not entail that Mary saw that the prime minister was naked.

Likewise, (B) and (B") are different. We need to clarify the times that are appealed to in (B") in order to be clear about the analysis. It will not do to let (B") be true just because John was naked *sometime,* for then (B") would automatically be true if Mary saw John for the first time the next day. This would not entail that she saw him naked. So suppose that we require in (B") that the time of being naked coincides with the time of seeing. This will not do either. For suppose that Mary did see John naked, but that she saw this on videotape. Then (B") is false, since the time of seeing is not the time of being under the tree, yet (B) is true. No tinkering with the times will make (B″) into an adequate analysis of (B).

What is required, I suggest, is that it is John's being naked ("John's nakedness") that is the object of Mary's perception. This is exactly what is required by the underlying state analysis.

10.3.2 Attributive Constructions

Attributive constructions are those in which adjectives modify nouns. They seem to be of at least two sorts. One is epitomized by words like 'former' that never occur predicatively; it is not English to say 'The king is former'. These adjectives seem to be best symbolized as operators on predicates. I do not discuss them here. The others occur predicatively with the copula. If I am correct, these adjectives furnish predicates of individuals that, even in attributive position, are analyzable in terms of underlying quantification over states.[11] For example,

x is a red book = Red(x) & Book(x),

where Red(x) has the further analysis

$(\exists s)[s$ is a state of being red & theme$(s,x)]$.

For syntactic reasons, iterated modifiers of such adjectives do not appear in these positions, and so there is little evidence for or against the underlying state hypothesis for them. A possible use for the underlying state is in constructions like

x is a brightly colored book,

which would have the form

$(\exists s)[s$ is a state of being red & Bright(s) & Theme$(s,x)]$ & Book(x).[12]

10.4 Locatives

A sentence whose predicate consists of the copula plus a locative is a clear example of a state sentence. For example,

Mary is in the garage.
John is home.

In this section I survey the nature of the evidence that these should receive logical forms containing underlying quantification over states.

10.4.1 Evidence from the Logic of Modifiers

Initially, sentences such as

A   Brutus is in the park under the tree
B   Brutus is in the park
C   Brutus is under the tree

might be seen as evidence *against* the underlying state view. For the underlying state view tells us that the conjunction of (B) and (C) does *not* entail (A). This is because there is nothing in the logical forms of (B) and (C) to tell us that the state of Brutus's being in the park is the very same state as the state of Brutus's being under the tree, and that is what is required by (A):

A′ ($\exists$s)[Subj(s,Brutus) & In(s,the park) & Under(s,the tree)]
B′ ($\exists$s)[Subj(s,Brutus) & In(s,the park)]
C′ ($\exists$s)[Subj(s,Brutus) & Under(s,the tree)]

Indeed, if the conjunction of (B) and (C) does entail (A), then that is evidence in favor of the standard logic textbook approach to these sentences: being in the park is simply a predicate of Brutus, as is being under the tree, and being in the park under the tree is just the conjunction of these.

Or so it seems. But, as Barry Schein has pointed out to me, this is not the correct view of the situation. The reason we infer (A) from the conjunction of (B) and (C) is that we make additional (*nonlogical*) assumptions: that Brutus is small relative to the region of the park and relative to the region under the tree, and that he is wholly contained in each of these regions. Without these assumptions the inference fails. To see this, consider an example in which the assumptions are not true:

D   IBM is in a hilly area in Paris.
E   IBM is in a hilly area.
F   IBM is in Paris.[13]

Clearly the conjunction of (E) and (F) does not entail (D). IBM may be in many places, some in Paris and some hilly, without any of the Paris locations being hilly ones. Seeing that (E) conjoined with (F) does not entail (D), we also realize, by parity of reasoning, that neither does the conjunction of (B) and (C) entail (A). Imagine that Brutus is temporarily scattered, with half of him under a tree outside a park and the other half a mile away inside the park. He would be under a tree, and he would be in the park, but he would not be under the tree in the park. This failure of the conjunctive analysis of modifiers is a remarkable phenomenon. Since the underlying state analysis explains this failure in a simple way, I take this to be evidence in its favor.

10.4.2 Evidence from Perceptual Idioms

The evidence here parallels that for adjectives. Although the following is not English,

G   Mary saw John be under the tree,

this is

H   Mary saw John under the tree.

Again, this is a construction whose semantics needs explanation. Sentence (H) clearly means something different from either

H′   Mary saw that John is (was) under the tree

or

H″   Mary saw John & John was under the tree.

Clearly (H) and (H′) are different; if Mary does not recognize John, or does not recognize the tree as a tree, then she may see him under the tree without seeing that he is under the tree.

We can also show that (H) and (H″) are different, paralleling the argumentation produced above for adjectives. Going back to IBM, it is easy to imagine a case in which (J) is false:

J   Mary saw IBM in Paris

even though (K) is true:

K   Mary saw IBM and IBM is in Paris.[14]

It is not essential to appeal to IBM, however, to show that (H) differs from (H″). First, we need to clarify the times that are appealed to in (H″). It will not do to let (H″) be true just because John was under the tree *sometime*, for then (H″) would be true if Mary saw John at any time whatsoever. This would not entail that she saw him under the tree. So suppose that we require in (H″) that the time of being under the tree coincide with the time of seeing. This will not do either. Suppose that Mary did see John under the tree, but that she saw this on videotape. Then (H″) is false, since the time of seeing is not the time of being under the tree, but (H) is true. No tinkering with the times will make (H″) into an adequate analysis of (H).

John's being under the tree is needed as the object of Mary's perception. This is exactly what the underlying state analysis requires.

10.4.3 Other Evidence

One further kind of evidence involving locatives is worth considering, since it seems initially to count against the analysis. Consider the following inference:

Mary was in the park.
Mary was running.
∴ Mary was running in the park.

This appears to be a good inference (if we assume that the times in question are the same). How to account for it? We might insist, contrary to the above analyses, that locatives apply to the subjects of sentences. The proposed inference would then be of this form:

In(Mary,park)
Running(Mary)
∴ Running(Mary) & In(Mary,park)

This, however, cannot be a general account. Suppose that Mary stands just inside a park and stabs Bill across a river outside the park using a knife tied to a long stick. Then this inference would appear to be invalid:

Mary was in the park
Mary stabbed Bill
∴ Mary stabbed Bill in the park.

The failure of this inference is accounted for by the theory under consideration. The first sentence locates a state of Mary as an in-the-park state. The conclusion locates a stabbing event of which she is the agent as an in-the-park event. The second premise says only that that event took place. So clearly the inference is invalid on this account, as it should be. But then why is the former inference (the one with Mary running) so persuasive?

Suppose we think of an event or state as being within a certain spatiotemporal region if and only if all its participants are in that region:

*   An event or state is in R iff each participant of the event or state is in R.[15]

Assume further that any running has a single participant: its Agent-Theme. Then the inference actually goes as follows: The premise, 'Mary was in the park', locates some state of Mary as being in the park. By (*) this locates all participants of that state, including Mary, in the park. The second premise gives us a running that has Mary as its only participant, and so (*) tells us that this running is located in the park, which is exactly what is needed for the conclusion.[16] The second argument fails because the premises do not locate Bill in the park. (This seems like the *right* reason for it to fail.)

Some people might question the data I have cited. For them, the argument

Mary was in the park
Mary stabbed Bill
∴ Mary stabbed Bill in the park.

is perfectly valid. They might hold that if Mary is in the park and stabbed Bill, then she stabbed him in the park, regardless of where he is. If they are right, then the theory can still get the data right, though its ability to do so provides no additional evidence in its favor; it merely avoids a counterexample. What is needed is a variant of the principle cited above:

** An event or state is in R if the subject of the event or state is in R.

This makes the argument valid.

I suspect that my remarks only scratch the surface of the topic of locatives within this framework. I have ignored the whole question of time, and the data are uncertain in some such cases (for example, when a participant is in a region for most but not all of the time in which the event occurs).

10.5 Explicit Reference to and Quantification over States

Evidence for underlying quantification over events was found when underlying quantification interacted with explicit event reference or with explicit event quantification in other sentences. An example of interaction with explicit reference to events is the near synonymy of these sentences:

After the singing of the song, they left.
After the song was sung, they left.

The first contains an explicit reference to a singing; the latter does not. The appeal to implicit quantification over singings in the second explains the relationship between the two sentences. The second type of evidence comes from relations between underlying quantification over events and explicit quantification, as in the following:

In every burning, oxygen is consumed.
Agatha burned some wood.
∴ Oxygen was consumed.

The validity of this argument was explained in terms of the interaction between the explicit quantification over burnings in the first premise and the implicit quantification over burnings in the second.

Can these same two sources of evidence for underlying quantification over events in event sentences carry over to states in state sentences?

Explicit Reference to States   Clear cases in English of quantification over states or of reference to states are difficult to find. Of course, there are technical philosophical locutions such as 'the state of being clever' or 'every state that Agatha is in now', but these do not resemble my earlier examples of constructions involving events, and they do not yield parallel arguments.

Parallel constructions exist in English phrases such as 'Mary's being clever', as in contexts like

Mary's being clever helped her get into graduate school.

And some philosophers take these constructions to refer to states. But this view, although respectable, is hardly forced on us. The sentence above seems to be synonymous with

That Mary was clever helped her get into graduate school,

and many would take the italicized clauses in both sentences to refer to facts or to propositions, not to states.[17]

Another construction that may very well refer to states (though this is difficult to prove) is the use of adjectives with 'ness' as a suffix, often along with possessives. Examples are

Brutus's nakedness.
Agatha's cleverness.

(I think that these refer to states, but I don't know how to prove it.)

Quantification over States   It is also difficult to find uncontroversial examples of quantification over states, though there are plenty of plausible ones. *Prima facie* cases of such examples seem to satisfy the patterns found earlier for quantification over events. Here are two examples:

In every owning of a dog, a license is required.
Mary owns a dog
∴ A license is required.

In every illness, blood pressure rises.
Mary was ill.
∴ Blood pressure rose.

This presumes that 'every owning' quantifies over states of ownership and that 'every illness' quantifies over states of being ill.[18]

10.6   Do Nouns Have Underlying States?

I have not been able to find evidence that ordinary nouns have logical forms containing quantification over states. They may, and there is no inconsistency in supposing that they do, but there is no evidence for it.

What is at issue is a choice between the standard textbook treatment of, for example, 'Fido is a giraffe'

Giraffe(Fido)

and the more complex form

($\exists$s)[s is a being-a-giraffe state & Theme(s,Fido)].

When nouns are used with quantifiers, it is a choice between the usual symbolization of 'Every giraffe is . . .' as

(x)[Giraffe(x) → . . .],

and the more complex form

(x)[($\exists$s)[s is a being-a-giraffe state & Theme(s,x)] → . . .].

Parallels to the Logic of Modifiers   No pattern of nouns is similar to the "logic of modifiers" pattern with verbs, since we do not have sentences such as

Agatha is a doctor through the house/cleverly/on the roof.

One might think to find a parallel that compares the modifying of nouns by adjectives with the modifying of verbs by adverbials. Such examples are easy to come by, but their logics differ. Recall the earlier paradigm with verbs, in which the following two sentences:

Brutus stabbed Caesar violently with a knife
Brutus stabbed Caesar gently with an icepick

do not entail the "mixing" of modifiers:

Brutus stabbed Caesar violently with an icepick.

A similar pattern with nouns and adjectives might be

This is a brass screwdriver with a long blade.
This is a heavy screwdriver with a serrated handle.
∴ This is a brass screwdriver with a serrated handle.

In this case, however, the inference goes through, so the example provides no evidence for the use of underlying states in symbolizing nouns. Indeed, if the underlying state analysis of nouns is relevant here, it will need to be supplemented by additional principles to validate the inference.[19]

It is possible to produce other examples that follow this pattern, but the explanation of why the inference fails cannot lie with underlying states. Here are two such:

This is a brass statue with a short arm.
This is a former statue with a long arm.
∴ This is a brass statue with a long arm.

She is a tall hockey player.
She is a short basketball player.
∴ She is a tall basketball player.

The first inference is clearly special because of the special nature of 'former'; for independent reasons this appears to be an operator in logical form. (See chapter 4.) The example is not relevant to the issue of underlying states, since it is invalid no matter how the nouns and other adjectives are treated. The second inference has two natural treatments. On one, 'tall' would be treated as an operator, on a par with 'former', and the argument would be invalid for this reason, no matter how the noun is treated. On the other analysis (defended in chapter 4) 'tall' is a predicate (perhaps a complex one) of the individual in question, but its extension is sensitive to context. Again, the argument has (context-dependent) readings on which it is invalid, no matter how the noun is treated.

I conclude tentatively that there is no evidence based on the logic of modifiers to favor the hypothesis that nouns stand for underlying states.[20]

Parallels to Perception Sentences   There are also no parallels to perception sentences for nouns:

*She saw him a basketball player.
*They heard him a singer.
*She felt him a doctor.

In conclusion, nouns may be viewed as standing for underlying states only if additional principles are invoked to account for some of the major inferences that this hypothesis misses. But there is no positive evidence at all for the hypothesis. Perhaps it is a major difference in our language between verbs and nouns that verbs automatically pick out kinds of events or states, and nouns (except for special cases) do not.

10.7 Participants of States

As conceived here, states have participants, just as do events. Whether the thematic roles that relate participants to their states are the same or different from those that relate them to events in which they also participate is an open question. My impression is that in the case of states we can make do with a very small number of roles, probably three, and that these can probably be identified with the roles Performer, Experiencer, and Theme that are used with events. The notion of Agent does not seem applicable to states, nor do those of Benefactive or Source.[21] The role of Instrument might possibly be relevant, in cases such as 'The board is grooved with chisel tracks'.

I assume that the notion of Theme applies to the subjects of adjectives and locatives and to the direct objects of state verbs. I also assume that the nonagentive notion of Performer applies to the subjects of transitive state verbs. The following sentences thus have the indicated forms (ignoring times):

Brutus is clever =
($\exists$s)[Being-clever(s) & Theme(s,Brutus)].

Mary believes that Carlos loves her =
($\exists$s)[Believing(s) & Experiencer(s,Mary) & Theme(s,that Carlos loves her)].

The statue stands on the grass =
($\exists$s)[Standing(s) & Theme(s,statue) & On(s,grass)].

It is not difficult to find evidence for some notion of participanthood in at least some cases of talk about states. For example, consider this inference:

Before every illness a bacterium enters the body.
Mary was ill.
∴ A bacterium entered her body.

The presence of 'the' in the first premise and 'her' in the conclusion is puzzling. Since the premise is a quantified claim (a false one), the phrase 'the body' is not referring to some particular body. What then is it doing? The obvious answer is that it alludes to the body of whatever person is ill, and that this applies in the conclusion as well. The argument appears to have this form (again, ignoring the tenses, and being sloppy about the parsing of 'a bacterium'):

(s)[s is a Being-ill → (∃e)[Entering(e) & Performer(e,bacterium) & Theme(e, the body of the Theme of s) & Before(e,s)]].

(∃s)[Being-ill(s) & Theme(s,Mary)].

(∃e)[Entering(e) & Performer(e,bacterium) & Theme(e,the body of Mary)].

The argument, so construed, is valid.

10.8 States in Arithmetic

Mathematical talk offers apparent counterexamples to the theory I am presenting. Some mathematical statements conform to my theoretical treatment of *event* sentences without conforming to my theoretical treatment of *state* sentences, yet the statements seem to concern eternal states, not events in time. Examples of this include

The first sequence converges to zero more rapidly than the second.

The curve declines over the origin and then ascends again.

When you get above 100 the curve is rising, whereas earlier it was falling.

The series sums to 4.9 as you go from zero to infinity.

This is puzzling talk, apparently full of motion through time. The sequence "converges," the curve "declines" and "ascends," "rises" and "falls," and the series "sums" as you go. But sequences, curves, and series don't really do anything at all; they are just there. And as for the series that "sums" as you go, does it fail to sum if you *don't* go? And who are *you?* And what if *you* don't go but somebody *else* goes? Does the series still sum to 4.9?

The air of paradox in all this arises from the assumption, originating with or before Plato, that mathematical objects inhabit an unchanging realm, one that contains *inter alia* no people. It is thus a realm in which nothing can converge, rise, or fall, and in which there is no "you" to "go" from zero to infinity. The statements above, if taken at face value, seem to be literally false on this view. But we use them, and we are apparently uttering truths.

The theory of language I am examining suggests that the sentences are literally false. The logical form of 'The series rises rapidly' is

(∃e)[e is a rising & Theme(e,the series) & Rapid(e)].

This requires an event of rising, an event that must literally be rapid, thus (apparently) ruling out our interpreting the "event" as really being a state.

It may help to consider what mathematicians actually say when they are being especially careful and rigorous. The informal talk reproduced above disappears, and it is replaced by "careful" statements.

The first sequence converges to zero more rapidly than the second

becomes

There is an n such that for every m>n, the mth term of the first sequence is closer to zero than the mth term of the second.

And

The series sums to 4.9 as you go from zero to infinity

becomes

For every d>0 there is some n such that the absolute value of (4.9 - the sum of the first n terms of the series) is less than d.

These statements eliminate all suggestion of change and time. Interestingly for my purpose, they also eliminate all adverbs and all event verbs.

These reconstruals are already what the mathematician intends. The logical form clearly suggested by the informal sentences is not taken at face value in careful treatments of the subject. In careful moments mathematicians *may* use the terminology of events, but they use it heuristically and not literally. For example, a mathematician who introduces by definition the phrase 'rapidly declining' to apply to a certain kind of sequence defines the phrase as a unit. It then takes a

proof that a rapidly declining sequence is a declining sequence. If the
adverb and the verb were given independent meanings, the adverb
could be dropped off automatically, and it could also be meaningfully
used with other verbs without further explanation. But it cannot be
dealt with in these ways. The complex phrase is defined as a unit; it
is not intended to be seen as having logical parts.

In short, "serious" mathematical talk, carefully and rigorously formulated, is plausibly construable as being about objects of an unchanging and unpeopled realm. It is also couched in language without event
verbs and without verbal modifiers appropriate to events. A vocabulary may be chosen that looks as though it includes event modifiers,
but this is for heuristic purposes only; the apparent modifiers are not
genuine units of the vocabulary. Construing adverbial event modifiers
for serious mathematical talk presents no problem; there are no such
modifiers to construe.

In a way this settles any worry that mathematical talk might cause
problems for the theory. But a subsidiary issue remains. How should
we construe the talk mathematicians use informally, even though they
abandon it in their rigorous formulations?

Most informal mathematical talk involves the supposed motion of
one or more agents in (mathematical) space. If the discourse is about
curves, we imagine that the agent moves along the curves (usually at
a constant rate in a given direction). Then the problematic talk about
what the curve does is easily reconstrued as accurate talk about what
the agent does:

The curve declines over the origin and then ascends again = as you
move along the curve, you decline when you pass over the origin
and then you ascend again.

When you get above 100 the curve is rising, whereas earlier it was
falling = when you get above 100 you are rising, whereas earlier you
were falling.

The series sums to 4.9 as you go from zero to infinity = if you add
up the terms of the series as you go from zero towards infinity, you
get closer to 4.9 at every step.[22]

I call this "accurate" talk about what the agent does, but I really have
in mind to straighten out the metaphor. Informal mathematical talk
often amounts to literal talk about the actions of an hypothetical agent
traveling in a strange realm. Reconstrued in this way, the sentences
of the story obey the theory of underlying events and states as I have

described it. The fact that the informal talk obeys the theory is additional weak evidence in favor of the theory.

The task of turning the heuristic informal story of the traveler in a strange realm into an accurate talk about a realm without travelers is a fascinating enterprise for philosophers of mathematics. I have not given general rules for carrying out this task. I have argued that such reconstruals are plausible, and that this kind of discourse does not threaten the theory of underlying events and states.

If my preceding remarks are correct for mathematics, they may also shed some light on the old conundrum about the road that goes both uphill and downhill. The problem is how to reconcile

The road from A to B goes uphill,

with

The road from B to A goes downhill,

when the road from A to B *is* the road from B to A. For substitutivity of identity appears to give us

The road from A to B goes downhill.

Here is the solution. Like the mathematical examples, the first sentence is construable as

You go uphill when you go from A to B.

This attributes uphillness to events that are goings from A to B; presumably, the goings from B to A differ from the goings from A to B, and so the problem disappears.

Some reconstrual is necessary, quite apart from the question of modifiers, since the unreconstrued versions entail that 'The road goes', and this cannot be literally correct, since roads don't "go." Or if they do, the sense of 'go' is synonymous with 'lead': "All roads lead to Rome." Since 'lead' naturally takes a direct object, this invites a reconstrual that is on a par with that suggested above: "The road leads *you* uphill whenever it leads *you* from A to B." Here, 'you' is the Theme of the leading, and so, on the principle about adverbs of motion suggested in chapter 5, it is you who end up "uphill" and "at B," not the road.

Chapter 11
Tenses and "Temporal" Adverbials

11.1 Overview of Tenses and "Temporal" Adverbials

This chapter surveys the treatment of tense and of "temporal" adverbials, and the ways in which they interact with underlying events and states. The word 'temporal' is here construed in the broadest possible way to include adverbials of point-time ('at noon'), interval-time ('between 2:00 and 3:30'), duration ('for 3 hours'), frequency ('every day', 'often'), and so on. There are also "spatial" adverbials, including adverbials of point-space ('at the corner'), region ('between New York and Chicago'), extent ('throughout China'), frequency ('everywhere'), and so on. The term 'temporal', or even 'spatiotemporal', is misleadingly narrow, since some of these adverbials have nothing to do with either space or time; an example is 'A country with a prime minister *often* has a parliament'.

The interaction of this vaguely delimited class of adverbials with tenses and with underlying events is complex, and I have no hope of presenting and justifying these matters in a systematic fashion by examining the evidence for each specific proposal on its own merits. This may not even be possible. I have opted instead for a general description of a theoretical treatment, accompanied by illustrations. The evidence in favor of the overall treatment will be that it gets the data right—if it does so. I do not have great confidence in the details that follow, but I think that they are promising enough to articulate, in the hope of provoking further research along these lines.

For simplicity I ignore context, including the embedding of sentences in narratives. I hope that I do not thereby distort the phenomena. I think that my account includes the ingredients that are needed to embed it in a sophisticated theory of discourse, even though I do not pursue that enterprise here.[1]

A Qualification about Noun Phrases   I assume that NP's are introduced after the core of a sentence is formed (as in Montague Grammar). For example, the sentence 'Everyone is happy' can be conceived as being constructed in these stages:

x be happy   Core
|
x is happy   Addition of Tense
|
Everyone is happy   NP Quantification

In this illustration the NP goes on last, which is why I have ignored NPs so far. But since NPs can interact with tense and with quantificational adverbs, things are now somewhat more complicated. (I illustrate this in sections 11.3 and 11.6.) For simplicity I avoid the use of quantified NPs in my examples wherever no question is begged by doing so.

11.1.1   A Simplified Overview

Temporal adverbials can introduce considerable complexity into logical forms. The ingredients of simple noncausative event sentences before frequency adverbials are introduced can be summed up as:

$Verb(e)$ & $Role(e)^n$ & $Mod(e)^m$ & $Cul(e,t)$,

where '$Verb(e)$' is the part contributed by the verb, '$Role(e)^n$' consists of one or more conjuncts relating the thematic role variables to the event, '$Mod(e)^m$' consists of zero or more conjuncts arising from adverbial verb modifiers, and '$Cul(e,t)$' relates the culmination of the event to the time in question. For the sentence 'Brutus stabbed Caesar violently', the parts are

$Verb(e)$ $Stabbing(e)$
$Role(e)^2$ $Agent(e,Brutus)$ & $Theme(e,Caesar)$
$Mod(e)^1$ $Violent(e)$
$Cul(e,t)$ $Cul(e,t)$

The logical form of a sentence expanded to include temporal adverbials (but still ignoring frequency adverbials) has this complexity:

Frame [$(\exists I)$[Tense(I) & Time-Constraint(I) &
$(\exists e)(\exists t)$[$t \in I$ & Verb(e) & Role(e)^n & Mod(e)^m & Cul(e,t) &
Temporal-Mod(e)]]].

The new items appearing in the form are Frame, Tense, Time-Constraint, and Temporal-Mod. I summarize them here in the order in which they appear in later sections of this chapter.

Frame   Many adverbials that are "temporal" or "locative" in appearance are frame adverbials, phrases that set a context within which the rest of the sentence is to be interpreted. 'During the war', 'on Tuesday', 'at noon', and so on, function in this way in sentences such as

During the war, Agatha ran every day in the afternoon.

Tense   The default form of a simple sentence contains a quantifier that contributes a period of time. Tenses are elements that constrain this period to the past, the present, or the future.[2] In logical form, the tenses contribute predicates of the time-period variable. In the following logical form for 'Brutus stabbed Caesar' the clause contributed by the past tense is '$I<$now':

$(\exists I)$[$I<$now & $(\exists e)(\exists t)$[$t \in I$ & Stabbing(e) & Agent(e,Brutus) & Theme(e,Caesar) & Cul(e,t)]]].

Time-Limiting Adverbials   The same period of time that is constrained by the tense of a sentence may also be constrained by temporal modifiers. In 'Yesterday, Brutus stabbed Caesar', the 'Yesterday' combines with the variable I, giving a (default) reading of

$(\exists I)$[$I<$now & $I \subset$ Yesterday & $(\exists e)(\exists t)$[$t \in I$ & Stabbing(e) & Agent(e,Brutus) & Theme(e,Caesar) & Cul(e,t)]].

If there are several such adverbials in the sentence, they all limit the same variable in the same way:

Yesterday at noon, Brutus stabbed Caesar =

$(\exists I)$[$I<$now & $I \subset$ Yesterday & $I \subset$ Noons & $(\exists e)(\exists t)$[$t \in I$ & Stabbing(e) & Agent(e,Brutus) & Theme(e,Caesar) & Cul(e,t)]],

where 'Noons' names the set of times that occur at some noon or other.

Temporal Event Modifiers   Some temporal modifiers can appear as predicates of events in logical form. This is a possible construal of any adverbial that can occur in the blank in

Did you ever run _____?

For example, in the question

Did you ever run at noon?

The question asks whether you have ever participated in an event of a certain sort. The answer, 'I ran at noon', will have this form:

$(\exists I)[I < now \ \& \ (\exists e)(\exists t)[t \in I \ \& \ Running(e) \ \& \ Agent\text{-}Theme(e,me) \ \& \ At(e,noon) \ \& \ Cul(e,t)]]$,

in which the temporal modifier appears as a predicate of events.

It is apparent that the same adverbials can occur in different places in a sentence and have different significance in those different places. For example, 'during the monsoon' can function as a Frame adverbial, as a Time-Constraining adverbial, or as a predicate of events. My view is more complex than those that classify adverbials primarily into the categories of point-time ('at noon'), interval-time ('from 2:00 to 3:00), duration ('for three hours'), and so on. These classifications are important, but they do not correlate in any simple way with the needed variety of application discussed here.

11.1.2 Frequency

The simple picture sketched above omitted adverbials of frequency, such as 'frequently', 'usually', 'once', 'twice', and 'often'. When these are absent, the event variable and the time variables are quantified, by default, by existential quantifiers. 'Brutus stabbed Caesar' in isolation means approximately 'There is a time period **I,** and there is an event e, such that **I** is in the past & e is a stabbing & . . .'. When frequency adverbials are present, however, they can replace the default quantifications by others. For example, 'At noon, Mary always runs' has as one of its readings

$(I)[I \subset Noons \rightarrow (\exists e)(\exists t)[t \in I \ \& \ Running(e) \ \& \ Agent\text{-}Theme(e,Mary) \ \& \ Cul(e,t)]]$,

in which 'always' has turned the default existential quantifier over periods of time into a universal. In other cases a frequency adverbial can affect the quantifier over particular times within the interval (the variable 't'), the quantifier over events or states, and even the quantification of various NPs that occur in the sentence.

I discuss frequency adverbials in section 11.6, along with subordinating adverbials such as 'before' or 'when'. Up to section 11.6, I assume the default existential quantifications in all examples.

11.2 Frame Adverbials

Some adverbials can establish a "frame of discussion"; I call them *frame* adverbials.[3] They include

In a dream
In this novel
In China
In 1939
During the war
Among the ancient Egyptians.

Since they include some time adverbials, I discuss them here, although I am uncertain about their function.

Frame adverbials seem to come in two sorts, exemplified in the list above. The first two set up unreal frames, and the rest do not. Perhaps the best way to treat them is as in the tradition of Montague 1973, namely, *generalize to the worst case,* and then add reduction principles (such as meaning postulates) to accommodate the more well-behaved ones. The "worst case" treatment for frame adverbials is to construe them as sentence modifiers; their logical forms map the meanings of sentences to other propositions, with no additional logical constraints assumed. This seems to be right for 'in a dream', since, for example, there is no logical connection between 'An orangutan assassinated the president' and 'In a dream, an orangutan assassinated the president'. But adverbials in the second group seem to have more specific meanings. They specify a region of space-time, and that region then gets tacked onto some later noun phrases via restrictive relative clauses. For example,

In 1939, Mary ran every day =
Mary ran every day-in-1939

During the war, Mary ran most afternoons =
most afternoons-during-the-war, Mary ran

In China, doctors are underpaid =
Doctors-in-China are underpaid

Last week, Mary ran at least once =
Mary ran at least one time-during-last-week.

This seems to be the right account for these frame adverbials, though it is not clear how best to formalize it.

Frame adverbials are difficult to recognize and to distinguish from others. The reason is that most modifiers functioning as frame adverbials can also function as predicates of eventualities or as predicates of time intervals:

A   Pred of event: Mary ran from 2:00 to 3:00.
B   Pred of interval: From 2:00 to 3:00, Mary ran.
C   Frame: From May to August Mary ran every day
                          (= Mary ran [on] every day-from-May-to
                          August).

In (A), the adverbials 'from 2:00' and 'to 3:00' are not frame adverbials; they indicate predicates of the event of Mary's running:

A' $(\exists I)[I<now$ & $(\exists e)(\exists t)[t \in I$ & Running(e) & Agent-
      Theme(e,Mary) & From(2:00,e) & To(3:00,e) & Cul(e,t)]]

These are discussed in section 11.5. In (B), the same adverbials constrain the interval:

B' $(\exists I)[I<now$ & From(2:00,I) & To(3:00,I) & $(\exists e)(\exists t)[t \in I$ &
      Running(e) & Agent-Theme(e,Mary) & Cul(e,t)]]

These are discussed in Section 11.4.

In (C), 'From May to August' is a frame adverbial whose effect is to constrain the NP 'every day':

C'   (x)[Day(x) & After(x,May) & Before(x,August) $\rightarrow$ $(\exists I)[I<now$
      & On(I,x) & $(\exists e)(\exists t)[t \in I$ & Running(e) & Agent-
      Theme(e,Mary) & Cul(e,t)]]].

I am not aware of any clear operational tests that would distinguish these three uses of "temporal" adverbials.

The proper treatment of frame adverbials is a matter of some complexity, and I do not develop it further here. I mention the topic primarily to distinguish the use of adverbials as frame adverbials from the other uses I discuss below.

11.3   Tenses

Tense logic typically employs two operators: PAST and FUT. PAST(S) is true at a time t if and only if S is true at some time before t, and FUT(S) is true at a time t if and only if S is true at some time after t. These operators can be used to define other notions; for example, one can define "always in the past" by $\neg$ PAST($\neg$ S), which is true at a time t if and only if S is true at every time before t.

What do these operators have to do with the English tenses? One sometimes gets the impression, because of the choice of terminology, that PAST(S) represents the past tense of S, and that FUT(S) represents the future tense of S (the use of S containing the auxiliary 'will'). This is a natural hypothesis, because it typically yields the correct truth conditions for the simplest of sentences (when context does not force a different reading): 'Brutus stabbed Caesar' is true if and only if there is some time in the past at which Brutus stabs Caesar. However, other constructions require a different time-quantification. For example, 'George Washington ate with a wooden spoon', on its most natural reading, is not made true by Washington's having eaten at least once with a wooden spoon.[4]

In order to represent English we need to distinguish two functions of the traditional tense operators of formal logic. One is that they have scopes that limit the significance of what lies within to the past or future. The other is their frequency aspect, the *at least once* in the past, or *at least once* in the future. In English the tenses have the former role of limiting times to the past, present, or future, but they do not have the additional role of indicating the frequency of an event or state; that role is carried by other elements in the sentence. The *at least once* is a default that appears in the absence of other indicators; it is not invariably contributed by the tense, and it is not required.

I shall use overt quantification over times and periods of time in clarifying the temporal aspects of sentences. Assuming that 'now' refers to the time of utterance, I represent the past, present, and future as constraining the interval of time during which events take place and states hold.[5] The forms are

Past   I<now
Pres   I=now
Fut   I>now

A typical use is in 'Brutus stabbed Caesar', where the time of the stabbing is said to be in the interval constrained by the past tense:

Brutus stabbed Caesar = ($\exists$I)[I<now & ($\exists$t)[t$\in$I & ($\exists$e)[Stabbing(e) & Agent(e,Brutus) & Theme(e,Caesar) & Cul(e,t)]]].

This is the default symbolization, in which the frequency is 'at least once', represented by the existential quantifier introducing the variable I (and in which we ignore any further restrictions on I due to context). The part of the sentence limiting I, namely 'I<now', is the part that is contributed by the tense. The next part, '($\exists$t)[t$\in$I & ...]' indicates the frequency of occurrence of the event within that period; it is the default reading 'at least once in the interval in question'. In this case the appeal to both interval and time-within-the-interval is redundant; the formalism is equivalent to

Brutus stabbed Caesar = ($\exists$t)[t<now & ($\exists$e)[Stabbing(e) & Agent(e,Brutus) & Theme(e,Caesar) & Cul(e,t)]],

where the use of the past interval is eliminated, and where the time part

($\exists$t)[t<now & ...]

gives the meaning of the usual operator PAST of tense logic. In this case, the proposed symbolization reduces to the standard one of tense logic. The interval I, however, will be employed in a nontrivial way in other examples. In particular, it will be subject to at least the following operations.

Discourse Discourse can provide additional constraints on I. For example, in a narrative, each event sentence describes an event that occurs after the preceding one. When occurring in a narrative, I will be subject to a condition that it be after the time of the preceding event (if the sentence is an event sentence). There are many aspects of this sort affecting I; they are not discussed in this book.

Frequency When the relevant frequency changes, the quantification of the I quantifier is affected, but the I-part remains constrained by the tense. For example, 'At noon, Mary always ran' has as one of its readings

(I)[I<now & I$\subset$Noon $\rightarrow$ ($\exists$e)($\exists$t)[t$\in$I & Running(e) & Agent-Theme(e,Mary) & Cul(e,t)]].

In other cases the I remains unchanged, and the frequency adverbial affects some other parts of the sentence. In 'Mary always walked with Bob' the meaning is

(∃I)[I<now & (t)[t∈I & Mary walks at t → Mary walks with Bob at t]].

This is discussed further in section 11.6.

Tenses and Scope   Tenses can interact with NPs in terms of their scopes. Two examples whose contents suggest different scopes for the tenses and NPs are

Every doctor at Hoag Memorial Hospital got his/her B.A. from Southern Missionary College.

(x)[(∃t)[t∈now & Doctor(x,t) & At(x,Hoag,t)] → (∃I)[I<now & (∃t)[t∈I & Get(x,B.A.,SMC,t)]]].

Every Orange County judge convicted at least one felon (before being disbarred).

(∃I)[I<now & (x)[(∃t)[t∈I & Judge(x,t)] → (∃t)[t∈I & Convict(x,felon,t)]]].

An ambiguous example is 'A doctor lived here':

(∃x)[(∃t)[t∈now & Doctor(x,t)] & (∃I)[I<now & (∃t)[t∈I & Live(x,here,t)]]].

(∃I)[I<now & (∃x)[(∃t)[t∈I & Doctor(x,t)] & (∃t)[t∈I & Live(x,here,t)]]].

It would be an interesting task to explore the constraints on the inter-actions of NP quantification with tenses, but that issue goes beyond the topic of underlying events and states, and I do not pursue it further here.[6]

11.4   Constraints on Times

11.4.1   The Modular Approach
One of the clearest and most natural kind of temporal adverbials is the kind that constrains the relevant time-period. Some cases include point-time ('at noon') and interval-time ('between 2:00 and 3:30') ad-verbials. One of their functions is to appear in logical form as predi-cates that apply to the interval of (space)-time that is also limited by the tense of the sentence. Earlier examples include

Yesterday at noon, Brutus stabbed Caesar = (∃I)[I<now & I⊂Yesterday & I⊂Noons & (∃e)(∃t)[t∈I & Stabbing(e) & Agent(e,Brutus) & Theme(e,Caesar) & Cul(e,t)]],

where 'Noons' names the set of times that occur at some noon or other, and 'Yesterday' picks out the set of all times during yesterday. The intersection of these two constraints will, in this case, make **I** effectively a unit interval, and this specifies exactly the identity of t, i.e., the time of the stabbing. In other cases the location of t is left partly open:

Tuesday afternoon between 2:00 and 3:00 Brutus stabbed Caesar =
$(\exists I)[I<now$ & $I \subset Tuesdays$ & $I \subset Afternoons$ & $I \subset Between(2:00,3:00)$ & $(\exists e)(\exists t)[t \in I$ & $Stabbing(e)$ & $Agent(e,Brutus)$ & $Theme(e,Caesar)$ & $Cul(e,t)]]$,

where 'Afternoons' names the set of times that occur during some afternoon or other, and, 'Tuesdays' picks out the set of all times on Tuesdays. In context 'Tuesday' might be limited to "next Tuesday" or "last Tuesday." But apart from context these words have meanings that are general, and the intersections of these general meanings contribute to constraints on the interval **I**. In the sentence 'Brutus stabbed Caesar on July 16, 1939 at 4:00 in the afternoon' the meaning is

$(\exists I)[I<now$ & $I \subset July$ & $I \subset 16th$ & $I \subset 1939$ & $I \subset 4:00$ & $I \subset afternoon$ & . . .]$,

where '16th' stands for the set of times on the 16th day of any month, and where '4:00' stands for any time of 4:00 (on any day, either A.M. or P.M.).

This treatment of time-constraining adverbials permits a modular account of such time indicators, the modularity extending even to certain adverbials that form natural pairs, as 'from . . . to . . .'. In particular, a sentence such as

Tuesday afternoon from 2:00 to 3:00 Brutus watched Caesar
should have the form

$(\exists I)[I<now$ & $I \subset Tuesdays$ & $I \subset Afternoons$ & $From(2:00,I)$ & $To(3:00,I)$ & $(\exists e)(\exists t)[t \in I$ & $Watching(e)$ & $Agent(e,Brutus)$ & $Theme(e,Caesar)$ & $Cul(e,t)]]$,

where '$From(2:00,I)$' indicates that **I** begins at some time of 2:00, and '$To(3:00,I)$' indicates that **I** ends at some time of 3:00.

Indeterminacy of Constructions   Certain constructions seem to have equally good alternative treatments on this view. The locution '2:00 P.M.' is paradigmatic. Does the 'P.M.' modify the '2:00', or is it an independent adverbial? That is, does the logical form of 'at 2:00 P.M.' contain

I⊂2:00 & I⊂P.M.

or

I⊂2:00 P.M.?

Both constructions seem equally viable. Other examples of such indeterminacy are 'Tuesday afternoon' (does 'Tuesday' say which afternoon, or does it mean 'Tuesday, in the afternoon'?), 'next week Friday', 'April the 14th', and so on.

An additional sort of indeterminacy is whether 'Tuesday' is to be construed as the set of all times that fall on some Tuesday, or whether 'Tuesday' is actually always short for *on* Tuesday, where the 'Tuesday' is either short for 'some Tuesday' or acts as a contextually determined name of a particular day. I suspect that both of these happen, with a typical use of 'Agatha always meditates on Tuesday' meaning 'on some Tuesday', and 'Bill will arrive Tuesday' meaning 'on next Tuesday'.

Spatial Locatives It is tempting to extend this treatment to include spatial locatives as well, thinking of all "locations" (both spatial and temporal) as on a par. Thus we might have

Yesterday in Rome Brutus stabbed Caesar = (∃I)[I<now & I⊂Yesterday & I⊂Rome & (∃e)(∃t)[t∈I & Stabbing(e) & Agent(e,Brutus) & Theme(e,Caesar) & Cul(e,t)]].

We then construe the I as ranging over spatiotemporal regions in general and the t as ranging over spatiotemporal points; 'Cul(e,t)' will then say *where and when* e culminates. This seems like an elegant amplification of the approach.

Constraining the Whole Event Once we add time-constraining adverbials to sentences, we face a new question about how the event relates to the period of time. If we merely have a sentence such as 'Brutus built a house', it is sufficient to say that there is some past period during which a house building by Brutus *culminated*. But now we can say 'Brutus built a house *yesterday*', and the question arises of the relation of the house building to yesterday. Is it enough to say that the house building culminated during yesterday? Much more than this would ordinarily be communicated by the use of such a sentence: we would typically communicate the information that most of the house building took place during yesterday. It is not clear to me whether this should be part of the logical form of the sentence, or whether it is merely a typical implication of its use. If it should be part of the logical form of the sentence, then we can easily conjoin to 'Cul(e,t)' an additional condition, say, 'e incl I', indicating that the total time that e holds is included in I. This would then require that if Brutus built a house yesterday afternoon, he both started and finished on yesterday afternoon. It would also require that if Brutus will build a house tomorrow, he can't start working on it today. I have not tried to introduce such a clause before, because I am uncertain whether it is correct, and because it introduces increased complexity into the logical forms.

11.4.2 Quantified Time-Constraining Adverbials

So far, I have considered only time-constraining adverbials that do not introduce additional complexity into the sentence due to quantification. But such quantification is rampant. Consider

sometime
every day (=daily)
every other day.

I assume that 'sometime' means 'at some time'. This 'some time' is a quantified NP that binds a variable, the variable that is the object of the preposition 'at'. So

. . . sometime . . .

means

For some time t, . . . at t. . . .

For example,

Mary will eat sometime

means

For some time t, Mary will eat at t.

On this account, adverbials like 'sometime' do not cause additional complexity in the treatment of atomic formulas of English; they are merely complexes of NPs whose scopes include those atomic formulas together with simple time-constraining adverbials whose semantics I have already discussed. Such NPs can add a great deal of complexity to the sentences in which they occur because of their scope interactions with other scope-bearing items. But they do not introduce new difficulties into the issue of time-constraint.

11.4.3 Durational Time Constraints

Durational adverbs also form a class of quantified time-constraining adverbials special enough to deserve separate comment. A classic case is the construction 'for three days'. This has two readings, one of which has already been discussed as being a simple quantification of a time-constraining 'on'. This is the relevant reading of 'For 3 days Mary awoke at sunrise; the days were Sunday, Monday, and Thursday'. On this reading the meaning of 'For 3 days' is 'For each of 3 days'; the first clause has the form

$(\exists 3y)[Day(y)$ & On y, Mary awoke at sunrise],

where 'on y' is a simple time-constraining adverbial of the first sort.

The other interpretation means 'for a period 3 days in length', which also involves quantification, though it is more complex. On this latter interpretation, the gross form of

. . . for 3 days . . .

is

$(\exists P)[P$ is some 3-day long period of time & (t)[t is a time in P $\rightarrow$ . . . at t . . .]].[7]

For example, the sentence 'For 3 days Mary was sick' would mean

$(\exists P)[P$ is some 3-day long period of time & (t)[t is a time in P $\rightarrow$ Mary was sick at t]].

The meaning of the process sentence 'Mary ran for 3 hours' is that there is a 3-hour period such that at each instant (always) in that period Mary runs:

$(\exists P)[P$ is 3 hours long & (t)[t$\in$P $\rightarrow$ $(\exists I)[I<$now & At(I,t) & $(\exists e)(\exists t')[t'\in I$ & Running(e) & Agent-theme(e,Mary) & Cul(e,t')]]]].

Since 'run' is a process verb, the above form makes sense; i.e., it is possible for Mary to run at each moment in some 3-hour interval. (A process verb, according to chapter 9, is one that, whenever it applies to an event, it also typically applies homogeneously to culminated subevents of that event.) Combining an event verb that is not a process verb with a duration adverbial of this sort yields anomaly. For example, 'Mary built a bookcase for three hours' means 'There is a bookcase such that for every time t during a certain three hour period Mary built it at t', which could not be true.[8]

11.4.4 Permutations

It is a marvel of the modularity of time-constraining adverbials and frame adverbials that permuting them in English sentences can have so little effect. Here, for example, are some permutations of the frame adverbial 'during the war' with several time-constraining adverbials, all but one of them quantified. All the following permutations seem to me equivalent:

During the war I ran every other day from 2 to 3 in the afternoon.
During the war I ran every other day in the afternoon from 2 to 3.
During the war I ran from 2 to 3 in the afternoon every other day.
During the war I ran from 2 to 3 every other day in the afternoon.
During the war I ran in the afternoon every other day from 2 to 3.
During the war I ran in the afternoon from 2 to 3 every other day.
Every other day during the war I ran from 2 to 3 in the afternoon.
Every other day during the war I ran in the afternoon from 2 to 3.
Every other day in the afternoon during the war I ran from 2 to 3.
During the war every other day I ran from 2 to 3 in the afternoon.
During the war every other day I ran in the afternoon from 2 to 3.
During the war every other day in the afternoon I ran from 2 to 3.
During the war every other day from 2 to 3 I ran in the afternoon.
I ran from 2 to 3 in the afternoon every other day during the war.
I ran from 2 to 3 in the afternoon during the war every other day.
I ran every other day during the war from 2 to 3 in the afternoon.
I ran every other day during the war in the afternoon from 2 to 3.
I ran every other day from 2 to 3 in the afternoon during the war.
I ran every other day from 2 to 3 during the war in the afternoon.
I ran every other day in the afternoon from 2 to 3 during the war.
I ran every other day in the afternoon during the war from 2 to 3.
I ran in the afternoon from 2 to 3 every other day during the war.
I ran in the afternoon from 2 to 3 during the war every other day.
I ran in the afternoon every other day from 2 to 3 during the war.
I ran in the afternoon every other day during the war from 2 to 3.
I ran in the afternoon during the war every other day from 2 to 3.
I ran in the afternoon during the war from 2 to 3 every other day.

Since there is ample room here for different quantifier scopes, and since some of these adverbials can potentially play other roles, it is unclear why there seems to be only one natural meaning for all these permutations:

For every other day, d, such that d is during the war, there is a time interval P such that P begins at some 2:00 and ends at (the immediately following) 3:00, and for every time t in P: $(\exists I)[I<now$ & $I \subset Afternoon$ & I is on d & I is at t & $(\exists e)(\exists t')[t' \in I$ & Running(e) & Agent-Theme(e,me) & Cul(e,t')]].

11.5 Temporal Modifiers of Events

Many of the time-constraining adverbials in the theory just sketched function as predicates of events. It is hard to prove this contention, but it seems to me that there is a difference between the construction

Did you ever run at noon?

and

At noon, Mary ran.

In the first, the adverbial functions as a predicate of events, whereas in the second it merely constrains the time. This opinion is based more on instinct than on evidence. Further, the proposal is problematic, since it introduces a possibly needless redundancy into the account of temporal modifiers. If it is correct, 'at noon' or 'for 3 hours' can characterize either a spatiotemporal region or an event, even though there is no obvious difference between these two options in terms of the overall import of what is said. If we assume that 'in the afternoon' constrains the time period, and that the period itself contains the event, we get a logical form with these parts:

$(\exists I)[\ldots$ & $I \subset Afternoon$ & $t \in I$ & Cul(e,t) & $e \subset I$ & $\ldots$].

If instead we assume that 'in the afternoon' applies directly to the event, we get a form like this:

$(\exists I)[\ldots$ & $e \subset Afternoon$ & $t \in I$ & Cul(e,t) & $e \subset I$ & $\ldots$],

(in which '$e \subset Afternoon$' means that the times at which e holds fall totally within an afternoon). It is hard to see under what circumstances the one would be true and not the other. Similarly, consideration of adverbials such as 'at noon', 'during the war', 'from 2:00 to 3:00' suggests a general equivalence between these two constructions. I am uncertain whether this equivalence is a needless redundancy or a far-reaching and useful principle.

There may be indirect evidence that temporal adverbials apply directly to events, since many constructions use the same or related lexical terminology in explicitly mentioning events. We have, for example, these constructions:

My *afternoon* drive soothed my nerves.
Yesterday's run tired her.
Their *midnight* meeting deprived them of needed sleep.
A *three week* backpack is rough on anyone.

Superficially, it would appear that the italicized phrases are predicates of events, and that they are related to

I drove *in the afternoon*.
She ran *yesterday*.
They met *at midnight*.
They backpacked *for three weeks*.

On the other hand, one might maintain that the adverbials in the latter sentences are not predicates of events, and that the predications in the former sentences can be explained by some theory of paraphrase. For example, 'My afternoon drive' might be decoded as 'My drive that took place in the afternoon', with a meaning something like

(the e)[Driving(e) & Agent(e,me) & ($\exists$I)[I$\subset$Afternoon & ($\exists$t)[t$\in$I & Cul(e,t) & e$\subset$I]]].

This gives the italicized phrases in the former sentences the status of complex predicates of events, analyzed in terms of predicates of periods of time, without making the italicized phrases in the latter group themselves be predicates of events. This analysis might be able to preserve the idea that real temporal adverbials never apply directly to events, though they are ingredients of complex constructions that do. On the other hand, it also provides the ingredients for developing the theory of temporal adverbials as predicates of events. That is, it offers the means of analyzing adverbials that act as temporal predicates of events in terms of their time-constraining homonyms, thereby explaining the equivalence between the two accounts.

Some additional evidence is relevant to this issue. The phrase 'a three-hour run' seems to mean 'a run that lasted for three hours'. This is *not* directly related to the construction 'for three hours' in 'For three hours, Agatha ran'. When 'for three hours' constrains the time, the sentence says that there was a three-hour period such that Agatha ran at each moment during it. This is different from saying that she engaged in a run that lasted for three hours. (Different, but equivalent, if the theory of process verbs discussed in the last chapter is correct. For the way in which Agatha runs for three hours is to engage in runnings continually throughout that interval; so she can't do one without the other.)

For event verbs, the details are a bit different. A three year house building is not picked out by the construction 'Agatha built a house for three years', which is anomalous (according to the account in the previous section). It seems to mean, instead, 'She built a house in three years', or, awkwardly, 'In three years she built a house'. That the phrase resists taking initial position in the sentence suggests it is a genuine verb modifier and perhaps therefore a predicate of events.

My temptation is to say that many temporal adverbials can directly modify events and states, and that these constructions are equivalent to the use of homonymal time-constraining adverbials in the case of process and state verbs, although not in the case of event verbs, since some such constructions with event verbs are anomalous when the adverbials are read as time-constrainers.[9]

My earlier suggestion that the past tense might require the whole event in question to fall within the time-period I arises with regard to a sentence such as 'Mary knew Agatha for three years'. We do not want this to be true just because Mary knew Agatha in the past and the total time she will know her is three years, since if she has known her for only one year that sentence is false, even though she will go on knowing her for two more. One way to get this to work out right is to require that a state sentence be true only if the whole state in question falls entirely within the interval I. We can accomplish this by adding a clause of the form 's incl I' in parallel with the proposed emendation for events from the last section. The other way is to make 'for three years' be sensitive to the time variable when it acts as a predicate of events or states, so that instead of 'For(3 years,e)' or 'For(3 years,s)', we should have 'For(3 years,e,t)' or 'For(3 years,s,t)', indicating that the three years in question directly preceded t. I do not decide between these, since the technicalities may be getting ahead of us. This sort of issue should be pursued when we are more certain about the overall form of the theory.

11.6   Frequency Adverbials and Subordinate Clauses

Adverbials of frequency appear to be related to time because of their form and sometimes their meaning: 'sometimes', 'usually', 'always', 'never', 'twice'. But over the past several years it has become apparent (as articulated in Lewis 1975) that they apply to other things as well. For example, 'sometimes' as used in my opening sentence here is clearly unrelated to time.

Frequency adverbials appear in logical form as quantifiers. *Cardinality adverbials* are typically unrestricted quantifiers that quantify either times or events. *Proportion adverbials* are restricted quantifiers that quantify times, events, or even NPs.

11.6.1   Cardinality Adverbials

These include 'twice', 'thrice', 'once' (in its meaning that parallels 'twice'), and 'often' (when it means "lots of times" as opposed to "a high proportion of times"). Their typical use is to quantify either times or events, and it is often unclear which. The sentence

Twice, Brutus stabbed Caesar

can be read as saying that there were two different times at which Brutus stabbed Caesar. 'Twice' is then simply a quantifier applied to a time-constraining adverbial. The logical form is

$(\exists 2t)$[Brutus stabbed Caesar at t],

that is,[10]

$(\exists 2t)(\exists I)[I < now$ & $At(I,t)$ & $(\exists e)(\exists t')[t' \in I$ & $Stabbing(e)$ & $Agent(e,Brutus)$ & $Theme(e,Caesar)$ & $Cul(e,t')]]$.

A similar sentence is

Brutus stabbed Caesar twice

which has a reading that allows the continuation 'But both stabbings were simultaneous; one was in the back and one in the thigh'. Clearly this cannot mean that there were two distinct times of stabbing. The logical form for this reading is one in which the cardinality adverb replaces the default existential quantifier over events by another:[11]

$(\exists I)[I < now$ & $(\exists 2e)(\exists t)[t \in I$ & $Stabbing(e)$ & $Agent(e,Brutus)$ & $Theme(e,Caesar)$ & $Cul(e,t)]]$.

11.6.2 Proportion Adverbials

Proportion adverbials include 'always', 'sometimes', 'usually', 'rarely', and 'often' (in certain of its uses). They are more complex than cardinality adverbials in two ways. First, they are restricted quantifiers, and so their logical forms need to include the restrictive clauses. 'Mary usually eats with her left hand' means something like 'Mary usually eats with her left hand *when she eats*'. The sentence says that times of Mary's eatings with her left hand form a large proportion of times when she eats. (Or perhaps, her left-handed eatings themselves are frequent among her eatings.) Part of the difficulty in formulating a theory of these adverbials is specifying the reference class that restricts the quantifier. The second way in which these adverbials are more complex than cardinality adverbials is that they can apparently quantify more things than just times or events (or states). In David Lewis's (1975) example,

A quadratic equation usually has two roots,

we appear to be saying that a majority of quadratic equations have two roots. That is, we appear to be quantifying over the quadratic equations themselves. The sentence seems to be saying

A quadratic equation usually has two roots = (Most x)[x is a quadratic equation, x has two roots].[12]

In this example, the quantification is equivalent to 'most', what is quantified is an NP position (the NP 'a quadratic equation'), and the quantifier is restricted to quadratic equations.[13] In other examples, these factors differ. Consider

Mary usually walks with John = (Most t)[Mary walks at t, Mary walks with John at t].

In this case the quantifier is still equivalent to 'most', but now times are quantified, and the quantifier is restricted to times at which Mary walks. That is, what is said is not that Mary walks with John a lot but that the proportion of times she walks with John to times when she walks is high. The sentence has a meaning equivalent to 'When Mary walks, she usually walks with John'.

It is no simple matter to determine what is being quantified, or what the restriction on the quantifier is.

Mary usually eats with her left hand

either asserts a high frequency of eatings with the left hand among eatings by Mary, or a high frequency of eatings by Mary among things done with her left hand, or, in certain contexts, a high frequency of eatings with her left hand among actions of some other sort (as in response to "How does Mary signal her readiness to pass over secret documents?"). Probably the best grammatical theory is to systematically produce all these as options. (I do not have such a systematic account.)

Part of the relevance for the theory of underlying events is that frequency adverbials sometimes quantify events themselves. Consider the following interchange:

"I must warn you that you are suspected of being the killer."
"That couldn't be. Whenever I stab anybody I do it with a knife.
These are icepick wounds. I may be a killer, but I'm not uncouth."

The sentence 'Whenever I stab anyone I do it with a knife' has to contain a quantification over stabbings, not over times of stabbings. Otherwise the sentence would not make its point, which is that all the speaker's stabbings are with a knife, not that all the speaker's stabbings are at a time when there is a (possibly different) stabbing with a knife. The default existential quantifier over events is here replaced by a universal quantifier.

The scopes of quantifications due to frequency adverbials can be fairly broad. For example, adverbials of frequency mix freely with quantifiers in

Occasionally I catch a fish.
There's a certain fish that I occasionally catch.
Everyone occasionally catches a fish.
Everyone occasionally catches a certain fish that I put there.
Occasionally, everyone catches a fish.
Occasionally, everyone catches a certain fish that . . .

Again, the details are not worked out here.

11.6.3 Temporal Subordinate Clauses
Some subordinate clauses are formed with a subordinating adverb, as in

When Mary leaves, Bill will be happy
After Sam leaves, Mary will return
Before Bill left, Mary berated him.

These constructions appear to have a single tense governing the whole construction. This explains the ungrammaticality of sentences such as

After Mary left, Bill will leave,

which is coherent but not English. The constructions are also subject to the sequence-of-tense rules of English, which require, for example, that a subordinate clause be in the present tense when the main clause is future:

Before Mary leaves, Bill will be unhappy.
*Before Mary will leave, Bill will be unhappy.

I suggest that these sentences are formed with a single tense, with the times of the constituent events/states being related by the adverb:[14]

Before Bill left, Mary berated him = $(\exists I)[I>now \ \& \ (\exists e)(\exists t_1)[t_1 \in I \ \&$
Berating(e) & Agent(e,Mary) & Theme(e,Bill) & Cul(e,t_1) &
$(\exists e)(\exists t_2)[t_2 \in I$ & Leaving(e) & Agent-Theme(e,Bill) & Cul(e,t_2) & t_1
is before t_2]]].

The subordinating adverbial can sometimes also affect the frequency, as in

Whenever Mary left, she sashayed = $(\exists I)[I<now \ \& \ (t_1)[t_1 \in I \ \&$
$(\exists e)[Leaving(e)$ & Agent-Theme(e,Mary) & Cul(e,t_1)] $\rightarrow$
$(\exists e)(\exists t_2)[t_2 \in I$ & Sashaying(e) & Agent-Theme(e,Mary) & Cul(e,t_2) &
t_1 is near t_2]]].

(In this example context is important in identifying the period **I**, spreading it out over a substantial period.) This also is one of the readings of 'When Mary left, she sashayed'.

In the examples just given, the adverb of proportionality is the same as the adverb that introduces the subordinate clause. But this need not be the case. Sometimes the subordinating adverbial merely identifies the restrictive clause for another proportional adverbial elsewhere, as in

When Mary runs she usually limps.

The word 'if' is especially good at introducing a subordinate clause in this manner while doing little else. (See Lewis 1975 for many such constructions.)

11.7 Interactions

I have sketched a theory that deals with a wide variety of components of language: simple verbs, causative and inchoative verbs, progressive and (in the next chapter) perfect forms of verbs, verb modifiers, tenses, "temporal" adverbials—as well as other linguistic forms that interact with these and that I have not presented, such as NP quantification. I have investigated most of these matters in isolation from the complications of the others, insofar as that is possible. It is not clear how they interact with each other, even though it is clear that they do. Investigation of such interactions is vital to assessing the adequacy of the underlying event approach, but it would require at least a book of its own.

Chapter 12
The Semantics of the Perfect and the Progressive in Modern and Old English

12.1   The Perfect in Modern English: Data

The perfect in English includes the present perfect, as in 'Mary has eaten', the past perfect (or pluperfect), as in 'Mary had eaten', and the future perfect, as in 'Mary will have eaten'. My goal is to sketch a positive account of the semantics of these constructions and to discuss their purported evolution from quite different constructions in Old English.[1] Along the way I discuss the progressive as well.

I begin with a puzzle that has long troubled semanticists. Linguistically, there seems to be an important difference between the simple past and the present perfect, yet it is difficult to see what the logical difference might be. Focusing on truth-conditions alone, it is hard to find any difference at all between

Simple Past   *Mary left.*
Present Perfect *Mary has left.*

They feel very different, yet they seem to be necessarily equivalent in what they say. If Mary left before the time of utterance, then both sentences are true; otherwise both are false. Any adequate theory should explain both the felt difference between them and their equivalence.

The simple past and the present perfect are only sometimes equivalent. The nonequivalence *in general* between the simple past and the present perfect is plain to see as soon as a temporal adverb is added to the sentences.[2] Consider

Simple Past   *Mary left yesterday.*
Present Perfect (?)*Mary has left yesterday.*

Here, the first sentence is fine, and the second seems anomalous. Now try a different adverb:

Simple Past   (?)*At present, Mary left.*
Present Perfect *At present, Mary has left.*

Here the first sentence is anomalous, and the second is fine.

The key to these peculiarities lies in the relation between the tenses and the temporal modifiers. The present perfect, after all, is a present tense construction, whereas the simple past is a past tense construction. And it is the tenses that interact with temporal modifiers, at least in the examples cited. Past and present tense sentences have semantical forms of this sort:

Past $(\exists I)[I < now \& \ldots]$
Pres $(\exists I)[I = now \& \ldots]$.

Temporal modifiers such as 'yesterday' constrain the same time-variables that the tenses constrain, so that part of the form of a sentence containing 'yesterday' will be

Past $(\exists I)[I < now \& I \subset Yesterday \& \ldots]$
Pres $(\exists I)[I = now \& I \subset Yesterday \& \ldots]$.

This explains why 'yesterday' produces anomaly when used with the present perfect; the "present" of the present perfect requires that the time in question be in the present, and the 'yesterday' contradicts this. Likewise, in the latter example above, 'at the present time' contradicts the constraint of the past tense.[3]

These comments do not solve the problem of how to analyze the present perfect, but they give us a first clue: however the perfect operates in a sentence, it works *in addition to* the tense. The tense, and the way it combines with temporal adverbials, is one module of the semantics, and the perfect is another. (The same holds for the progressive.) The present perfect must be a present tense sentence; its semantic pastness comes from something in addition to the tense, whereas the semantic pastness of a simple past tense sentence arises from the tense alone.

The second clue to the treatment of the perfect is that it is a construction that produces a state description from an event (or state) description. This idea is implicit in much of the nonformal literature on the topic; it is also employed, e.g., by Kamp and Rohrer 1983 in their analysis of tense and aspect in texts.[4] The simple past construction 'Mary ate' says that a certain *event* took place *in the past*. The perfect construction 'Mary has eaten' says that Mary is *now* in a certain *state*, a state of having eaten at some time in the past. 'Have eaten' is thus true of a "resultant state"—a state that holds at a given time if and only if the agent in question is the agent of an eating event that culminated earlier than that time. The "time" attributed to the resultant state in a sentence is determined in the ordinary way by tense operators and temporal adverbs. Because the state in question is a resultant state, the sentence requires for its truth that some event have happened prior to the time indicated by the tense of the sentence; this is the origin of the occasional equivalence of the present perfect with the simple past.

The perfect also has another use in English: it is sometimes used as a stylistic variant of the simple past. Immigrant speakers commonly do this, especially those whose native tongues (such as German) properly use the perfect where English uses the simple past, and those whose native tongues lack the construction altogether. This is not the whole story, since such uses go all the way back to Old English (see McCoard 1978 for a critical review of the literature on this issue). I shall focus on the use of the perfect that is distinctively different from the simple past.

12.2   The Semantical Framework of Underlying Events and States

I begin by reviewing some parts of the semantical framework within which I shall offer an account of the perfect in terms of resultant states. Because of the detailed treatment in earlier chapters, I merely give paradigm illustrations here, using a simplified treatment of the tenses.

12.2.1   Paradigms

Paradigm Analysis of Event Verb Sentences

Brutus stabbed Caesar =   For some event e:
                          e is a stabbing,
                          the agent of e is Brutus,
                          the theme of e is Caesar, and
                          e culminates before now.

This indicates a logical form associated with the sentence 'Brutus stabbed Caesar'. In formal notation the form is

($\exists$e)[Stabbing(e) & Agent(e,Brutus) & Theme(e,Caesar) & ($\exists$t)[t<now & Cul(e,t)]].

This is the common pattern for all noncausative event sentences. Each such sentence asserts that there is an event of a certain sort. The verb tells us what sort of event it is. The subject and object of the verb relate their denotata to that event via certain thematic roles, discussed in chapter 5.[5] Finally, the tense of the verb tells us either that the event in question already culminated in the past, or that it culminates right now, or that it will culminate in the future.

Paradigm Analysis of State Adjectives Used as Predicates The same pattern is obeyed by state sentences, except that they assert the existence of a certain kind of state instead of a certain kind of event. (Also, states do not "culminate"; at any given moment they either do or do not "hold".) For my later convenience, I use an adjectival sentence to illustrate the underlying form of a state sentence:

Mary was clever =   For some state s:
                    s is a state-of-being-clever,
                    Mary is the theme of s, and
                    s holds before now.

In formal notation

($\exists$s)[Being-clever(s) & Theme(s,Mary) & ($\exists$t)[t<now & Hold(s,t)]].

Paradigm Analysis of State Adjectives Used Attributively Finally, it will be useful to articulate how adjectives function when they occur attributively, before a noun:

The clever woman =
The woman such that there is a state s which is such that:
        s is a state-of-being-clever,
        she is the theme of s, and
        s holds now/then.

In predicate calculus notation:

(The x)[Woman(x) & ($\exists$s)[Being-clever(s) & Theme(s,x) & Hold(s,t)]].

Paradigm Analysis of Perception Sentences Modern perception sentences are useful in explaining the historical development of the perfect. In sentences such as:

Mary saw Brutus stab Caesar.
Sam heard Mary shoot Bill.
Agatha felt Samantha rock the boat,

the analysis (from chapter 2) assumes that the verb 'see' has the same meaning as in other sentences when it takes a concrete object. 'Mary saw _____' has as its standard analysis

Mary saw _____ = For some event e:
         e is a seeing,
         the agent of e is Mary,
         the theme of e is _____, and
         e culminates before now.

We then analyze simple sentences by filling in the blank. For 'Mary saw Brutus' we fill it in with 'Brutus', and for 'Mary saw the stabbing of Caesar by Brutus' we fill it in with 'the stabbing of Caesar by Brutus'. The key to handling the sentences above is to see the embedded clauses as containing indefinite references to events; for 'Mary saw Brutus stab Caesar' we fill in the blank with 'a stabbing of Caesar by Brutus'. This then yields the analysis

Mary saw Brutus stab Caesar = For some event e':
         e' is a stabbing,
         the Agent of e' is Brutus,
         the Theme of e' is Caesar, and
         Mary saw _____e'_____,

where the last conjunct, 'Mary saw _____e'_____' has the further analysis given above. The form of the whole sentence, in symbols, is

$(\exists e')$[Stabbing(e') & Agent(e',Brutus) & Theme(e',Caesar) & $(\exists e)$[Seeing(e) & Agent(e,Mary) & Theme(e,e') & Cul(e,before now)]].

12.3 The Progressive and Perfect in Modern English

The semantics of the progressive and the perfect in Modern English require only some new principles about how events and states are related to one another. I state the analyses, and then illustrate how they work. First the progressive, then the perfect.

12.3.1 The Progressive

I make the following theoretical assumption: whenever an event e is in progress, there is a corresponding state of affairs, "that e is in progress." This is a state that holds while e is in progress (and at no other time). Call this the "in-progress state" of the event e, or "e's IP-state." For example, if Mary is hanging a picture, then there is a state that holds during the picture hanging—the state of this particular picture hanging. It holds now, and it stops holding when Mary stops hanging the picture—either because she gets the picture hung, or because she is interrupted or just loses interest. In the former case the event culminates, in the latter it does not; the In-progress state holds in either case. This In-progress state is the state that is relevant to the analysis of the progressive[6] sentence, 'Mary is hanging the picture'.

Semantically, the progressive in Modern English is a verb-form. Sentences containing the progressive are to be analyzed in the same manner as those without the progressive, except that instead of saying that the event picked out by the verb culminates at the time in question, we say that its corresponding "in-progress" state holds at that time:

NonProgressive

Mary runs (now) =
For some event e:
e is a running,
the theme of e is Mary, and
e culminates now.

Progressive

Mary is running (now) =
For some event e:
e is a running,
the theme of e is Mary, and
e's IP-state holds now.

For purposes of the applications discussed below, I need to add one principle for IP-states:

1 For any event e, the theme of e's IP-state = the theme of e.

12.3.2 The Perfect

For every event e that culminates, there is a corresponding state that holds forever after. This is "the state of e's having culminated," which I call the "Resultant state of e," or "e's R-state." If Mary eats lunch, then there is a state that holds forever after: the state of Mary's having eaten lunch.[7] The notion of resultant state is clearly subject to the defining principle[8]

2 e's R-state holds at t $\equiv$ e culminates at some time at or before t.

It is important not to identify the Resultant-state of an event with its "target" state. If I throw a ball onto the roof, the target state of this event is the ball's being on the roof, a state that may or may not last for a long time. What I am calling the Resultant-state is different; it is the state of my having thrown the ball onto the roof, and it is a state that cannot cease holding at some later time.

For general purposes "resultant state" needs to apply to states as well as to events; if Mary knows John, then "Mary's having known John" is a state that holds forever after:

2′   s's R-state holds at t ≡ the period of time for which s holds terminates at or before t.

Now for the analysis of the perfect. Semantically, the perfect in Modern English is a verb form. Sentences containing it are to be analyzed in the same manner as those without it, except that instead of saying that the event e culminates we say that e's resultant state holds:[9]

Simple Present	Present Perfect
Mary runs =	*Mary has run* =
For some event e:	For some event e:
e is a running,	e is a running,
the theme of e is Mary, and	the theme of e is Mary, and
e culminates now.	e's R-state holds now.

As with the progressive, we shall later need one additional principle:

3   For any event e, the theme of e's R-state = the theme of e. (And likewise for states.)

I have introduced the notion of a Resultant-state without providing a philosophical analysis or definition of it. Although such an analysis might be useful, it is not necessary for any of the results discussed here; they all follow from the stated principles. An example is the equivalence of the present perfect and the simple past.

12.3.3   Equivalence of the Present Perfect and the Simple Past
I am now in a position to show the equivalence (according to the theory) of the present perfect with the simple past in simple cases when temporal modifiers are absent. The equivalence is illustrated by these analyses:

Mary has eaten the apple =   *Mary ate the apple* =
For some event e: For some event e:
e is an eating,   e is an eating,
the agent of e is Mary,   the agent of e is Mary,
the theme of e is the apple, and   the theme of e is the apple, and
e's R-state holds now.   e culminates before now.

Principle (2) above yields the equivalence. The equivalence disappears as soon as temporal adverbs are added that interact with the tense.[10] The results are similar for state sentences.

12.3.4 The Perfect Progressive
By combining the analyses of the perfect and the progressive, I obtain the analysis of the perfect progressive. E.g.,

Mary has been running =
For some event e:
    e is a running,
    the theme of e is Mary, and
    the R-state of the IP-state of e holds now.

12.3.5 The Progressive Perfect
On the analysis I have given, "IP-state" is either not defined at all for states, or else it applies to them redundantly. The theory thus requires that "progressives of perfects" are either undefined or redundant. This conforms to the data: there is no "progressive perfect" in English, no use of phrases such as 'Mary is having eaten lunch'.

12.4 Participles as Adjectives

An issue crucial to the historical derivation of the progressive and perfect in Modern English is the use of participles as adjectives. The *American Heritage Dictionary* contains this entry:

participle: A nominal form of a verb that is used with an auxiliary verb to indicate certain tenses, and that can also function independently as an adjective. In the expressions *a glowing coal* and *a beaten dog, glowing* and *beaten* are participles.

Participles occur in English, at least superficially, in most of the places in which nondegree adjectives occur, such as prenominal positions. In this section I investigate the hypothesis that it is possible to treat participles, semantically, as adjectives when they occur in these positions. For example, in the phrase 'a glowing coal', the word 'glowing' is a participle used as an adjective. I am uncertain whether this hypothesis is correct for Modern English but it appears to be correct for Old English, and it is easier to explain it for Modern English, since readers will understand the examples without explanation. I do *not* assume that participles are adjectives when used to form the progressive or the perfect; 'glowing' is not an adjective (in Modern English) in 'the candle is glowing brightly'.

First some terminology. I use 'PresP-Adj(verb)' to stand for the present participle of a verb when used as an adjective. For example, 'PresP-Adj(sleep)' stands for 'sleeping' as it is used in a construction such as 'the sleeping child'. Similarly, 'PastP-Adj(cool)' stands for 'cooled' as it occurs in 'the cooled soup'. Since I am assuming that any participle-used-as-an-adjective *is* an adjective, the participle must conform to the account of adjectives as sketched above. In particular, particles must pick out states. Since a participle is derived from a verb, its meaning as an adjective must have something to do with the meaning of the verb from which it is derived. The needed proposal will therefore explain what it means for the adjective to apply to a state, couched in terms of what the verb does when applied to an event (assuming that the verb is an event verb).

Following are the connections that seem to yield the right results, stated both in English and in predicate calculus notation.

4   PresP-Adj(Verb) is true of a state s if and only if s is the In-progress state of an event of which Verb is true.
    PresP-Adj(Verb)(s) $\equiv$ ($\exists$e)[Verb(e) & s = e's IP-state].

5   PastP-Adj(Verb) is true of a state s if and only if s is the resultant state of an event of which Verb is true.
    PastP-Adj(Verb)(s) $\equiv$ ($\exists$e)[Verb(e) & s = e's R-state].

Both of these proposals have straightforward applications. A simple and tantalizing illustration of the present-participle-used-as-an-adjective is this. If the present participle could occur as an adjective anywhere that a nondegree adjective can occur, then a sentence of Modern English of the form

The child is sleeping

would be ambiguous. On the one hand, its predicate could be read in the natural way as containing the progressive form of the verb 'sleep';

on this reading we are talking about what the child is doing; the child is sleeping. This reading is analyzed as

*The child [is sleeping]*PROGRESSIVE VERB
>   For some event e:
>>   e is a sleeping,
>>   the theme of e is the child, and
>>   e's IP-state holds now.

On the other hand, the predicate might be read as containing a copula plus an adjective; on this reading we are describing the child: it is in a sleeping state. The theory then yields this analysis:

*The child is [sleeping]*ADJECTIVE
>   For some state s:
>>   s is a PresP-Adj('sleep') state,
>>   the theme of s is the child, and
>>   s holds now.

(Again, if you think that this second reading does not exist in Modern English, bear with me. It apparently existed in Old English.) These two readings are intimately related and difficult to distinguish. I take this to show that any correct theory ought to demonstrate an equivalence of some kind between them. The present theory does so. Principle (4) reduces the second analysis to

*The child is [sleeping]*ADJECTIVE:
>   For some state s:
>>   For some event e:
>>   e is a sleeping & s = e's IP-state,
>>   the theme of s is the child, and
>>   s holds now,

which is logically equivalent to

*The child is [sleeping]*ADJECTIVE:
>   For some event e:
>>   e is a sleeping,
>>   the theme of e's IP-state is the child, and
>>   e's IP-state holds now.

And principle (1) reduces this to the progressive analysis. This shows that whenever the progressive-verb reading of the sentence is true, so is the present-participle-adjective reading of the sentence, and vice versa. The two readings are necessarily equivalent in truth-value in all circumstances, so there would never be any reason to prefer one to the other on grounds of content.

Another consequence of this account is that 'the sleeping child' is equivalent to 'the child that is sleeping' (where 'sleeping' is an adjective in the first phrase and part of the progressive verb-form in the second phrase).[11]

Past Participles   An apparent example of a past participle used as an adjective is 'cooled' as in 'the cooled soup'. On the analysis I propose, 'the cooled soup' receives a form that is equivalent to 'the soup that has been cooled' (where 'cooled' is an adjective in the first phrase and part of the perfect verb-form in the second phrase):

*The [cooled]*PAST PART USED AS ADJ *soup* =
(The x)[Soup(x) & ($\exists$s)[PastP-Adj(Cool)(s) & Theme(s,x) & Hold(s,now)]]

*The soup that [has been cooled]*PERFECT =
(The x)[Soup(x) & ($\exists$e)[Cooling(e) & Theme(e,x) & Hold(e's R-state,now)]].

Principles (3) and (5) together yield the equivalence.[12]

12.5   The Progressive and the Perfect in Old English

The topic of diachronic change in the history of our language is an area we seem to know little about. The older secondary literature focuses informally on the causes of diachronic change and is highly speculative. I want to address instead the formal preconditions for linguistic change, in particular, the issue of what syntactic and semantic conditions are required for such change to be possible. I shall focus on an example of the very easiest sort, which I call "Conservative Restructuring."[13] If the standard historical accounts of the origins of the perfect and the progressive are right, then the evolution of the modern progressive and the modern perfect have involved a conservative restructuring, a change in which sentences with one syntactic form came to be viewed as having a different syntactic form, albeit a form that already existed in the language. The words in the sentences did not change—except that some inflectional endings on the adjectives indicating number and case agreement disappeared. The condition that made the restructuring possible was that the resulting sentences, viewed as having the new forms, automatically had meanings that were necessarily equivalent to the original forms. The syntax changed, and so did the semantics, but the transition was eased because (1) the same words appear, in the same order,[14] (2) no new syntactic forms were introduced, and (3) the new meanings were necessarily equivalent to the old ones.

12.5.1   Historical Accounts

According to standard accounts, modern uses of the progressive and the perfect as verb forms originated from quite different constructions, adjectival constructions, in Old English. Specifically, the "source" constructions in question contained participles used as adjectives, and the change was to a system resembling the modern one in which participles are parts of complex verb forms. In terms of the units of syntactic analysis, the original forms consist of a verb plus an adjective:

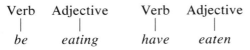

whereas the new forms are complex verbs:

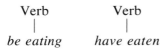

In the old form, the participle ending is a way to make adjectives out of verbs; in the new form it marks the fact that the verb is part of a complex form with 'have' or with 'be'. The standard account of the history of these words says that the new verb forms were already evolving from adjectival forms in Old English, and the corpus of OE texts gives us a snapshot of this transition.[15]

The terms 'adjectival' and 'verbal' may mean different things to different people, but I think that what scholars of OE mean when they use these terms connects sufficiently with certain of the theoretical constructions in the semantics I am using to make comparison useful. One theme shared between my theory and the scholarly literature on OE is the contrast between "event" sentences and "state" sentences (the terms in the literature tend to be 'action' and 'state'), together with the assumption that adjectival readings must be stative whereas most verbal readings are eventive. An additional aid in telling adjectives from verbs is that Old English has a distinctive system of adjectival inflections, which identify words as adjectives in certain contexts. The general rule of thumb in the secondary literature seems to be that when a participle (1) is inflected as an adjective, and (2) conveys a stative meaning when the verb from which it is derived is an event verb, then the word is being used as an adjective. If instead the word (1) is not inflected as an adjective in a context in which overt adjectival inflections would be required if it were an adjective, and (2) conveys an eventive sense, then the word is being used as a verb. Additional evidence for adjectival constructions sometimes comes from constructions in parallel with clear cases of adjectives.

Unfortunately, there are plenty of known problems with the data. Sometimes it is unclear whether a given sentence is eventive or stative. Often, adjectives take the null inflection, so that looking at the spelling does not determine whether the adjective is inflected. In later Old English the inflections were often reduced or omitted, they were never uniform across all dialects to begin with, and both the dates and the dialects of many of the texts we have are uncertain. Further, in the poetry the presence or absence of inflections could be influenced by metrical considerations, and the meaning was often metaphorical. To top it all off, only a few million words of Old English survive, most in the West Saxon dialect, which is not the main dialect (the Anglian) from which Modern English evolved. In addition, a significant part of the surviving literature consists of translations from the Latin, raising the possibility that the syntax merely imitates the Latin, and is not genuine native English at all. Nor do we have any native informants for OE. So there is reason to be cautious about accepting the standard account of Old English. Having said this, I shall speak as if the standard account is correct. Any uncertainty I indicate is uncertainty about the data from the point of view of the standard account, not skepticism about the standard account itself. I return to reservations about the standard account itself in section 12.7.

My task in this section is to use the theory of underlying events and states to formalize the standard account of the historical development of the progressive and the perfect in English and to show this development as an example of Conservative Restructuring.

12.5.2   The Progressive
There are many examples that scholars analyze as a present participle used as an adjective with 'beon'/'wesan' ("be"/"was") or some related

verb. For example, Kisbye (1970, b1-23) states that 'scinende' is an adjective in[16]

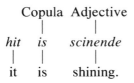

Copula Adjective

hit   is   scinende

it   is   shining.

Alongside examples of this sort there are others in which the participle loses its status as an adjective and is treated as part of a verbal complex, as in

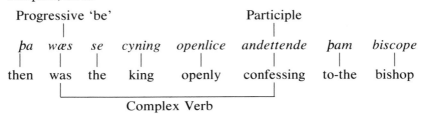

Progressive 'be'   Participle

þa   wæs   se   cyning   openlice   andettende   þam   biscope

then   was   the   king   openly   confessing   to-the   bishop

Complex Verb

It is clear that these examples are like the ones in Modern English that compare the two readings of 'the child is sleeping', except that most people do not "get" the adjectival reading in Modern English. But even if you can't "get" it, you know what it means. So the examples for Modern English correspond exactly to the relevant constructions in Old English, with the adjectival reading generally held to be the original one from which the other developed by what I have called Conservative Restructuring. The conditions for Conservative Restructuring apply to the transition from one to the other.[17]

12.5.3 The Perfect
The perfect is more complicated. It comes from two different sources. The first is constructions using 'beon'/'wesan' ("be"/"was") or 'weorþan' ("become") plus the past participle of an intransitive verb. The second is constructions using 'habban' ("have") plus the past participle of a transitive verb. These have different semantical accounts. The one using 'be' plus the past participle of an intransitive verb is easier to see, since it is still with us in a small number of cases, such as,

The Lord is risen,

in which 'risen' can be read as an adjective.

The contrast between adjectival and verbal forms in Old English is illustrated by that between

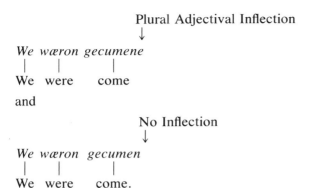

Plural Adjectival Inflection
↓

We wæron gecumene
 | | |
We were   come

and

No Inflection
↓

We wæron gecumen
 | | |
We were   come.

If we treat 'beon'/'wesan' as the ordinary copula of Modern English that occurs with adjectives, and if we treat the past participle as an adjective with the same meaning that it has in Modern English, we get an account in which this adjectival construction of Old English is equivalent to the perfect in Modern English—except that we now use the word 'have' instead of 'is' as the helping verb. (That change occurred over the course of several centuries, and is still going on.)[18]

The perfect with 'have' is more complex. A sentence in the perfect using 'have' plus a transitive verb is supposed to have originated from a sentence containing 'have' as a main verb, with an embedded adjectival clause containing the participle of the verb used as an adjective. An example that gives the flavor of the Old English is

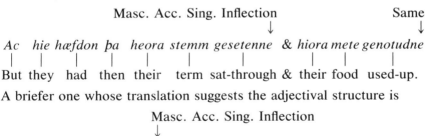

Masc. Acc. Sing. Inflection   Same
↓   ↓

Ac hie hæfdon þa heora stemm gesetenne & hiora mete genotudne
 | | | | | | | | | |
But they had then their   term sat-through & their food used-up.

A briefer one whose translation suggests the adjectival structure is

Masc. Acc. Sing. Inflection
↓

Ic hæbbe hine gebundenne
 | | | |
I have him   bound.

I propose to exploit the fact that this construction—'I have him bound'—seems to be identical in structure with that of a perception sentence, such as

I see him bound.[19]

I suggest that the OE constructions with 'habban' be given the same structural analysis as modern perception sentences, so that the semantical analysis of

I have him bound

would be

For some state s:
    s is a state of being-bound,
    the Theme of s is him, and
    I have s (now).

Is this construction equivalent to the Modern English perfect? It certainly looks very different from the modern perfect

I have bound him,

whose analysis would be

For some event e:
    e is a binding,
    the Agent of e is me,
    the Theme of e is him, and
    e's R-state holds now.

To make the analyses equivalent, I need several assumptions, most of which I have already used for other purposes. To begin, principle (5) is an account of the meaning of the Past-Participle-used-as-an-adjective. 's is a being-bound' thereby becomes '$(\exists e)$[e is a binding and s = e's R-state]', and the analysis of the embedded adjectival reading is equivalent to

For some state s:
    For some event e: e is a binding & s = e's R-state,
    the Theme of s is him, and
    I have s (now),

which simplifies to

For some event e:
    e is a binding,
    the Theme of e's R-state is him, and
    I have e's R-state now.

Next, principle (3) identifies "him" in the former analysis as the Theme of e. At this point the modern reading compares with the embedded adjectival reading as follows:

Modern Perfect	Embedded Adjectival
I have bound him =	*I have him bound* =
For some event e:	For some event e:
e is a binding,	e is a binding,
the Agent of e is me,	
the Theme of e is him, and	the Theme of e is him, and
e's R-state holds now.	I have e's R-state now.

But the analyses are still not equivalent. According to OE specialists, and also according to what is apparent by reading the translations into Modern English, not every sentence of the form 'x have (Embedded Clause)' *is* equivalent to the modern perfect, even with the more detailed form 'x have (NP PastP-Adj)'. So it is wrong to expect the two forms to be equivalent *in general*. 'Have' can mean a wide variety of things here, and only certain of them will yield a meaning that is equivalent to the perfect. Here are some Modern English examples where the equivalence is missing:

General Examples

I had the maid cleaning the parlor.
We have our bedroom on the second floor.

Examples with Past Participles

I had my engine cleaned.
(Implication: cleaned by someone else)[20]
I have the barbecue lit and ready to go.
(No implication as to identity of lighter)

The source of the modern Perfect in 'I have him bound' lies in the meaning of 'have' that makes me responsible for his present state of bindedness in the most direct way. I have to be responsible for the state by being the agent of the binding that gives rise to the state; no other meaning will be equivalent to the Perfect. The embedded adjectival sentences will be equivalent to the Perfect only when the content of 'have' identifies me as the agent of the previous binding.[21] If we formalize this constraint we get a special meaning for 'have'

6   x *has* e's R-state at t ≡ (e culminates before t & x = the agent of e)

If 'have' is used in this way, then the embedded adjectival form is equivalent to the perfect form with no further assumptions needed beyond principle (2).[22]

12.5.4   The Perfect Progressive in Old English

The analyses of the Modern English perfect and progressive combine naturally with one another to yield an analysis of the perfect progressive. I see no simple way to combine the analyses of the original adjectival forms of the progressive and of the perfect in OE so as to yield an account of the perfect progressive. Fortunately, the perfect progressive did not occur in OE.

12.6   Unsolved Problems

It is unfortunate that this straightforward formalization of the standard account does not yet explain all of the data. It works adequately in simple cases but not in more complicated ones. It works nicely, for example, for

ac   hi   hæfdon   þa   heora   stemn   gestenne   and   hiora   mete   genotudne
| | | | | | | | | |
but they   had   then   their   term   finished   and   their   food   used-up.

But it does not work when the examples include occurrences of additional thematic roles and adverbials. Consider the following sentence:

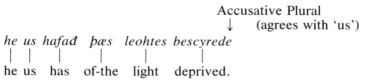

Accusative Plural
↓   (agrees with 'us')

he us hafað   þæs   leohtes   bescyrede
| | | | | |
he us   has   of-the   light   deprived.

The proposed syntactical analysis contains an embedded adjectival clause:

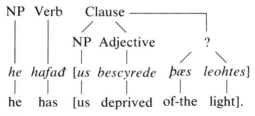

NP   Verb   Clause
                    ╱ ╲
                NP   Adjective   ?
                                         ╱ ╲
he   hafað   [us   bescyrede   þæs   leohtes]
| | | | | |
he   has   [us   deprived   of-the   light].

The problem lies with how we are to treat the occurrence of '*þæs leohtes*'.

In Modern English, adjectives do not subcategorize NPs. Except for a few examples of what are called "quirky case" (as in 'proud of Agatha'), our adjectives do not take direct or indirect objects. The problem, then, is how to explain the relation between 'bescyrede' and 'þæs leohtes'. If 'bescyrede' is really an adjective, as the standard account suggests, and if adjectives do not take objects, then we are in the dark about 'þæs leohtes'. Formally, the theory does not yet account for this occurrence of 'þæs leohtes'. If 'bescyrede' is an adjective, the theory does not show that the sentence quoted above is equivalent to a restructured version of it in which 'hafaď' and 'bescyrede' together make up the modern Perfect.

A similar theoretical issue is raised by the apparent modification of the adjective 'cumene' by the *motion* adverbial[23] 'to-Craccuse', as in

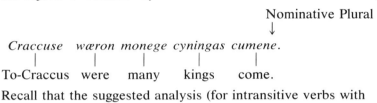

Recall that the suggested analysis (for intransitive verbs with 'beon/wæron') gave this the form

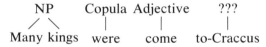

Normally, adjectives cannot be modified by motion adverbials, so the embedded adjectival clause analysis needs to explain how this seems to happen. I see three possible responses to such examples.

Response 1.   We can insist that adjectives do not take objects. Then, in the examples quoted above 'bescyrede' and 'cumene' are not adjectives, in spite of their adjectival endings. Instead, we construe them as examples of the modern perfect. Generalizing, we insist that the only examples of genuine adjectival sources of the modern progressive/ perfect lack expressed objects and motion adverbials.

This hypothesis appears to destroy the whole approach, since it involves rejecting too much of the putative data on which the evolution of the progressive/perfect is based. It is also theoretically incomplete as an account of the source of the modern progressive and perfect since, for example, if present participles of transitive verbs with expressed objects were never adjectival, we do not yet have a diachronic account of their source.

In the end, however, this may turn out to be the right approach to take. The majority view seems to be that something approximating the modern forms of the perfect and progressive had already evolved by the time of the earliest surviving Old English texts, and that the evolution of these forms from adjectival sources took place earlier. Since we have no data concerning the variety of these sources, we do not know whether the problems cited above occur in the pristine adjectival sources of the perfect and the progressive. Conceivably, the modern forms all originated from uses in which the participle had no apparent expressed object and occurred without adverbial modifiers. The existing corpus of Old English constructions would then be viewed in transition between the old and modern constructions. As unclear and speculative as this is, it has a ring of truth to it.[24] It leaves the exact status of the theory I have sketched rather unclear.

Response 2.   We can decide that adjectives in Old English take the same objects as verbs, are modified by the same adverbials as verbs, and, in general, can fit into the same structures as event verbs.

This is intuitively awkward, since if an adjective picks out a state it is hard to see how the state can be modified by a motion adverbial. But if we must live with this option, the theoretical account given so far needs to be expanded by a variety of meaning postulates. In particular, the earlier principles would need to be generalized. Principles (1) and (3)

1   For any event e, the theme of e's IP-state = the theme of e.

3   For any event e, the theme of e's R-state = the theme of e.

would be generalized to

1'   For any event e, $X(e\text{'s IP-state}) \equiv X(e)$.

and

3'   For any event e, $X(e\text{'s R-state}) \equiv X(e)$.

where X stands for the denotation of any thematic role or adverbial. That is, in addition to e's R-state having the same theme as e, it must also have the same instrument and same agent. Furthermore, it must be subject to all the same adverbial modifiers as e; for example, either both or neither must be "to Craccus," "in the park," "violent," etc. This is clumsy and theoretically worrisome, since we do not have a clear idea of the possible range of the X in (1') and (3'); if it ranges over *all* properties of events, then we cannot distinguish between e and e's IP-state and its R-state. Yet these must be distinct for the theory to work correctly. Further, the principles still fail to address further complications, such as the occurrence of 'to fultume' in

Nominative Plural
↓

Craccuse   waeron   monege   cyningas   to   fultume   cumene.
| | | | | | |
To-Craccus   were   many   kings   as   a help   come.

So it is unclear how this proposal is to be fully articulated.

Response 3.   We could hold that participial phrases are formed, not from verbs alone, but from whole VP's. Semantically, these phrases are handled by generalizing principles (4) and (5) to verb phrases. In case the VP consists of a single verb, this account coincides with the traditional account. Otherwise, it produces "adjectival" participial phrases, such as 'teaching Mary' or 'eaten with a spoon'.

This is probably the most theoretically satisfactory solution. As an example, it would start with

stab swiftly with y

and generate the past participial phrase

stabbed swiftly with y,

which would be a predicate that holds of a state s if and only if

$$(\exists e)[s = e\text{'s R-state \& Stabbing}(e) \text{ \& Swift}(e) \text{ \& With}(e,y)].$$

When fed into the theory above this fills in all the needed gaps—even including the treatment of 'to fultume' in the last major example cited.

The significance of this hypothesis for OE is that instead of supposing that participles are adjectives that are formed in a regular way from verbs, with other ingredients of the VP being independent of this process, we suppose that participles are the heads of adjective phrases that are formed in a regular way from verb phrases. These adjective phrases thus serve as the inputs to the restructuring, not just their heads.

How could any evidence be found that might bear on this hypothesis? A popular *speculation* about the origin of OE might be relevant. Proto-Indo-European (PIE) is the supposed language from which all Indo-European languages originated. Some scholars hold that PIE consisted entirely of simple sentences, where meanings we now express by embeddings of clauses were figured out from the context surrounding sequences of sentences. Instead of the relative clause in

The boy who played loves Mary,

PIE would have something like

boy played. boy loves Mary.

After a while, the subordinate-clause-to-be became distinguished by an anaphoric demonstrative

boy loves Mary. that boy played,

or

boy loves Mary. he played.

Eventually the subordinate clause was incorporated into the main one, with the anaphoric element evolved into a relative pronoun:

boy he played loves Mary

or

boy that played loves Mary.

Other embeddings were supposed to have worked differently, but they originated similarly from independent clauses.[25] In certain languages, for example, some embedded clauses are marked not by a relative pronoun but by the verb's taking an infinitival or a participial form. Lehmann 1980 cites a Sanskrit example that literally translates: 'you-know not me standing-near' (='you do not know that I am near'), where the participial ending on 'standing' singles out its clause ('me standing-near') as the one that modern English would embed. If something like this lay in the background of Old English, then we could construe the participial endings on verbs in embedded "adjectival" clauses as being, in part, indicators of semantic embeddedness. The participial ending would thereby have significance for the clause as a whole! And that is the key idea behind Response 3.

Response 3 may even apply to Modern English, in explaining the use of 'smoothly' in 'the smoothly shaved leg', or 'deftly' in 'the deftly broken egg'. If 'shaved' is an adjective in 'the smoothly shaved leg', then some account needs to be given of the status of 'smoothly', whose normal use is to modify a verb, not a noun or adjective.

12.7 Skeptical Reflections on Participles

I wish now to express some reservations about the standard account of the evolution of modern verb-forms from purported adjectival sources in Old English. I am concerned by the difficulty in distinguishing participles used as adjectives from completely independent adjectives that happen to be spelled the same way. This matter is at the heart of the standard discussions of the origin of the Modern perfect and progressive. It also affects the testing of theories about participles in Modern English.

12.7.1 Problems Concerning Past Participles

It is sometimes easy to distinguish past participles used as adjectives from other adjectives which are not past participles at all. Nobody will confuse 'an open door' with 'an opened door'. The former denotes a door that is in a certain state—it isn't closed. The latter denotes a door that has been opened. If a door is opened and then closed, it is then an opened door but not an open door. Likewise, if the door were built in an open position, then it would be an open door but not an opened door. The two words 'open' and 'opened', are almost completely independent of one another. I call 'open' an "autonomous" adjective, to distinguish it from the past participle 'opened' when it is used as an adjective.

It is, however, easy to confuse the autonomous adjective 'closed' with the past participle 'closed', since they are homonyms. They are different words that are related as are 'open' and 'opened'. Another example of this is 'broken', which is used both as an autonomous adjective and, adjectivally, as a past participle. "Which leg is the broken one?" "The left one." "It looks fine now." "Yes, it isn't broken anymore; it's fully healed." If a leg is broken and then heals, it is still a broken leg in one sense (in the past-participle-used-as-an-adjective sense) but it is no longer a broken leg in another sense (in the autonomous adjective sense).

Adjectives and past participles can be related in at least two ways when they are homonyms. Sometimes they are completely independent of one another; neither sense entails the other, as with the senses of 'closed'. And sometimes the autonomous adjective sense seems to entail the participle sense, but not vice versa. This may be true with 'broken'—that is, it may be true that anything that is ever in a broken state got that way by having been broken—though that is arguable. Certainly 'marooned' works in this way. If you are a sailor who is marooned (autonomous adjective) on an island, then you must be a marooned (participle) sailor; if you are rescued you are still a marooned (participle) sailor though you are no longer marooned (autonomous adjective).

Such pairs of homonyms are quite common in Modern English, perhaps as the product of two distinct and partially productive processes. The first is that adjectives generate causative transitive verbs. From our adjective 'open' we naturally form a transitive verb 'open', meaning something like 'cause to become open (adjective)'. This is quite common in English, and once children catch on to it they try to overgeneralize it: "I deaded him." Usually the adjective does not look like a participle, so the past participle of the causative transitive is not confused with the adjective; 'cooled' is not confused with 'cool'. But whenever the adjective looks like a participle, the past participle of the causative transitive verb may be pronounced and spelled just like the adjective.

A second semiproductive process may also be at work. For a large number of verbs, there is a "typical" independently identifiable state that its object is in after the verb is true of it. If the state is transitory, then we come to use the adjective form of the past participle to stand for the transitory state instead of for the permanent resultant state. For example, anything that is cracked and then not repaired is in a state that is easy to identify—until the repair. One could imagine the verb as existing before the adjective, and then the (past-participle) adjective's coming to be used for the unrepaired state, even when the "crack" may not have originated by cracking (the mirror may have been designed that way). This would naturally give rise to adjectives with different meanings than the past participles from which they evolved.

These two processes work in opposite directions; one produces causative verbs (and thus their participles) from adjectives, and the other produces adjectives from participles of verbs. Once the processes get going they may very well reinforce one another. Unless historical research can shed some light on this, we may face a chicken-and-egg issue. (It is known, for example, that the adjective 'open' and the past participle 'opened' both go back to Old English. It is more difficult to trace the origin of the adjective 'closed' versus the participle 'closed', since spelling is no guide.)

This is my first difficulty about the data that lies behind the derivation of the modern perfect. If, indeed, the perfect is derived from purported adjectival uses *of the past participle,* how can we be sure whether the examples are uses *of the past participle,* when so many adjectives are spelled exactly like past participles? How can we be sure that we are seeing a past participle and not an autonomous adjective?[26] Perhaps past participles were never used as adjectives in the supposed sources of modern perfects. Perhaps the supposed examples are all examples in which *autonomous adjectives* occur. Indeed, perhaps the modern perfect existed throughout the origins of our language, and the speculation that it originated from adjectival sources is generated from attributing the wrong significance to the fact that there is a similarity of spelling between the past participle used with the perfect and adjectives that occur elsewhere in the sentences.

12.7.2 Problems Concerning Present Participles

My second qualm about the data is whether present participles were ever generally used as adjectives after the copula? As in Modern English, OE seems to have used present participles as adjectives in prenominal position (at least they sometimes appear there with adjectival inflections), but they seem hardly ever to have adjectival inflections when they follow the copula. Yet this position is supposed to have been the *adjectival* source of the modern progressive. Perhaps neither Old English nor Modern English uses present participles as adjectives after the copula. If not, the origin of the progressive remains unknown.

12.8 Temporal Adverbials

Probably one of the most important and least understood phenomena related to the perfect is its interrelations with adverbials. In the case of perfects, adverbials may modify either the past event or the resultant state. My suggesting that ordinary (nontemporal) verb modifiers apply to the past event adds to the plausibility of considering the perfect as just another form of the past. 'Violently' in 'Brutus has stabbed Caesar violently' appears in logical form as a predicate of the event of Brutus's stabbing of Caesar, not as a predicate of the resultant state. In fact, in the favored treatment, there seem to be no cases in which an ordinary verb modifier applies to the resultant state, as opposed to the previous event.

But there are also temporal modifiers to consider. The theory would let them appear as constraints on the time interval that is also constrained by the tense, as predicates of the past event, or as predicates of the resultant state. I am not aware of any need for them to apply to the resultant state, but the other two options are fulfilled. In short, I propose that temporal adverbials in perfective sentences work exactly the same as in nonperfectives. The resultant state of the perfect therefore adds no new options. Some illustrations follow.

Some adverbials constrain only the time and do not apply to the event; they include 'now', 'yesterday', and 'tomorrow' (though not 'today'). With them we get anomaly or non-anomaly, depending only on the tense. Thus we have

OK   Agatha ran yesterday
*   Agatha runs yesterday
OK   Agatha had run yesterday
*   Agatha has run yesterday

If the adverbial could apply to the resultant state, then the following ought to be acceptable:

*   Agatha will have run yesterday.

It is not.

Other adverbials can apply to either the tense-time or to the event; each of the following has two readings, depending on whether the adverbial governs the tense-time or the event:

Time   *Event*

OK   OK   Agatha ran at noon
OK   OK   Agatha runs at noon (*Reportive Usage*)
OK   OK   Agatha had run at noon
OK   OK   Agatha has run at noon (*Reportive Usage*)

Durational adverbials like 'for three years' are anomalous with the present tense when read as time-constraining, since this would require the time to simultaneously span three years. Therefore, for the present tense only the event/state modifier reading remains. We then have

Time *Event*

*   OK   I have lived in New York for three years
OK   OK   I lived in New York for three years.

The modified-event readings of the two sentences turn out to be equivalent, except that the past tense version requires the state in question to be over at the time of utterance and the perfect does not. (If we change the example to 'exactly three years' then the sentences might diverge in truth-value when uttered exactly at the end of a three-year residence in New York.)[27]

12.8.1   The Perfect Progressive; Repairing the Progressive

When the perfect is combined with the progressive, things mostly work fine. But a slight repair is needed in one area of the account. Consider the sentence

Mary has been building a house for three years.

Now suppose that the house building has been going on for three years and that it will continue for another two before the house is completed. (It does not matter for present purposes whether it gets completed.) The question is how to handle the adverbial 'for three years'. Potentially, it can apply to any of four possible things:

the time that is constrained by the tense,
the event of house building,
the result-state of the in-progress state (supplied by the perfect), or
the in-progress state of house-building (supplied by the progressive).

Clearly the time constrained by the tense is inappropriate to combine with the adverbial, since that time is the present time, and it does not span three years. ('For three years' never combines with the present tense.) Nor is the house building event itself the proper thing of which to predicate 'for three years', since that event lasts for five years. (I assume that 'for three years' is understood for present purposes as 'for exactly three years'.) Further, the result-state is equally inappropriate as a subject of that predication, since it will go on forever. We are left with the building-state that is supplied by the progressive. But according to the theory, there is only one in-progress state, and that coincides with the entire house building itself, which lasts five years, not three. It is this last part of the account—concerning the progressive—that needs alteration.

If a state verb applies to a state that holds over a certain interval, that same verb also applies to substates of the larger state. If Mary knows Fred for three years, then many shorter Mary-knowing-Fred states hold within that interval of time. The progressive ought to work like this as well; if 'be building a house' applies to a certain long-lasting state, then it ought to apply also to substates of that state that hold for arbitrary subintervals of the original interval. The error in my earlier treatment of the progressive was to posit only a single, large in-progress state, without positing the smaller substates as well. Accordingly, my notation should change '*the* in-progress state of e' to '*an* in-progress state of e', and we should assume that there is such a state for each subinterval of time that e is going on.

We can now resolve the applicability of the temporal adverbial 'for three years' in the example above. It applies to the requisite in-progress state of house building. That is, the sentence has roughly this form:[28]

Mary has been building a house for three years =
($\exists$I)[I=now & ($\exists$e)($\exists$t)[t$\in$I & Building(e) & Agent(e,Mary) & Theme(e,house) & ($\exists$s)[s is an in-progress state of e & s lasts for 3 years & Cul(the result-state of s,t)]]].

The overall consequence is that the progressive does indeed introduce new states that are available for adverbial modification, but the perfect does not.

Chapter 13

Eventlish—A Fragment of English

13.1 Introduction

The purpose of this chapter is to show in detail how to generate the syntax and semantics of atomic formulas of English, by producing a fragment of English that I call "Eventlish." This fragment illustrates what a part of English would be like if the theory I have developed were true.

The task here is limited in various ways. First, it is limited to generating atomic formulas, such as 'x stabbed y with z'. Clearly, these atomic formulas need to be embellished in many ways to produce the full range of English sentences. For example, the variables in the atomic formulas must be replaced by names and quantified NPs, to yield, e.g., 'Mary stabbed everyone with an icepick'. This is a whole topic in itself, and I totally ignore it here. I also ignore infinitives (as in 'want to eat'), that-clauses, conjoined sentences, and a host of other constructions. The task of producing the atomic sentences is itself only partially complete, because I also ignore "temporal" adverbials. A full and adequate treatment of these words and phrases in all of their complexity is beyond my ability at present. The fragment consists entirely of what I call "default" constructions (see chapter 11); they produce the readings of sentences that occur with no influence from context and no influence from temporal adverbials such as 'for three days' or 'twice'. The readings are all of the "reportive" kind. This must be kept in mind when evaluating my treatment of the present tense forms, where the reportive usage is less frequent than other usages (such as "generic" readings, which I do not include).

I present a Lexicon and a series of Templates. These two together are meant to be empirically adequate (with the qualifications indicated above). They are, however, open to the accusation that they "miss linguistic generalizations." There are many different ways to generalize in accordance with the templates, and various schools of linguists will prefer to do so differently. My goal is to produce a treatment that is clear enough for each person to incorporate the results into his/her favorite framework. It would be fascinating to combine these results with Government-Binding theory,[1] Lexical Functional Grammar, Generalized Phrase Structure Grammar, Categorial Grammar, Montague Grammar, or something else along these lines, but I do not attempt this.

Each template may be filled in any way possible with ingredients from the Lexicon, subject to certain constraints. Some constraints are stated with the template itself: they are to be construed as part of the defining characteristics of the template. Other constraints arise from the verb selected from the Lexicon; they are indicated in the Lexicon along with the verb entries. Some directly constrain the syntax, such as the general condition that intransitive verbs may not occur with direct objects, and some are purely semantic, such as the fact that the choice of verb determines the choice of (semantic) thematic relations that are available for interpreting its subject and objects.

Each template has two correlated parts; one characterizes the syntactic form, and one produces a logical form associated with that syntactic form. The syntactic forms are stated in terms of a sequence of morphemes, and I assume that it is clear how to produce real sentences from them. For example, a structure of the form 'Pres+run' with a singular third-person subject is supposed to produce the third person singular present tense form of the verb: 'runs'. I also take for granted the principles that will yield the correct person and number for the verb, as well as principles of syntactic case assignment (i.e., principles that make the surface subject nominative, the direct object accusative, and so on). These are fascinating issues, but I am not concerned with them here.

The logical forms utilized are expressed in the familiar terminology of the first-order predicate calculus with function symbols and lambda abstracts.[2] I do not believe that this symbolism is adequate to represent all of English, but it is adequate for the parts I am studying, and its semantics is well understood. Some constructions that require enhancement of the predicate calculus symbolism are discussed in chapters 3 and 4.

I need to explain one subtlety. The templates directly produce what I call "blocks," sequences that look exactly like atomic formulas of English and have the appropriate semantics for such formulas. From my point of view, there is no particular reason why these blocks should not be the direct bases of sentences of a language. However, English has a Subject-Predicate form, which is not addressed semantically in the process of block-formation. In particular, VPs have a life of their own, both syntactically and semantically. The most natural way to accommodate this is not to use blocks directly to yield formulas of English but rather to use them to produce VPs ("grammatical predicates") and then to combine these with subject-variables to produce the atomic formulas. I shall return briefly to the details of this process after introducing the first templates, when we have more material to work with. For most purposes, no semantic harm will come from confusing blocks with atomic formulas of English.

My exposition begins in section 13.2 with a simple template, section 13.3 gives the Lexicon, and sections 13.5-12 provide the remaining templates.

13.2   The Templates

A template shows how to produce both the syntax[3] of a block and its associated logical form. This is based on the fact that there is a straightforward correlation between simple parts of the block and parts of a standardized logical form.

Template #1 is available for use by all noncausative noninchoative nonperception verbs, that is, by ordinary intransitive, transitive, and double-object verbs, such as 'fall', 'date', 'give'. Specifically, it is available for all verbs labeled "IV," "TV," or "2TV" in the Lexicon.

Template #1: Simple Active Sentences

Syntax

$$x_{Subj} \quad \text{Tns} \quad \textbf{Perf} \quad \textbf{Prog} \quad \text{Verb} \quad z_{Indir} \quad y_{Dir} \quad AdV^n$$
$$\uparrow \qquad\quad \uparrow \qquad\qquad\qquad\qquad\quad \uparrow$$
$$* \qquad\quad * \qquad\qquad\qquad\qquad\quad *$$

Explanation   A block is produced from a template by (1) erasing all subscripts, and (2) substituting items from the lexicon for each nonbold item in the string. The bold items are terminal symbols, that is, they may not be replaced by other symbols from the Lexicon, but must be used "as is." The nonbold items stand for categories of terminal symbols that can be filled in from the Lexicon in various ways. The items indicated by arrows must be chosen; the others are optional[4] (except that in Template #1 if z_{Indir} is chosen, y_{Dir} must be chosen as well). The superscript 'n' on 'AdV^n' indicates that there may be several AdVs in a row here. All the choices of items from the Lexicon are subject to constraints that are stated in the Lexicon associated with the verb that is chosen.

Logical form

$(\exists I)(\exists t)(\exists \alpha)[t \in I \ \& \ SUBJ(\alpha,x) \ \& \ I \blacklozenge now \ \& \ OCCUR(r(p(\alpha)),t) \ \&$
$Verb'(\alpha) \ \& \ INDIR(\alpha,z) \ \& \ DIR(\alpha,y) \ \& \ AdV'(\alpha)^n]$

Explanation   The logical form associated with a block is produced by filling in various items, depending on the choices that were made to produce the block itself. The variable 'α' ranges over events, states, and processes. The three relations 'SUBJ', 'INDIR' and 'DIR' are dummy places for thematic relations, the choice of which will be determined by information given in the Lexicon along with the verb that is chosen. The symbol '$\blacklozenge$' in 'I$\blacklozenge$now' is to be replaced by '$<$', '$\approx$', or '$>$', depending on whether the past, present, or future tense is chosen for "Tns." As stated in the Lexicon, 'r' denotes the function that maps each event or state to its resultant-state[5]; it is to be omitted if Perf is not chosen. Similarly, 'p' denotes the function that maps each event to its In-Progress state;[6] it is present only if Prog is chosen. 'OCCUR' is a dummy symbol to be replaced by 'Cul' if the chosen verb is an event verb and if neither Perf nor Prog is chosen; otherwise it is replaced by 'Hold'.[7] The superscript 'n' in 'AdV'$(\alpha)^n$' here indicates a conjunction of formulas, one for each AdV that was chosen in the block. Both 'Verb'' and 'AdV'' are placeholders for the predicates assigned to the verb and adverbial in the Lexicon.

The association between parts of the block and parts of the associated logical form can be displayed graphically as follows:

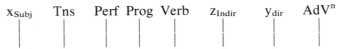

x_{Subj} Tns   Perf Prog Verb z_{Indir} y_{dir} AdV^n

$(\exists I,t,\alpha)[t \in I \ \& \ SUBJ(\alpha,x) \ \& \ I\blacklozenge now \ \& \ OCCUR(r(p(\alpha)),t) \ \& \ Verb'(\alpha) \ \& \ INDIR(\alpha,z) \ \& \ DIR(\alpha,y) \ \& \ AdV'^n(\alpha)]$

In all of the remaining templates these correlations will be taken for granted, and only newly introduced ones will be explained.

Some examples of the use of this template are

x stabbed y violently with u.

x will have run.

x is giving z y. ("John is giving Mary the book.")

Template #1a

Template #1a differs from Template #1 only in reversing the order of the direct and indirect objects and inserting 'to' or 'for' to mark the indirect object:

Syntax

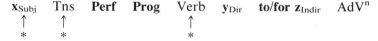

x_{Subj} Tns   **Perf**   **Prog**   Verb y_{Dir} **to/for** z_{Indir} AdV^n

Logical Form   Same as in Template #1. If 'to' is selected then the dummy INDIR must be replaced by Goal, and if 'for' is selected then INDIR must be replaced by Benefactive.

Example:

x has given y to z.

13.2.1   Blocks and Atomic Formulas of English

Previously I noted that the "blocks" that are produced by the templates are not themselves atomic formulas of English; they are used indirectly to produce those formulas. To illustrate, Template #1 will allow us to generate the block:

x stab y violently with u,

with a logical form (ignoring times) something like:

$(\exists e)[Subj(e,x)$ & $Obj(e,y)$ & $Stabbing(e)$ & $Cul(e)$ & $Violent(e)$ & $With(e,u)]$.

From this block we then remove its apparent subject, thus producing the VP

stab y violently with u.

The logical form of this VP is produced by lambda abstraction on the logical form of the block, using the "removed" variable

$\lambda x[(\exists e)[Subj(e,x) \& Obj(e,y) \& Stabbing(e) \& Cul(e) \& Violent(e) \& With(e,u)]]$,

which is a predicate true of any person x just in case a stabbing culminates, whose agent is x, whose object is y, which is violent, and which is with u. This generation of VPs from blocks is something like Partee's "derived verb phrase" rule in Montague Grammar (see Partee 1976a), except that in the present framework it is applied uniformly in every case, and it is applied before any of the variables in the block are quantified.

At this point, any of various things can happen to the VP. It can be combined with a subject variable to reintroduce the syntactic string that looks exactly like the block we started with:

x stab y violently with u.

Semantically, the lambda abstract is applied to the re-introduced variable, to yield a meaning logically equivalent to that of the original block:

$\lambda x[(\exists e)[Subj(e,x) \& Obj(e,y) \& Stabbing(e) \& Cul(e) \& Violent(e) \& With(e,u)]](x)$.

One application of lambda-elimination to this form yields the original logical form again, getting us right back where we started. This is why confusing blocks with atomic formulas of English is semantically harmless for many purposes.

However, other things can happen to the VP before it gets its subject variable, and then the results are different. For example, the VP 'stab y violently with u' can be augmented into 'want to stab y violently with u', which then combines with a subject to produce an atomic formula unlike the original block. The many ways of producing complex VPs are not studied at all here, but a place needs to be available for them. This is why I have chosen to generate atomic formulas from VP's which are themselves generated from blocks.[8]

In summary, atomic formulas of English that contain simple VPs are semantically equivalent to the blocks from which they are generated; others may not be.

13.3 The Lexicon

The Lexicon includes all the syntactic vocabulary that does not already appear in the templates, as well as all the items that appear in logical forms but that are not specified in the templates. Additional constraints on the use of the vocabulary is also included here.

13.3.1 Tense
The choices for Tns are 'Past', 'Pres', and 'Fut'. I suppose that 'Past+run' surfaces as 'ran', and I suppose that 'Fut+run' surfaces as 'will run'. The tense choice locates the period of time in question to be before, the same as, or after the "speech-time" of a simple sentence.[9] This is accomplished in the logical forms by selecting '<', '≈', or '>' for the symbol '♦' that is correlated with Tns in each template. The formula '$I < t$' means that every moment in the interval I precedes t, and similarly for '$I > t$'. '$I ≈ t$' means that I is a unit interval consisting entirely of t.

13.3.2 Perf and Prog
Each of these, when selected, contributes a function symbol to the logical form. **Perf** contributes the symbol 'r', where 'r(α)' stands for the resultant-state of α (see chapter 12). **Prog** contributes the symbol 'p', where 'p(α)' stands for the in-progress state of α. This is the alternative account of the progressive mentioned in section 9.2; its use is discussed in detail in portions of chapter 12.

13.3.3 Pass
This is a syntactic morpheme that combines with a verb to produce its passive form preceded by 'be', such as 'be eaten'. It has no representation in the logical forms. (The effect of its presence is described in Templates #2 and #2a.)

13.3.4 Thematic Relations
The available thematic relations are Agent, Performer, Experiencer, Theme, Goal, and Benefactive, as well as Agent-Theme, Experiencer-Theme, and Performer-Theme. These replace the dummy terms SUBJ, INDIR, and DIR in the logical forms displayed in the templates; the choices are made in accordance with constraints associated with the verb that is chosen. In the logical notation, 'Agent-Theme(α,x)' is an

abbreviation for 'Agent(α,x) & Theme(α,x)', and similarly for the other hyphenated options. These notions are discussed throughout chapter 5. "Performer" includes cases that are usually called "Instrument" in the linguistic literature (see section 5.4).

13.3.5 Noncausative Noninchoative Verbs

The simple categories of Intransitive Verbs (IV), Transitive Verbs (TV), and Double-Object Verbs (2TV) are expressly limited to noncausative noninchoative verbs; causatives and inchoatives are treated separately, as are higher-order verbs. Each IV, TV or 2TV contributes to logical form a predicate of events or states. By custom, the predicate in logical form is represented by the gerund form of the verb, capitalized; this predicate replaces the 'Verb'' in the logical form portion of the template.

According to the theory, process verbs are just a special case of event verbs, and process phrases (such as 'run') can be converted into nonprocess phrases (such as 'run to the store') by expansion with modifiers (see section 9.5). For intuitive naturalness, I classify process verbs as such, but it should be kept in mind that they appear in the templates officially as event verbs.

Since most verbs have multiple homonyms, I often provide examples to suggest the particular meaning that I have in mind. The verb lists below are chosen partly at random, as are those of adverbials and adjectives.

13.3.6 Intransitive Verbs (IVs)

General constraints: IVs do not take direct or indirect objects, and so they may not occur in a block along with a variable subscripted as Dir or Indir. IVs may not occur in passives. Available subjects are limited to Theme (T), Agent-Theme (A-T), Performer-Theme (P-T), Experiencer-Theme (E-T).

Verb	Event/State	Subj	Example
arrive	Event	T, A-T	The package (woman) arrived late.
burn	Process	T	The paper burned.
clatter	Event	T	The plate clattered on the floor.
fall	Event	T	The brick fell.
fly	Process	T, A-T	He (the kite) flew over the north pole

hunger	State	E-T	She hungers for his love.
leave	Event	T, A-T	She (the letter) already left.
look	Process	A	I looked, but I saw nothing.
move	Event	T, A-T	That leaf (man) just moved.
run	Process	A-T	She ran for 3 hours.
sing	Process	A-T	She sang all day.
sit	Process	A-T, P-T	She sat there all day.
sit	State	T	(= "be located")
sleep	Process	E-T	He slept like a log.
stand	Process	A-T, P-T	Dennis (the statue) stood in the corner.
stand	State	T	(= "be located")
talk	Process	A-T	He talks like Jimmy Durante.
walk	Process	T, A-T	He (the robot) walked like a duck.

13.3.7 Transitive Verbs (TVs)

General constraints: TVs do not take indirect objects, and so they may not occur in a block along with a variable subscripted as Indir. Available subjects are limited to Agent (A), Performer (P), Agent-Performer (A-P), Experiencer (E). DIR is always Theme.

Verb	Event/State	Subj	Example
beat	Event	A	She beat him at chess.
chase	Process	A	He chased her for days.
consume	Process	A, P	The fire consumed O_2.
cross	Event	A, P	She (the wagon) crossed the street.
cut	Event	A, P	He (the knife) cut the cheese.
date	Event	A	Mary dated Bill.
eat	Event	A	She ate the apple.
feel	Event	E	I felt her smooth skin.
find	Event	E	I found the book.
flip	Event	A, P	I flipped the switch.
follow	Process	A-P, P	The small ball followed the large one down the ramp.

have	State	E	I have a dog.
hear	Event	E	She heard the crash.
hit	Event	A, P	The hammer hit the nail.
kiss	Event	A	She kissed me.
know	State	E	She knows Fred.
know	State	E	She knows the answer.
like	State	E	like mathematics.
load	Process	A, P	load hay in the barn
load	Event	A, P	load the wagon
look	Process	A	I looked, but I saw nothing.
love	State	E	I love you.
murder	Event	A	She murdered her.
own	State	E	I own a shack on a lake.
pay	Event	A	He paid the bill.
push	Process	A, P	push the cart
reach	Event	A, P	They reached the summit.
salute	Event	A	salute the flag
see	State	E	see the giraffe
shoot	Event	A	shoot the king
shoot	Event	A	shoot the gun
sing	Event	A	sing the song
stab	Event	A, P	stab Caesar
think	State	E	think that she is ill
throw	Event	A	throw the ball
understand	State	E	understand mathematics
win	Event	A	win the game

13.3.8 Double-Object Verbs (2TVs)

General constraints: SUBJ must be Agent, and DIR must be Theme. INDIR must be Benefactive (B) or Goal (G). The examples illustrate cases with indirect objects, all of which are optional.

Verb	Event/State	Indir	Examples
build	Event	B	build her a bookcase
buy	Event	B	buy her a car
find	Event	B	find him a taxi
give	Event	G	give him five dollars
give	Event	B	give her a party
make	Event	B	make her a doily
pay	Event	G	pay her the money
sell	Event	G	sell her a computer
steal	Event	B	steal you a car

throw	Event	B	throw him a party
write	Event	B	write her a check
write	Event	G	write her a memo

13.3.9 Perception Verbs

These feed into the template for perception verbs as 'Verb$_{PER}$'. They all take Experiencer for SUBJ. A sample list is:

'see', 'feel', 'hear', 'watch', 'catch', 'detect', 'discern', 'find', 'glimpse', 'notice', 'observe'.

Certain of these ('catch', 'detect', 'discern', 'find', 'glimpse') seem to require that the embedded clause be in the progressive. (A verb that has the same syntax and semantics as perception verbs is 'make', as in 'I made him stand still'.)

13.3.10 Inchoatives and Causative-Inchoatives

An inchoative is an intransitive verb whose meaning is based on that of an adjective; the meaning of the verb is roughly to "become Adj," where 'Adj' represents the adjective in question. For example, 'The door opened' means, roughly, "The door became open." In the templates for inchoatives, a predicate operator 'BECOME#' converts the logical form representation of the adjective (a predicate of states) into a representation for the verb (a predicate of events). Most inchoatives take Theme as SUBJ; a few (such as 'sit') take Agent-Theme.

Causative-Inchoatives are transitive verbs whose meanings are similarly based on adjectives; the meaning of the verb is roughly "to cause to become Adj." For example, 'Mary opened the door' means, roughly, "Mary did something that caused the door to become open." The template for causative-inchoatives uses both the predicate operator 'BECOME#' and the two-place predicate 'CAUSE' to analyze these verbs.

In each case, the lexical entry for the verb need only cite the adjective on which the meaning of the verb is based. A list of triads follows. The entries in the first column are causative-inchoative transitive verbs, and the entries in the second column are inchoative intransitive verbs. The third column, denoted "V-Adj," gives the adjective that determines the meaning of the verb.

Trans.	Intrans.	V-Adj	Examples of Transitive Verb
alert	—	alert	alert the burglar
awaken	awaken	awake	awaken the child
break	break	broken	break the window
brighten	brighten	bright	brighten the color
close	close	closed	close the door
cool	cool	cool	cool the soup
dirty	—	dirty	dirty the rug
empty	empty?	empty	empty the ashtray
fatten	—	fat	fatten the cattle
fell	fall	fallen	fell the tree
fill	fill	full	fill the tank
flatten	—	flat	flatten the pillow
harden	harden	hard	harden the metal
kill	die	dead	kill the intruder
lighten	lighten?	light	lighten the load
load	—	loaded	load the wagon
load	—	loaded	load the hay
melt	melt	molten	melt the wax
open	open	open	open the door
randomize	—	random	randomize the digits
redden	redden	red	redden the solution
seat	sit	seated	seat the couple
sink	sink	sunken	sink the Bismarck
solidify	solidify	solid	solidify the emulsion
wet	—	wet	wet the towel

13.3.11 Causatives of Noninchoatives

Some causative transitive verbs are based on intransitive verbs that are not themselves inchoatives. Although these are not implemented here, their forms can be generated by simplifying the pattern for causative-inchoatives. Some examples are

Trans.	Intrans.	V-Adj	Examples of Transitive Verb
burn	burn	—	burn the wood
explode	explode	—	explode the bomb
flip	flip	—	flip the switch
fly	fly	—	fly the kite
rock	rock	—	rock the boat
rotate	rotate	—	rotate the wheel
run	run	—	run the machine

set	sit	—	set the cup (on the rug)
shuffle	shuffle	—	shuffle her feet
walk	walk	—	walk the dog

13.3.12 Higher-Order Verbs

Intransitive higher-order verbs contribute no predicates or operators to logical form. Some examples are 'occur', 'happen', and 'take place'. The only transitive higher-order verb implemented here is 'cause'. This contributes the predicate 'Cause' to logical form; it is a two-place predicate of events or states.

13.3.13 Adverbials (AdVs):

I abbreviate these "AdV" in order to emphasize that they modify verbs; they are "ad-verbs" (see chapter 4). They all contribute predicates of events or states to logical form. They come in two forms: adverbs and prepositional phrases. By custom, I use the adjectival form of an adverb for the predicate of events that the adverb contributes to logical form. A preposition combines with a variable to produce a predicate of events or states, and I construe these as relations between the thing denoted by the variable and the event or state. Thus I treat 'violently' and 'with u' on a par syntactically, and I write the formulas that they contribute to logical form 'Violent(α)' and 'With(α,u)'. I schematize each of these as 'AdV$'(\alpha)$'.

General constraints: Only one adverbial of each type is permitted in each block, except for locatives. In addition, instrumental 'with' is permitted only with a verb that takes Agent, and then only when it applies to the same event variable as Agent. (It may also occur with a verb that takes Agent when Agent and Performer are both absent— in "agentless passives." Thus we have 'The door was opened with a key', but not 'The key opened the door with a thong'.)

In the following list, adverbs precede prepositions.

Instrumental with
Locative home, here, there, away, in, on, on top of, at, outside of, away from, under, behind, off, above, over, alongside, across, in front of, upon, against, below, between, among
Motion home, here, there, away, up, down, sideways, into, onto, to, from, out of, across, away from, under, behind, off, uphill, through, at, in, towards, between, among

Direction   home, here, there, away, up, down, sideways, into,
                   to, from, out of, away from, under, behind, off,
                   uphill, through, at, in, towards, between, across
Orientation   crosswise, upright, vertical, across
Manner   violently, gently, slowly, quickly, calmly, loudly,
                   quietly, happily, rudely, easily, carefully.
Miscellaneous   in_TARGET ("in the back"), in_INVOLVEMENT ("in every
                   killing"), with_ACCOMPANIMENT (= in the company of),
                   with_ORNAMENT ("loaded with hay", "black with soot").

(Beware of confusing non-ad-verb homonyms of ad-verbs with the ad-verbs themselves; e.g. of confusing 'Rudely, she answered the queen' with 'She answered the queen rudely_Adv'. The former are not implemented in this fragment; see chapter 4).

13.3.14 Adjectives

Each adjective contributes a predicate of states to logical form. For heuristic purposes the predicate is spelled by adding 'ness' to the end of the adjective. 'Cleverness(α)' may be read "α is a state of cleverness." All the adjectives listed in the Causative-Inchoative Triads above count as adjectives, as well as

'clever', 'tall', 'tight', 'naked', 'heavy'.

13.3.15 Other Primitives

The following additional terminology (discussed in chapter 6) appears in the templates for causatives and inchoatives; they are listed here for completeness:

CAUSE   (a two-place predicate of events/states)
BECOME#   (a predicate operator).

13.4 Miscellaneous Matters

3.4.1 Context

Context affects the interpretation of logical forms in two principal ways. First, the actual denotation of any English word (such as 'love') can vary from context to context, in addition to shifts due to ambiguity. Because morphemes of English correlate fairly precisely with items in the logical forms, the shift of denotation of English words can be precisely reflected in shifts of denotation of the corresponding item in logical form.

Context is also of key importance in interpreting temporal "reference" (cf. Partee 1973). For example, a typical utterance of 'I ran' is not thought to be true just because I have run at least once before in my life, perhaps several years previously; context imposes further constraints on the period in question, as does embedding of the sentence within a narrative discourse. I assume that contextual constraints of this sort turn up as constraints on the variable 'I' in logical form, in addition to the constraints imposed by the logical form itself. Thus the actual interpretation of 'I ran' could be reflected by the form

$$(\exists I)(\exists t)(\exists \alpha)[t \in I \ \& \ \text{Agent-Theme}(\alpha,\text{me}) \ \& \ I < \text{now} \ \& \ \text{Context}(I) \ \& \ \text{Cul}(\alpha,t) \ \& \ \text{Running}(\alpha)]$$

where 'Context(I)' represents the constraint due to context; this constraint is in addition to the tense, which places I only sometime in the past. Since context similarly affects all predicates and all quantifier+variable combinations, I omit explicit mention of it in the symbolism.

13.4.2 Adverbial Transportation

The templates given here all place adverbials at the ends of their blocks. Some should be allowed to appear in other positions. For example, in addition to 'She stroked the baby fondly' we have 'She fondly stroked the baby'. Adverb position is difficult to evaluate, since key tests (such as those discussed in Jackendoff 1972) depend heavily on examples whose acceptability differs from person to person, and because matters of style and matters of grammar are unusually difficult to disentangle here. I assume that the templates must be supplemented by something like Keyser's (1968) "Principle of Transportation," which moves adverbs to other positions in the sentence. I am not able to formulate such a principle myself.

13.4.3 Conjunctions and Disjunctions

Many cases of apparent conjunctions and disjunctions of subsentential parts have the semantics of conjunctions and disjunctions of blocks. For example, as discussed in chapter 4, 'Kim drove to the store and to the laundromat' should come from a conjunction of blocks, or of VPs, not from a conjunction of modifiers within a single block. The form should be something like[10]

(∃I)[I<now & (∃t₁)(∃α)[t₁∈I & Agent(α,Kim) & Cul(α,t₁) &
Driving(α) & To(α,store)] & (∃t₂)(∃β)[t₂∈I & Agent(β,Kim) &
Cul(β,t₂) & Driving(β) & To(β,laundromat)]],

as opposed to

(∃I)(∃t)(∃α)[t∈I & Agent(α,Kim) & I<now & Cul(α,t) & Driving(α)
& To(α,store) & To(α,laundromat)].

The reason is that two possibly distinct drivings, and not one, are
involved. This is something like the old principle of "conjunction
reduction," although it takes place at a very early stage of derivation,
before NP scopes get into the picture.

   To give another example, I think that 'John saw Mary walk and
Susan run' can mean only that 'John saw Mary walk and saw Susan
run'. Likewise, 'John saw Mary walk or Susan run' means only 'John
saw Mary walk or saw Susan run'. Of course, NPs can quantify into
such constructions. So 'Everybody saw Mary walk or Susan run'
means 'Each person is such that he or she saw Mary walk or he or
she saw Susan run'.

   I have not attempted to formulate the principles of "modifier conjunction" in this fragment.

13.5   Simple Passives

The template for passives of blocks with noncausative noninchoative
verbs (IVs, TVs, 2TVs) is

Template #2 (Simple Passives)

Syntax

y_{Dir}	Tns	**Perf**	**Prog**	**Pass**	Verb	z_{Indir}	**by** x_{Subj}	AdV^n
↑	↑			↑	↑			
*	*			*	*			

Again, the indicated items must be selected, and the others are optional. In addition, either 'to' or 'for' may precede z_{Indir}.

Logical Form (same as the active form)

(∃I)(∃t)(∃α)[t∈I & SUBJ(α,x) & I◆now & OCCUR(r(p(α)),t) &
Verb'(α) & INDIR(α,z) & DIR(α,y) & AdV'(α)ⁿ].

Constraint: If 'to' is inserted before z_{Indir} then INDIR must be Goal, and if 'for' is chosen then it must be Benefactive. If z_{Indir} is present with no preposition, then INDIR must be Goal. (Considerations of style may prohibit the occurrence of z_{Indir} without a preceding preposition.)

Examples

y was stabbed violently
y will be stabbed by x with u
y was given to z
y is given to z by x

Template #2a (Simple Passives—Second Form)

Syntax

z_{Indir}	Tns	**Perf**	**Prog**	**Pass**	Verb	y_{Dir}	**by** x_{Subj}	AdV^n
↑	↑			↑	↑	↑		
*	*			*	*	*		

Again, the indicated items must be selected and the others are optional. The logical form is the same as in Template #2.

Examples

z was given y by x
z will be sold y

13.5.1 Other Passives (Not Implemented)

Passives for causative and inchoative and higher-order verbs can be generated by similar templates. The challenge is to get the right words in the right order. To do so elegantly requires a sophisticated theory of syntax, the complications of which I am avoiding by the use of these templates. In all cases, the use of the passive yields the same logical form as the active.

13.6 Perception Sentences

There are two templates for sample perception sentences.

Template #3 (Perception Sentences)

Syntax

u_{Subj} Tns **Perf Prog** Verb$_{PER}$ x_{Subj} **Prog** Verb z_{Indir} y_{Dir} AdV$_2^n$ AdV$_1^n$

Note that this is of the form

u_{Subj} Tns **Perf Prog** Verb$_{PER}$ [. . . . .] AdV$_1^n$,

where the embedded [. . . . .] has the form of a tenseless clause. An example is

Mary has seen [. . . . .] with her telescope,

where the [. . . . .] may be occupied, e.g., by 'Brutus stab Caesar'.

Logical Form

$(\exists I)(\exists t)(\exists \alpha)[t \in I$ & SUBJ(α,u) & $I \blacklozenge$ now & OCCUR$(r(p(\alpha)),t)$ &
Verb$_{PER}'(\alpha)$ & AdV$_1'(\alpha)^n$ & $(\exists t_2)(\exists \beta)[$SUBJ$(\beta,x)$ & OCCUR$(p(\beta),t_2)$
& Verb$'(\beta)$ & INDIR(β,z) & DIR(β,y) & AdV$_2'(\beta)^n$ & Theme$(\alpha,\beta)]]$

Exception: Whenever the main verb is in the progressive, the embedded verb must be treated as if it were progressive, even if it is syntactically nonprogressive.

Examples

u saw x stab y violently
u will see x give y to z
u is watching x eat y with w

(Note the ambiguity of 'with w' in the last example; this may modify either the watching ("with u's telescope") or the eating.)

Template #3a (Perception Sentences with Missing Copulas)

Syntax

u_{Subj} Tns **Perf** Verb$_{PER}$ x_{Subj} Adj AdV$_2^n$ AdV$_2^n$

Logical Form

$(\exists I)(\exists t)(\exists \alpha)[t \in I$ & $SUBJ(\alpha,u)$ & $I \blacklozenge now$ & $OCCUR(r(\alpha),t)$ &
$Verb_{PER}'(\alpha)$ & $AdV_1'(\alpha)^n$ & $(\exists t_2)(\exists \beta)[SUBJ(\beta,x)$ & $OCCUR(\beta,t_2)$ &
$Adj'(\beta)$ & $Theme(\alpha,\beta)]]$

Examples

u saw x naked
u will see x naked in w

(Note the ambiguity of 'in w' in the last example; this may modify either the seeing or the being naked.)

13.6.1 Forms not Implemented

When causatives, and inchoatives, and sentences with "higher-order" event verbs are added, their clauses should be able to appear as the objects of perception verbs. This is easily done along the pattern of Template #3. It is an interesting question whether the unmodified results of such a treatment are semantically correct. And do additional options become available when causatives are involved? Does 'Mary heard the door opened' say that she heard the event that caused the door to open? Or does it (instead, or also) mean that she heard the door's opening (with 'open' read intransitively)? What does she have to hear in order to hear the door be opened by Kim?

In addition, perception verbs themselves should be allowed to appear as the objects of other perception verbs, as in 'Mary noticed Bill observing Sally watch the dog'. Semantically this construction is unproblematic, but the crudity of the template approach makes it awkward to capture it in this fragment.

13.7 Inchoatives

Ordinary inchoatives are just like simple intransitive verbs except that they contribute complex predicates to logical form. E.g., 'The door opened' can be produced by Template #1, by treating the predicate associated with 'open$_{INTRANS}$' as 'BECOME#(open$_{ADJ}$)'. However, inchoatives can also have "resultative tags"; examples are the intransitive readings of 'open wide', 'close tight', 'freeze solid'. These adjectives need to be incorporated into the scope of the BECOME#. A general treatment of (intransitive) inchoatives is thus yielded by

Template #4 (Inchoatives)

Syntax

x_{Subj} Tns   **Perf**   **Prog**   Verb   Adj AdV^n
  ↑   ↑   ↑
  *   *   *

Logical Form

$(\exists I)(\exists t)(\exists \alpha)[t \in I$ & $SUBJ(\alpha,x)$ & $I \blacklozenge now$ & $OCCUR(r(p(\alpha)),t)$ & $BECOME\#(\lambda s[V\text{-}Adj'(s)$ & $Adj'(s)])(\alpha)$ & $AdV'(\alpha)^n]$

where 'V-Adj'' is the predicate of states associated with the adjective that the verb is lexically derived from (this information is included in the lexical entry for the verb), and 'Adj'' comes from the Adj indicated in the syntactical form. In case there is no such Adj, the form in question reduces to that of an ordinary sentence whose intransitive verb has the meaning BECOME#(V-Adj).

Examples

the door is opening
the soup cooled
the bough will break
the water froze solid

13.8 Resultative Tags

Resultative tag sentences are sentences whose verbs are not causative but that contain an adjective indicating a resulting state. Classic examples include 'hammer the metal flat', 'paint it red', 'chop the onions fine', and even 'chop the onions coarsely', where the 'ly' ending is present by hypercorrection. Their syntax is exactly like that of ordinary TVs, except that they contain an extra adjective; semantically, they give rise to a final state.

Template #5 (Resultative Tags)

Syntax

x_{Subj}	Tns	**Perf**	**Prog**	Verb	y_{Dir}	Adj	AdV^n
↑	↑			↑			
*	*			*			

Logical Form

$(\exists I)(\exists t)(\exists \alpha)[t \in I$ & $SUBJ(\alpha,x)$ & $I \blacklozenge now$ & $OCCUR(r(p(\alpha)),t)$ &
$Verb'(\alpha)$ & $DIR(\alpha,y)$ & $AdV'(\alpha)^n$ & $(\exists \beta)(\exists t')[t' \in I$ &
$BECOME\#(Adj')(\beta)$ & $Theme(\beta,y)$ & $OCCUR(r(p(\beta)),t')$ &
$CAUSE(\alpha,\beta)]]$

Examples[11]

he chopped the onion fine
she hammered the metal flat

13.9 Causatives

Because they involve two underlying events plus an underlying state,
and because modifiers can modify any of these three, causatives are
the most complex cases. I give the general form for causative-inchoatives; causatives (such as '$rock_{TRANS}$', as in 'rock the boat') that are
related to noninchoative intransitive verbs can be treated similarly.
The format allows optional tag adjectives.

Template #6 (Causative-Inchoatives)

Syntax

x_{Subj}	Tns	**Perf**	**Prog**	Verb	y_{Dir}	Adj	AdV_2^n	AdV_1^n
↑	↑			↑	↑			
*	*			*	*			

Logical Form

$(\exists I)(\exists t)(\exists \alpha)[t \in I$ & $Agent(\alpha,x)$ & $I \blacklozenge now$ & $OCCUR(r(p(\alpha)),t)$ &
$AdV_1'(\alpha)^n$ & $(\exists \beta)(\exists t')[t' \in I$ & $BECOME\#(\lambda s[V\text{-}Adj'(s)$ &

$Adj'(s)])(\beta)$ & $Theme(\beta,y)$ & $AdV_2'(\beta)^n$ & $OCCUR(r(p(\beta)),t')$ & $CAUSE(\alpha,\beta)]]$

Constraints: AdV_1 may not include Adverbials of Motion, Direction, and Miscellaneous, and AdV_2 may not include Instrumental adverbials. (Adverbials of manner and location may occur in either.) The ordering of AdV_1 and AdV_2 in the syntactical form is of no particular import. In some cases 'Performer' can replace 'Agent' (as in 'The wind opened the door'). The 'V-Adj'' is the same as in Template #5; it comes from the adjective associated with the intransitive verb that is (in this case) associated with the causative transitive verb in its lexical entry.

Examples

x closed y tight with u
x froze y solid
x closed y loudly   (note the ambiguous application of 'loudly')

13.10   Higher-Order Constructions with Causative Verbs

These constructions use causative-inchoative verbs but take subjects that denote events. The event reference in the subject takes the place of 'α' in Template #6. For this reason, the logical forms themselves can be simpler than those used in regular causatives.

Template #7 (Higher-Order Causatives)

Syntax

e_{Subj}	Tns	**Perf**	**Prog**	Verb	y_{Dir}	Adj	AdV_2^n
↑	↑			↑	↑		
*	*			*	*		

Logical form

$(\exists I)(\exists t)[t \in I$ & $I \blacklozenge now$ & $OCCUR(r(p(e)),t)$ &
$(\exists\beta)[BECOME\#(\lambda s[V\text{-}Adj'(s)$ & $Adj'(s)])(\beta)$ & $Theme(\beta,y)$ &
$AdV_2'(\beta)^n$ & $CAUSE(e,\beta)]]$

Examples

e broke the glass   ("Mary's singing broke the glass.")

13.11   Higher-Order Verbs

These are verbs such as 'happen' (intransitive) or 'cause' (transitive) when they take events as their explicit subjects. Examples are 'The fight happened at noon' and 'Her singing caused the breaking of the glass'.

Template #8 (Higher-Order Intransitives)
Syntax

e_{Subj} Tns   **Perf**   **Prog**   Verb AdV^n
↑   ↑   ↑
*   *   *

Logical form

$(\exists I)(\exists t)[t \in I \ \& \ I \blacklozenge now \ \& \ OCCUR(r(p(e)),t) \ \& \ AdV'(e)^n]$

Template #9 (Higher-Order Transitives)

Syntax

e_{Subj} Tns   **Perf**   **Prog**   Verb e'_{Dir}
↑   ↑   ↑
*   *   *

Logical form

$(\exists I)(\exists t)[t \in I \ \& \ I \blacklozenge now \ \& \ OCCUR(r(p(e)),t) \ \& \ (\exists t_2)[t \in I \ \&$
$OCCUR(r(p(e')),t_2) \ \& \ Verb'(e,e')]]$

13.12   Copular Sentences

I assume that copular sentences are state sentences, where the states in questions are picked out by the adjective or locative phrase following the copula.

Template #10 (be+adj)

Syntax

x_{Subj}   Tns   **Perf**   **be**   Adj
↑   ↑   ↑   ↑
*   *   *   *

Logical Form

$(\exists I)(\exists t)(\exists \sigma)[t \in I \; \& \; SUBJ(\sigma,x) \; \& \; I \blacklozenge now \; \& \; Hold(r(\sigma),t) \; \& \; Adj'(\sigma)]$

Examples

x is clever
x has been red

Template #11 (be+adv_{LOC})

Syntax

x_{Subj}   Tns   **Perf**   **be** AdV^n_{LOC}
↑   ↑   ↑   ↑
*   *   *   *

Logical Form

$(\exists I)(\exists t)(\exists \sigma)[t \in I \; \& \; SUBJ(\sigma,x) \; \& \; I \blacklozenge now \; \& \; Hold(r(\sigma),t) \; \& \; AdV'(\sigma)^n]$

Examples

x is (at) home
x is in w under u ("in the park under a tree")

13.12.1   The 'be' of Activity (Not Implemented)

The 'be' of activity is not implemented here. It would produce constructions like 'Mary is being silly', in the sense of 'Mary is acting silly'. Probably this can be captured by giving 'be' the meaning of 'act', although its precise syntax and semantics are uncertain.

Afterword

I have described a theory that links events, states, and processes with sentences of English in such a way as to account for a wide variety of semantic phenomena. The real test of the theory, and also the measure of its explanatory fruitfulness, is its robustness: the extent to which its various components, each well-motivated and apparently successful in its own domain, combine with one another to apply in those areas where the domains overlap. We need to look at examples in which tenses combine with perception verbs, in which the progressive and the perfect combine with causatives, in which perception verbs combine with inchoatives, in which verb modifiers interact with temporal modifiers, in which sentences explicitly about events and states figure in arguments with others that do not, and so on. I am optimistic about these further applications of the approach, and certain that numerous adjustments will be needed along the way.

The most obvious technical gap that must now be filled is to link the "templates" of the last chapter with a clearly formulated syntactic theory that will let us project the semantics of the templates to more interesting sentences of English. Most of the pertinent examples that come naturally to the minds of philosophers and linguists concerned with events are couched in syntactic terminology that far transcends "Brutus stabbed Caesar in the back with a knife." So any searching scrutiny of the theory will inevitably involve us in hosts of other issues—of NP scopes, of nonextensionality, of floating quantifiers, of the semantics of indefinites, of the effects of context, and so on. Those are the working conditions; the pleasure lies in facing them. Everyone is invited.

Notes

Chapter 1

1. See, for example, Davidson's (1967) critique of Reichenbach's theory. For one thing, the same verb 'hit' occurs with a wide variety of different agents and objects. If 'hit' is to be understood as referring to a particular action, then the action will be different in different sentences, since the actions in 'Mary hits John' and 'Sam hits Fred' are different. (E.g., one might be violent, the other not.) How, then, to tell which action the verb stands for in a particular sentence? Things get even more complicated if the sentence in question is false. Suppose I say 'Mary hit Fred' but that I am wrong. Then what does 'hit' refer to in my sentence? There are two natural options. We can say that 'hit' fails to refer when it occurs in a false sentence, or that it refers to an action that does not occur. Either view might be developed into a viable account, but we have now left far behind the simple idea that we started with, an idea that purported to explain the unique functioning of verbs in terms of their association with actions and states. I also suspect that if either of these views were to be made adequate, the resulting theory would be equivalent to the one I discuss. I explore the former view in detail in Parsons (forthcoming).

2. Plato (*Sophist*, 261D-262C) says ". . . we have two kinds of vocal indications of being. . . . One called nouns, the other verbs. . . . The indication which relates to action we may call a verb. . . . And the vocal sign applied to those who perform the actions in question we call a noun." He goes on to refer to ". . . 'walks,' 'runs,' 'sleeps' and the other verbs which denote actions."

3. For example, "Those verbs which signify actions which are transmitted beyond the agent, such as to beat, to break, to heal, to love, to hate, have subjects which receive these actions, or objects which these actions concern. For if one beats, one beats someone; if one loves, one loves something, etc. And thus these verbs require that they be followed by a noun which will be either the subject or the object of the action which the verbs signify." Arnauld 1660, 83.

4. "When . . . we hear the sentence, 'Charles I's head was cut off', we may naturally enough think of Charles I, of Charles I's head, and of the operation

of cutting off *his* head, which are all particulars; but we do not naturally dwell on what is meant by the word 'head' or the word 'cut', which is a universal." Russell 1912, 94.

5. Something like this account was proposed as an improvement by Hector Castañeda (1967) on Davidson 1967.

6. A more elegant explanation can be given using lambda abstracts. The predicate 'D' of the logic text account then has the structure '$\lambda x(\exists e)[\text{Dying}(e)$ & Object$(e,x)]$'. The logic text account is thus completely accurate as it stands (for such simple examples); it just fails to exhibit the additional structure encapsulated in the lambda abstract.

7. 'NP' and 'VP' stand for 'Noun Phrase' and 'Verb Phrase' respectively. NPs include proper names along with the sorts of phrases Russell called "denoting phrases": 'every man', 'no woman', 'the tallest spy', and so on. VPs are, roughly, "predicates" of sentences, minus tense and helping verbs. In illustrating VPs I often (inaccurately) use tensed forms of the verb.

8. In the informal literature the term used is usually 'action', though this is understood broadly to include such things as 'the action of the flywheel on the shaft'. I use the term 'event' instead of 'action' because of the tradition in philosophy of limiting 'action' to events performed by intentional agents. I make no appeal to "passions" in addition to actions; I think that passive sentences are related to the same events as active ones.

9. I include some of my own earlier work in this criticism.

10. This is why I am doubtful about the possibility of a "truth-definition for English," and even more doubtful about the value of trying to produce one.

11. Strictly, it is utterances of words that are in question, not word types. The distinction between words and their utterances, and the relevance of context to semantics, are important, but not specially germane to the issue I discuss, so I often ignore these matters.

12. It would be acceptable to me to use Montague-style analysis trees (as in Montague 1973) instead of forms from symbolic logic. I avoid them because of their unfamiliarity. It might also be possible to use the forms that contemporary linguists generate under the title "LF"; this is the thrust of much recent work by James Higginbotham (1985a and 1985b).

13. Perry & Barwise (1983) attack the use of logical forms in semantics. They insist that the meaning of a sentence ought to be a relation, not a proposition of the sort normally associated with logical forms. However, I see this as primarily a matter of how the theory is presented, not as part of its substance. For example, in their work, someone wishing to identify when a sentence is true (in a context) applies a certain procedure to it (in the metalanguage). The result of this procedure, if formulated in predicate calculus notation, would yield something very closely resembling the logical forms I employ. A similar remark applies to Montague's (1973) account where meanings turn out to be functional relations of the sort insisted on by Barwise and Perry. When certain of the parameters are specified in Montague's meanings, one obtains forms of

the sort I employ. Throughout this work I ignore the context of utterance for simplicity only. Standard appeals to the notion of context can be grafted onto the theory I discuss.

14. An exception is section 2 of chapter 4.

Chapter 2

1. I have purposely chosen an example containing two modifiers instead of just one. This is vital if we are to understand the logic of modifiers. I pattern my methodology here on that of Frege, Russell, and Peirce in their pioneering investigations of the logic of quantifiers. So long as we confine ourselves to simple sentences that contain a single quantifier it is hard to find fault with sophisticated versions of Aristotelian logic; it is principally when we begin to address the interactions among quantifiers that more complicated analyses are needed. I suspect that the same is true of grammatical modifiers.

2. There seems to be a conversational implication that if x sees y V, then x sees y. I am not sure how to account for it, but it needs to be acknowledged somehow in the theory. I hope that this implication will account for the differences noted by Vlach (1981) between 'I saw Oswald shoot Kennedy' and 'I saw Kennedy shot by Oswald'.

3. One of the phenomena Barwise and Perry note is that 'x sees A and B' seems to entail 'x sees A and x sees B', and that 'x sees A or B' entails 'x sees A or x sees B'. I think that perception verbs never take sententially complex objects, so, 'x sees A or B' just *is* a shortened form of 'x sees A or x sees B'; the former entails the latter because they are synonymous. That 'x sees A or B' cannot be read except as equivalent to 'x sees A or x sees B' is evidence for the view that the former is just a surface manifestation of the latter. This view is complicated in the case of conjunction because we tend to think of two related events as somehow constituting a third complex event made up of them. We naturally use 'and' to indicate this construction, as we use 'and' to indicate "addition" elsewhere in the language. I do not discuss this invoking of complex events in certain special circumstances, but it is one of the chief areas needing further exploration.

4. Great care must be taken in interpreting gerundive constructions, because many of them are ambiguous. If the sample construction 'the singing of the *Marseillaise*' is embedded in this sentence:

The singing of the *Marseillaise* surprised me,

then it has a quite different meaning than in

The singing of the *Marseillaise* hurt my ears.

In the former construction the gerundive has a meaning similar to a that-clause:

That the *Marseillaise* was sung surprised me.

These "propositional" constructions have quite different logical forms; they cannot be interpreted as implicitly referring to events. For example, such constructions occur entirely in opaque contexts. From the "propositional" construction

Mary predicted the beheading of the king,

it does not follow that Mary predicted the beheading of the tallest spy, even if the king *is* the tallest spy. But from the "event" construction,

The beheading of the king occurred at noon,

it does follow that the beheading of the tallest spy occurred at noon, given that the king is the tallest spy. These issues are discussed in chapter 7.

5. The same is also true for sentence modifiers; for example, 'necessarily' and 'necessary' contribute the same predicates to logical form; see Parsons 1970.

Chapter 3

1. This particular argument depends on the use of logical forms that separates out the participants, placing the subject and object in separate conjuncts. The argument is not valid on the version of the theory that lumps the subject and object with the verb in a single three-place predicate. The same point could be made without this assumption, however, by using examples employing modifiers of the sort discussed previously. Suppose that Brutus stabbed Caesar in the back with a knife, and in the thigh with an icepick. Then we have

(∃e)[Stabbing(e,Brutus,Caesar) & In(e,back) & With(e,knife)]
(∃e)[Stabbing(e,Brutus,Caesar) & In(e,thigh) & With(e,pick)].

If the events were the same, we could combine the modifier conjuncts and simplify, getting

(∃e)[Stabbing(e,Brutus,Caesar) & In(e,back) & With(e,pick)],

which is the logical form of 'Brutus stabbed Caesar in the back with an icepick'.

2. We might be able to explain both sides of the dispute by holding that "true" Achievement verbs pick out events that essentially lack development portions, but that there is a productive mechanism for using such verbs in another sense, to pick out related verbs that have development portions. In this case the Achievement verb 'win', which does not occur meaningfully in the progressive, has a homonym that means 'leads', so that 'Henry is winning' has a reading that means 'Henry is leading' or 'Henry is ahead'. This too is consistent with the framework under discussion, though it is an odd view since, as was noted above, there is no *non*progressive use of 'wins' to mean 'leads'.

3. For simplicity, I suppose that if e is an eventuality then the set of times at which e holds forms a continuous interval, and I further suppose that if e culminates it does so at the end of that interval (that is, at its least upper bound). This presumes that there are no "gappy" eventualities, those that hold for a while, then fail to hold for a while, and then hold again. The main problem this addresses has to do with a sentence such as 'Mary is running', uttered at a time in the middle of her workout when she is taking a rest. There seem to be two different ways to take the sentence; in one way the answer is *Yes,* and in the other way the answer is *No.* The same phenomenon is illustrated by the question "Is someone sitting there?" accompanied by pointing to an empty seat. I would account for the *Yes* answers to these questions by

supposing that the running (or the sitting) is an extended gapless process that holds even during the "lulls."

4. Certain sentences require more complex forms than are indicated here, particularly causatives (such as 'Kim opened the door' [= caused the door to open]) and inchoatives (such as 'The door opened' [= became open]), which are discussed in chapter 6, and sentences involving explicit discourse about events ('The flight occurred over the park', as opposed to 'The bird flew over the park'), which are discussed in chapter 7.

5. As part of a general theory of language, this form is an idealization. A good general account of English will have to focus on *discourse* (sequences of utterances) as the primary unit of analysis. A theory of discourse may resemble that of Hendrix 1978, Kamp 1981, and Heim 1983 by (in effect) leaving certain variables free in certain places in sentences; these free variables would become implicitly bound in various ways, depending on the context in which they occur. In simple isolated sentences, however, the effect should be that of an existential quantifier, as I have used it. This would be achieved within Heim's theory, for example, by treating the event variable as an indefinite. (Since I deal always with isolated sentences, this is equivalent to starting with an "empty file.") In longer stretches of discourse the event place might get bound in some different way, in keeping with principles of discourse theory. This offers an interesting line of investigation but not one that I shall develop in this book.

6. It is also consistent to view the "direction" of generation as being in the opposite direction; the NPs start out "in place" and are then moved out front, leaving variables (= coindexed "traces") in their places. Or one can ignore directionality altogether.

7. Kenny also objects that tense operators cannot be used to express the inference for performance-verbs from 'A is Xing' to 'A has Xed'. This is discussed in chapter 9.

8. This isn't quite right, since news reports, especially headlines, are often written in the "narrative present," that is, using the words that a contemporaneous observer would use to describe the scene. The import of this usage is that the sentences are not to be understood as telling you what is true now but as sentences originating from on-the-scene reporting. (Even more interesting, a recent *Los Angeles Times* photograph bore this caption: "Rep. Mickey Leland speaks with Sudanese refugees at a camp in Ethiopia last April.")

9. Without most of the problematic additions incorrectly attributed to Frege by modern critics, such as the view that all names are disguised descriptions, or that the entire content of a Fregean proposition ("thought") must contain no senses with *de re* force.

10. I assume here the contemporary view about reference. Russell (1903) held that disjunctive terms could refer to disjunctive individuals. I defend the coherence of his views in Parsons 1988, but his theory is not better than the current view, which I adopt here.

11. Dowty takes on the task of analyzing the Aristotelian categories in terms of more basic notions. I do not address the question of whether such analyses are possible (except for Processes, which are explained in terms of events).

12. For a representative sample of the literature see Kenny 1963, Vendler 1967, Mourelatos 1978, Dowty 1979, Ritchie 1979, Bach 1981, Bennett 1981, Dahl 1981, Vlach 1981, Taylor 1985.

13. Schachter (1985) suggests that the copula is unambiguous but that the adjectives in question have "active" readings. This avoids the problem under discussion as well as the proposal for a 'be' of action.

14. Dowty (personal communication) mentions 'want', 'need', 'feel', 'think', 'hear', 'see', 'taste'.

15. Dowty suggests that the progressive version, though not the nonprogressive, implies that the state in question is temporary. My intuitions are unclear on this.

16. Perhaps x could even have built that very same birdbath before. Certainly if the example is changed to 'paint a house', then x could have painted the very same house before. The "sameness" of the object is not relevant to the test.

17. For discussions see Kenny 1963, Vendler 1967, Dowty 1979, Ritchie 1979, Bach 1981, Bennett 1981, Dahl 1981, Mourelatos 1978, Vlach 1981.

18. The choice of subject or object can also affect the distinction. 'Weigh the nail' is an event VP, but 'weigh gold' seems to be a process VP.

Chapter 4

1. Compare remarks in Jackendoff 1972, section 3.12.

2. This view differs from that of Stalnaker and Thomason (1973), who treat prepositional phrases as semantical units that are also modifiers. They argue that 'in several restaurants' creates opaque contexts, citing as evidence the fact that 'In several restaurants the maitre d' wears a tuxedo' may be true even if there is no one who wears a tuxedo in several restaurants. I do not recognize 'in several restaurants' as being a modifier at all; it is a complex phrase consisting of a modifier 'in x' together with a quantificational NP 'several restaurants'. The "opacity" cited is merely a matter of the scope of 'the maitre d'' coming inside the scope of 'several restaurants', so that the overall form is 'For several restaurants x: (the maitre d' in x wears a tuxedo in x)'. This explains the phenomenon in question without attributing scope to the modifier 'in x' and without recognizing 'in several restaurants' as a semantical unit.

3. Some of the relevant literature is Clark 1970, Kamp 1975, Montague 1974, Parsons 1970, Siegel 1979, Wheeler 1972.

4. Generally such modifiers are taken to operate on predicates, not on formulas. (Parsons 1970 unfortunately blurs this distinction.) 'Formerly', I think, operates on formulas. A discussion of this issue would take us far afield.

5. There is also a question of *degree* that can vary independently of these. This works the same on either account.

6. Barry Taylor (1985) proposes a different way to accommodate group readings. He symbolizes the group reading as:

($\exists$e)(x)(Boot(x) $\rightarrow$ e is a quick polishing of x by Samantha).

This seems to me to be wrong, since it entails that if Samantha quickly polished all the A's, then she quickly polished the B's, whenever the B's are a subset of the A's. (The counterexample may be clearer with 'slowly' instead of 'quickly'.)

7. Or one might pursue a more detailed option where the availability of forms depends on the kinds of modifiers used. For example, in English it is usually not grammatical to iterate adverbs of manner (*'She ran quickly smoothly'), so in these cases if we wish to indicate that one running was both quick and smooth the only option is to use surface conjunction. Perhaps in the case of adverbs of manner, surface conjunction sometimes means conjunction of predicates of (the same) event, whereas in the case of other modifiers, where we can either iterate the modifiers or link them with 'and', the latter option automatically requires two event quantifications, with modifiers available to each.

8. I have in mind constructions such as

(*) They met in a park in a cabin in a strange country . . . ,

which suggests that the number of places in a simple sentence may be increased without limit merely by iterating certain prepositions. Note that we should need several meaning postulates for 'in' alone, just to insure that (*) entails each of

They met in a park in a cabin.
They met in a park in a strange country.
They met in a cabin in a strange country.
They met in a park.
They met in a cabin.
They met in a strange country.
They met.

Each of these complex sentences is ambiguous, since each modifier following the first can be read either as a reiterated modification or as a relative clause modifying the noun at the end of the preceding modifier. I am discussing only the reiterated modification readings.

9. For discussion, see Materna and Sgall 1984.

10. Kenny 1963 was apparently the first to focus on this issue.

11. It is easy to generate an arbitrary number of modifiers for a wide array of verbs but not necessarily in a manner that refutes the idea I am examining. For example, it is possible to reiterate adverbials of location indefinitely:

Brutus stabbed Caesar in the Lyceum in front of the statue on the bridge under the arch. . . .

But reiterations of this kind might be handled by means of a single preposition of location, with a variety of specifiers, something as follows:

$(\exists x)(\exists y)(\exists z)(\exists u)[x$ is in the Lyceum & y is in front of the statue & z is on the bridge & u is under the arch & $P(b,c,x)$ & $P(b,c,y)$ & $P(b,c,z)$ & $P(b,c,u)]$,

where '$P(x,y,z)$' means something like 'x stabbed y at location z'.

I think that this is incorrect, because it would make the conjunction of (1) and (2) entail (3)

1 The crowd swarmed over the bridge.
2 The crowd swarmed in the park.
3 The crowd swarmed over the bridge in the park.

(1) and (2) would both be true if a large crowd were swarming over the bridge just outside the park, and also swarming through the park, though (3) need not be true in this circumstance. This type of example is discussed in more detail in chapter 10.

12. For a discussion of this issue, see Materna and Sgall 1984.

13. This proposal is discussed further in Chapter 5.

14. See Kamp 1975, Montague 1970, Parsons 1970, Stalnaker and Thomason 1973.

15. When I speak here of a property of *individuals* I mean only to specify properties of the things that, in the case of event sentences, enter into the events in question. In the case of 'Mary runs', Mary is the individual and the event itself is not. I do not suggest that events are not themselves individuals in some metaphysical sense. In fact, in the sentence, 'In every burning, oxygen is consumed', I call the burnings the individuals. My point is that, in the standard treatments of modifiers as operators, the property operated on by "slowly" is the property of being a thing that runs, not the property of being an event of running.

16. There is no consensus in the "operator" literature as to whether an adverb like 'slowly' always operates on one-place properties, or sometimes (for example, when combined with a transitive verb) on many-place predicates (as in Montague 1970)—or even whether it can consistently be treated as a whole sentence operator within a theory of fine-grained meaning. For simplicity, I suppose that the operator theory holds that adverbs such as 'slowly' always operate on one-place predicates. The logical form of 'Agatha slowly sharpened every knife' is then

$(x)[knife(x)\ [slowly(sharpen(x))](Agatha)]$.

But within the framework of Montague 1973 the logical behavior of adverbs like 'slowly' leads to considerable unexpected complexity and unsolved problems, having to do with how 'slowly' interacts with direct objects of transitive verbs. See Zimmermann 1987. I do not know whether these are general problems for the operator account, or whether they depend on easily modifiable details of Montague's framework. My discussion of the operator account focuses on quite different issues.

17. Earlier (Parsons 1970) I was inclined to defend the operator account and I tried to find examples in which there was a scope ambiguity in the English. This proved to be quite difficult, and the best I could come up with was the ambiguity in 'John painstakingly wrote illegibly'. I now realize that on the

interpretation required for the scoped reading of 'painstakingly', the word 'painstakingly' functions as a subject-oriented or a sentence adverb, and so the example is beside the point. There are also apparent (but illusory) scope ambiguities created by the use of attributives ('Mary swam *slowly*') and group constructions ('Seymour sliced *the bagels* quickly'); I discuss these in previous sections.

18. Earlier, I explored (Parsons 1980) a different way to combine a variant of the operator account with the underlying event account. Contrary to the usual version of the operator approach, I supposed that all verbs stand for properties of events, construing operators as operating on *these* properties. The underlying event account is then seen as a refinement of this variant of the operator account. Indeed, this kind of operator theory is mainly an alternate symbolization of the underlying event theory, not a competing approach requiring assessment.

19. I so construe her account in McConnell-Ginet 1982 on the basis of her example number (59) (p. 170). Her specific proposals in (57) through (59) differ somewhat from the version discussed here. I bear responsibility for the interpretation.

20. I do not take issue with analyzing 'quickly' as something like 'at a quick rate'. On the underlying event account, this amounts to replacing 'Quick(e)' in logical forms throughout by '$(\exists r)[\text{Quick}'(r) \ \& \ \text{At}(e,r)]$', which preserves the overall structure of the theory. This is different from McConnell-Ginet's account.

21. To avoid the problem with the second proposal we might try giving 'x V's A-ly B-ly' the form
$(\exists z)[Q^A(z) \ \& \ (\exists z)[Q^B(z) \ \& \ R^A(x,z)]]$.
But this is not consistent with the idea that motivates the proposal. For example, for the "z" to be violent, z must be a manner, but for it to be "with a knife" it must be something else. This proposal would identify manners with rates, and with locations, and so on.

22. Parsons 1970 criticized Reichenbach's account on the grounds that it does not correctly represent the logical form of 'x painstakingly wrote illegibly'. I now believe that Reichenbach's theory does not capture the reading of this phrase in which 'painstakingly' is a Sentence modifier or Subject-oriented modifier, as opposed to a Verb modifier, and so my former criticism is groundless.

23. The underlying specific property account is parasitic on the underlying event account (and not vice versa) because the predicates used to represent modifiers on the underlying specific property account need to be explained in terms of the predicates of the underlying event account. As noted above, it is incorrect to call a specific property 'slow', as Reichenbach suggests. We could try calling a specific property "slow'" if and only if the specific property is the conjunction of all ordinary properties of an event that is slow. We can

then define all of the primitive terms needed in the underlying specific property account by means of the terms of ordinary English (such as 'slow') that the underlying event account uses. (The relation between 'slow' and 'slowly' is discussed in more detail in Chapter 8.)

24. I am indebted here to Bellert 1977. She also includes a category of "domain" modifiers, such as 'aesthetically', 'mathematically', 'morally'.

25. This is not quite the right way to put it, since in each case we have dual assertions. There is a kind of category mistake involved in calling both 'Fortunately, Mary ran home' and 'Mary ran home quickly' "factive" in the same sense on the grounds that each "entails" that Mary ran home. But the point is clear enough.

26. So-called epistemic logic studies the adjectival forms of epistemic modifiers, constructions such as 'It is possible for all x knows that . . .'.

27. To be contrasted with the natural readings of 'She invested wisely', and 'She spoke rudely'; these latter are VP modifiers.

28. This form by itself does not account for the factivity of the construction. A better representation might be 'Rude(x, ↑ [x insults y])', where ' ↑ S' refers to the (propositional) fact that S, as opposed to '^S', which refers to the proposition that S. (This requires a development of the semantics of reference to propositional facts, not given here.) It might be the case that Subject-oriented adverbs can have their scopes limited to only part of the VP in question. For example, Stalnaker and Thomason (1973) argue that 'John carefully carried the eggs in his left hand to the wrong house' is three ways ambiguous, depending on how much is included in the scope of 'carefully'. (I assume that it is the subject-oriented reading of 'carefully' that is relevant to their example, the reading in which 'carefully carried' can be paraphrased by 'took care to carry'. The VP modifier reading is a fourth one, in which it is the manner of the carrying that is careful.)

29. Much of this stems from Stalnaker and Thomason 1973.

30. When I speak of "VP-internal" position I mean positions inside the VP that can be occupied by adverbs; I do not include Determiner positions, such as that occupied by 'only' in 'Mary loves only Bill', or positions in which a word modifies an adjective, as in 'The book is very heavy'.

31. More specifically, if a quantifierless sentence containing an adverb in Aux position is ambiguous, and if moving the adverb to Initial position yields an unambiguous sentence with one of the readings of the original sentence, and moving it to VP-internal position yields an unambiguous sentence with the other reading of the original sentence, then the adverb is ambiguous between a VP adverb and a Speech-act or Subject-oriented or Sentence adverb. (This should be compared with Criterion 2 of Stalnaker and Thomason 1973, according to which if there is a semantic contrast between 'Q-ly someone F's' and 'Someone F's Q-ly' then 'Q-ly' is a sentence modifier. This is a test for quantifier scope ambiguities.)

32. Jackendoff (1972) even suggests this as the solution to a problem that has puzzled many people: the ambiguity of certain adverbs in passives. For example, the sentence:

Mary was willingly examined by the doctor

can either attribute willingness to Mary or to the doctor. Jackendoff assumes that 'willingly' is homonymous between a Subject-oriented and a VP adverb, and that "subject-orientation" always refers to the surface subject. This accounts nicely for the ambiguity of the passive. However, this explanation must also account for the apparent lack of ambiguity in the active; this would consist of showing an equivalence between the Subject-oriented 'Willing(x,ˆ[x VP])' and the reading 'x VP willingly'. McConnell-Ginet (1982) has a proposal for this, though not within the framework of underlying events.

The other popular account of the ambiguity of such passives assumes that 'willingly' is just a Subject-oriented adverb, but that in the passive it has two subjects to orient toward: the surface subject, and the "deep" subject. This proposal is highly sensitive to the theory of syntax employed; it is criticized in McConnell-Ginet 1982.

33. 'I didn't fly in my dream' can be felicitously followed by either 'I crawled (in my dream)' or 'I flew in actuality'. The sentence 'That isn't right according to the church' can be followed by either 'It's wrong (according to the church)' or by 'It's right according to the government; the church takes no position on it'. (Though this might possibly be an ambiguity of focus, and not one of scope.) The alethic modals hardly ever show ambiguity with negation in English, because the position of the negation usually disambiguates them. Compare 'Necessarily she won't arrive on time' (or 'She necessarily won't arrive on time') with 'She won't necessarily arrive on time'. The symbolism of modal logic can easily capture scope ambiguity if it occurs, but scope orderings (of modals, as opposed to negation) are usually illustrated in English with two distinct sentences, neither of which is ambiguous, or with that-clauses and adjectival forms of modals.

34. Although I believe the view defended here, nothing in the underlying event account commits one to it. If one wishes to construe 'Sally didn't move quickly' as having an interpretation in which there is one assertion made, with the meaning of 'Sally moved not-quickly' then the theory easily accommodates it. The logical form would be $(\exists e)[\text{Moving}(e) \ \& \ \text{Subject}(e,\text{Sally}) \ \& \ \neg\text{Quick}(e)]$.

Chapter 5

1. The rules also allow us to produce 'Brutus stabbed'. This appears to be correct; we need to be able to say 'Brutus stabbed, but he missed'.

2. Panini's own account allows more flexibility in correlating thematic roles and semantic relations. For example, he would correlate these two sentences with the indicated thematic roles:

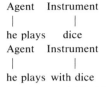

he plays with dice

But he would hold that the relations between the dice and the event indicated in the first sentence by Theme and in the second sentence by Instrument are one and the same. Thus a single semantic relation corresponds to two distinct thematic roles. In other cases, two distinct semantic relations are represented linguistically by the same thematic role; an example is 'he plays dice' versus 'they inhabit the village'. Both points just cited are from Kiparsky & Staal 1969, 85–6. They refer to the semantic relation as 'Instrument' and to the two thematic roles with Panini's terms 'karman' and 'karana'.

Nothing in Panini's general approach forces us to identify the semantic relations in the first pair of sentences (I do not identify them), nor does his theory require that there be two different semantic relations in the second pair (I identify them).

3. Any given preposition corresponds to a variety of prepositions in other languages, even among Indo-European languages. If surface prepositions in English were unambiguous, then those in German would not be—an odd situation indeed. The common view seems to be that each preposition has a small number of meanings; translating a preposition in use depends on identifying the relevant reading and then finding a preposition in the other language that, in the given context, will express that reading. At least this is the way language instruction books are written. This assumption deserves scrutiny, but I shall not pursue it.

4. In terms of Fillmore's classic discussion, I am ignoring the roles Factitive (for that-clauses) and Locative. In omitting the role Locative from discussion I may be going against my policy of including all roles that show up at the surface unmarked by prepositions. It is Fillmore's thesis that in a sentence such as 'The studio is hot' the subject of the sentence indicates a *location,* as opposed to a thing, and thus has the Locative role. (It does this in its usual meaning, which is roughly 'It is hot in the studio'. The sentence has another reading, which makes the studio the Theme; this is the reading suggested by 'The studio is hot to the touch, though it is not hot inside'.)

Writers since Fillmore have expanded the array of thematic roles that may appear in subject and object position well beyond his; I am therefore ignoring a great deal of literature, although I touch on some of it in section 5.4.

5. This requirement of uniqueness is practically forced on us by the type of logical forms employed. Without it, the theory tends to fall into falsehood. For example, suppose we were to label as Themes both the direct and indirect objects. Then the logical form of a sentence containing both such items would be logically equivalent to the sentence with the direct and indirect objects interchanged. If you gave a fish to Mary, you would thereby give Mary to a fish.

6. The apparent exceptions are a small class of "psychological" verbs, including 'please', as in 'Roses please Mary', in which the subject ('Roses') seems to be the Theme and the object ('Mary') the Experiencer, as well as a class of psychological interaction verbs such as 'annoy', 'anger', 'irritate', which also seem to take Experiencer as direct object. N. McCawley 1976 argues that these are in fact causative constructions. If so, they are not counterexamples to the classification of direct objects as Theme. However these psychological verbs are to be analyzed, they have always been seen as rather idiosyncratic, and so I feel justified in not addressing them here.

7. It is arguable whether 'see' passes the "persuade test." Most writers on the topic assume that it does not, and this is the rationale for classifying 'see' as Experiencer.

8. In the case of cities, states, and countries, the locational 'at' should be replaced by 'in'. There are other details of this sort that I ignore for simplicity.

9. It might be desirable to limit this edict to verbs other than 'is', since it is unclear whether to classify x as a Theme in 'x is pleased' (where 'pleased' is read as the adjective). Also, the principle may not apply to "subjectless" verbs, as in 'It rained'.

10. See Traugott 1972, 89.

11. The trickiness in formulating the principle has to do with the density of time and the possibility of infinite processes that converge at a given instant. If a cup rolls onto and then off a rug repeatedly, taking a minute for the first cycle, a half minute for the next, then a quarter minute, and so on, and then ends up on the rug at the end of two minutes, it is not clear what to say about its being off the rug "just before" its finally being on the rug.

12. In the case of 'across' and 'cross', both come from a common source, the noun 'cross'. Most of the cases discussed by Gruber 1976 cannot be treated in a parallel manner. For example, he also discusses the relation between 'pierce' and 'through', where 'pierce through' is not redundant (since something can be pierced without being pierced through). Gruber proposes that such pairs share "semantic markers."

13. Dowty (1979) proposes, for example, that 'into' is a verb modifier that acts differently on transitive and intransitive verbs; it requires motion of the subjects of intransitives and of the direct objects of transitives. This gets the same effect as our principle about Themes without appeal to the notion of "theme" (or any kind of thematic role) at all. Clearly, more justification for the use of thematic roles in semantics is needed than I have given it so far.

14. The theory under discussion is not a panacea for addressing all important issues about modifiers, for example, some relationships between adverbs and prepositions of Direction and those of Motion. There is some interesting relation between looking across a room and moving across the room, between looking through a curtain and moving through it, although exactly what this relationship should be is very difficult to state. To look through something is to look in a direction in which one might move if one were to move through

that thing, and, in addition, to see the location at which one would be at if one were to so move. To move through something is (sometimes) to move along the line of sight of someone who is looking through that thing, and to move so as to arrive at the place of something seen by that person looking through the thing. Or something like this. The semantical framework I propose might make such principles easier to state than certain other frameworks, since it allows the prepositions to occur in isolation from the verbs they modify, but this still leaves most of the job undone.

15. Presumably Kim is also the Goal of the selling, and Sheehan is related to the buying by the "from" relation, which some authors would include as an additional thematic relation, called "Source". These additional classifications are not relevant to the puzzle under discussion.

16. Dowty's (1979) view is that one should dispense with thematic roles, and explain the 'onto'-'on' phenomenon by the simpler principle that in the case of motion verbs what moves is the (denotation of the) subject in the case of intransitive motion verbs and the (denotation of the) direct object in the case of transitive motion verbs. This explains the anomaly of sentence (6): 'I emptied the tank of water into the sink', because its meaning is that the water moves, not the tank, yet the principle just cited requires the tank to move. That is, the ungrammaticalness is explained by a conflict between the principle and the understood meaning of the verb. This cannot be the complete story, however, since the same explanation would make sentence (2) anomalous: 'I emptied the tank into the sink'. But (2) is not anomalous.

17. This gives much the same effect as the logical operation of producing the converse of a relation, except that instead of changing the relation to its converse, we interchange its argument places. We then produce a sentence equivalent to the original by reversing the order of the terms that go in the (reversed) places.

18. A popular view is that the set of thematic roles themselves occurs in a language-independent ordering called the "thematic hierarchy," and that each individual language exploits this hierarchy in its own distinctive way to position NPs at the surface. For example, part of this hierarchy is the ordering, Agent>Instrument>Theme, and one view is that every language will choose an Agent as subject of an active sentence if the Agent is present, and will choose Instrument as subject if it is present without Agent, and so on. There are too many versions of this idea to examine here.

19. This is ignoring further options, such as VP scope quantification of NPs. The point is the same, though it needs to be worded more carefully: the parts of the VPs *prior to quantification* are the same.

20. The issue discussed in this section is also addressed in various ways in Dowty 1989, which marshals a number of arguments against appeals to thematic roles.

21. Castañeda proposed the use of thematic roles as separate conjuncts in order to explain why 'I flew my spaceship to the morning star' entails 'My spaceship flew to the morning star', but does not entail 'I flew to the morning

star' (because, e.g., I might have flown the spaceship by remote control). This can easily be explained if the logical forms of the sentences are:

I flew my spaceship to the morning star:
(∃e)[Flying(e) & Agent(e,me) & Theme(e,spaceship) & To(e,morning star)].
I flew to the morning star:
(∃e)[Flying(e) & Theme(e,me) & To(e,morning star)].
My spaceship flew to the morning star:
(∃e)[Flying(e) & Theme(e,spaceship) & To(e,morning star)].

However, the first sentence is a causative construction, and these inferences are readily explicable in terms of the account of causatives developed in chapter 6. Since the causative analysis provides an explanation of this phenomenon that is better than the explanation in terms of thematic roles, the phenomenon does not by itself provide good evidence for the use of the roles. For the rest of this chapter I focus on examples that do not depend on the special nature of causatives. That is, I confine myself to non-causative examples, or to examples in which the causative status is irrelevant to the point at issue.

22. David Dowty has proposed that the use of roles versus modifiers corresponds to a traditional distinction between the "arguments" of a verb and its "adjuncts." This is a distinction within syntax. The arguments of a verb are those NP places that must be present in order to have a well-formed sentence, whereas adjuncts are syntactically optional. This distinction is completely neutral as to how the arguments of the verb are indicated—by word order, spelling, inflections, prepositions, and so on. As an illustration, we are supposed to see 'Caesar' as being an argument of 'stab' in 'Brutus stabbed Caesar with a knife in the marketplace', whereas 'a knife' and 'the marketplace' are adjuncts.

The difficulty with using this distinction to separate thematic roles from others is that it is highly theoretical. If employed superficially, nothing is an argument, because almost nothing must be present in the surface sentence. For example, the Theme is missing in

Brutus stabbed, but he missed,

and the Agent is missing in

Caesar was stabbed.

The distinction, if it is to be viable, must appeal to a level of syntax with elements that are invisible at the surface, and whose presence can be revealed only by subtle means. Partly for this reason I shall not pursue the issue. I also set it aside because I think the test discussed in the next subsection is more basic. But that test may be as inconclusive as it is basic, and in the end we may require subtle syntactic tests for an answer.

23. The same also holds when the sentences are embedded within perception verbs after having their tenses removed. 'Mary saw Brutus stab Caesar in the back' entails 'Mary saw Brutus stab Caesar'.

24. Or to Dowty's similar distinction between arguments of the verb and adjuncts.

25. The following objections were raised at a conference on Thematic Roles held at Cornell in spring 1988. Dreams can be so incoherent that they cannot be described by the linguistic means at our disposal, so we improvise. We use words in unusual ways, and our hearers understand this. We communicate effectively by using language, but we do not use it with its normal meaning. Our hearers catch on to this fact because we *are* contradicting ourselves when we say things like 'I was stabbed, but not by anybody (or anything)'. Hearing contradictions from rational people, they figure out what we are trying to communicate, taking into account the fact that it is something sufficiently problematic as to strain our linguistic resources.

This proposed explanation, by itself, is not adequate. It needs to explain in more detail how the trick is done. David Dowty (personal communication) has proposed one such fleshing out. He notes that stabbings have typical outcomes, and that although it is difficult to specify them, people's assumptions about what they are like are fairly uniform. When we say that we were stabbed, we succeed in communicating that the dream placed us in such a typical state. It is consistent to be in that state without having been stabbed, and so we communicate something coherent. This proposal indicates a direction in which to look for a more general account of dream reports that would be consistent with the incorporation analysis. I leave this as one of many open questions.

26. This question is independent of the one discussed in the last section, in which we compared the incorporation analysis with the independent conjunct analysis. A similar question is addressed within a variety of different frameworks in Dowty 1989. For convenience I adhere to the terminology of the independent conjunct analysis in giving examples, but the incorporation analysis is equally relevant if supplemented as above.

Chapter 6

1. For a discussion of the development of analyses of causatives and inchoatives in Generative Semantics see Dowty 1979, 38–51.

2. I skip over a great deal of discussion in the philosophical literature on this point.

Dowty (1979) argues for what he calls a "bisentential analysis of CAUSE." But all the examples he cites are equally good evidence for a "bievent analysis of CAUSE." The examples suggest that CAUSE must link *two things that are intimately associated with simple sentences,* but they do not require that the things linked be sentences (or propositions). Because of the ways in which we refer to events, it is often easy to mistake reference to events for reference to propositions. All Dowty's examples may be accounted for within the theory of underlying events, with CAUSE linking events.

3. Dowty (1979, 81, 87) discusses two phenomena in which he claims to find a use for the purported scope of 'BECOME'. One depends on Carlson's analysis of bare plurals coupled with an analysis of 'discover' as 'come to know that'. I doubt that this is a correct analysis of 'discover'. Even if it is,

the underlying event approach accounts for the same data when BECOME operates directly on the verb 'know'.

A second pattern of argument Dowty gives is that 'BECOME' must take scope over negation in order to successfully analyze the causative verb 'uncrate' (as in 'She uncrated the bicycle'). I discuss this example in section 6.7.1.

4. My favored opinion about the data accords with the forms assigned to the causative sentences by the analysis I have given. The past and future versions of 'Mary break the window' are

PAST(∃e)[Agent(e, Mary) & Cul(e) & (∃e′)[Breaking(e′) & Cul(e′) & Theme(e′, window) & CAUSE(e,e′)]],

and

FUTURE(∃e)[Agent(e, Mary) & Cul(e) & (∃e′)[Breaking(e′) & Cul(e′) & Theme(e′, window) & CAUSE(e,e′)]].

When this shorthand notation is expanded, the PAST and FUTURE operators require a totally past (or future) interval of time, and 'Cul(e)' means that e culminates sometime during this interval. Thus the former sentence first becomes true when the caused event culminates, and the latter is true at any time before the causing event culminates (assuming that it culminates sometime). (This is so unless the cause precedes the effect, as in a time travel story or in certain theories of physics or parapsychology. Understanding these often involves assuming alternative time-lines, a complication I ignore.)

5. See Traugott 1972, 75, note 7.

6. See Dowty 1979, 308. The general form of 'blocking' is attributed to Arnoff 1976. If a pattern is blocked, the derived word is available to be used with another meaning: 'deaden' = 'cause to become numb'.

7. Dowty suggests that 'send' might be a causative, meaning 'cause to go'. This does not seem to be correct, since you don't send something if you cause it to go by carrying it with you. Another suggestion is that 'x reminds y of z' means something like 'x causes y to remember z'. This may be a correct account of one of the readings of 'remind', which is etymologically related to 'remember'.

There might also be causative-inchoative triads in the case of double-object-verb/transitive-verb/transitive-state-verbs:

x give z to y   y get/receive z   y have z
x take z   x get/receive z   x have z

However, these seem implausible; one can come to have something without being given it by anyone, or without taking it. But perhaps there is a sense of 'get' that means 'come to have'?

8. Strictly, the proposal is not to derive 'Floyd melted the glass' from 'Floyd caused the glass to melt' but rather to derive the former sentence from an underlying structure that is strongly suggested by the surface structure of the latter. Fodor uses the notation '(Floyd caused (the glass melt))' for this structure. I use the former wording for simplicity; none of the arguments depend on this point.

9. Actually it is ambiguous but not in the relevant way. One reading is that John walked the dog by John's moving John's legs sideways; the other is that John walked the dog by John's moving the dog's legs sideways. This ambiguity turns on whose legs John moved sideways. But there is no ambiguity in who is the agent of the moving; it must be John, not the dog. It is this latter ambiguity in who the agent is that is relevant to Fodor's example.

10. There are also objections to a corresponding treatment of Inchoatives within the deep case theory based on the identity of similarly spelled words. Fillmore proposed that intransitive verbs and adjectives have the same forms, the difference being that the use of an adjective requires the addition of a verb such as 'be'. The "optional case" idea for inchoatives would be that the intransitive verb and the adjective (with copula) are identical in meaning. But this is wrong. If the adjective 'closed' and the intransitive 'close' were to receive the same forms, then there would be no difference at all in the forms attributed to 'The door closed' and 'The door was closed (ADJ)'. This is incorrect, since the latter could be true without the former's ever being true.

11. Note that it is too strong to require that if x becomes Adj then x is not Adj prior to the becoming, since a window can break even if it is already broken, a stick can burn even if it is already burnt, a color can brighten even if it is already bright, and so on. It over-generalizes some nonlogical facts, such as the fact that one cannot awaken without being asleep, one cannot fill a tank unless it is not yet full, and so on.

12. This is not quite right, since the "just before" needs further analysis.

13. The following is not a causative-inchoative triad:
x dressed y—y dressed—y is dressed.
The difference is that although the transitive is a causative-inchoative form on the adjective, the intransitive is not an inchoative on the adjective—or, at least, not an ordinary one, and the transitive is not a causative on the intransitive. This is explained by the proposal that the intransitive adds agenthood to its inchoativeness, and that the transitive does not presuppose this. (In fact, it practically guarantees the opposite, though causality by duress may provide an example of dressing y by causing y to dress.)

14. There are complications. Some uses of adverbs with apparently "intransitive" verbs are related to causatives in which the causing event must be present for a given adverb to make sense. This happens, for example, in 'The can opens easily'. It also happens in one reading of the ambiguous 'This dog walks easily'. In these cases, we have a transitive causative verb without its normal subject, in which case the normal direct object migrates to subject position. There are even cases in which the "intransitive" exists only as a reduced causative transitive; an example is 'Greedy people fool easily'. The only meaning of "intransitive" 'fool' is 'to be fooled' in its causative interpretation, that is, to be such that someone causes you to become fooled, where 'fooled' is an independent adjective.

15. The wagon does not end up in the state "loaded with pitchforks" when 'loaded' has its adjectival reading. If 'loaded' is read as a past participle, then

it may be true to describe it as "loaded with pitchforks." This reading is not relevant to the analysis of causative-inchoatives. (Confusion may arise because the adjective 'loaded' is spelled the same as the past participle 'loaded'.) I discuss the contrast more fully in chapter 12.

16. Angelika Kratzer has raised questions concerning the treatment of similar words that end in 'ly' and thus appear to be verb modifiers. I attribute this to the process commonly called "hypercorrection," where writers overcompensate for the widespread tendency to omit 'ly' when it should be present. We see this in 'chop the onions coarsely', and even sometimes in 'chop the onions finely'. The "proper" forms are the ones lacking the 'ly' on the end; but propriety aside, the semantics of these constructions clearly requires the modifiers to apply to the final states, not to the events that cause them.

17. Where 'closed' is the adjective, not the past participle.

18. The analysis also appears to validate this inference: if I shoot him dead through the heart, I kill him through the heart. This seems awkward. I think the awkwardness lies in the latter sentence all by itself; it seems to be borderline English to say "I killed him through the heart." If it is not English, then the theory is not in trouble, since the semantic theory does not predict that the sentence is grammatical. It predicts only that, if it is grammatical, then it is entailed by 'I shot him through the heart'. Insofar as I am able to force a meaning on the sentence, it seems to me that the entailment should be there.

19. Specifically, what is accounted for is that if something is uncrated, it had to start out "not uncrated." This is not a logical truth; see Section 6.6.

20. This is relevant to Dowty's argument that BECOME must be a sentential operator with scope, in order to govern '¬(x is crated)'.

21. Where 'uncrated' is interpreted as the independent adjective. If 'uncrated' is interpreted as the past participle in its adjectival use then an uncrated bicycle is precisely a bicycle that has previously been taken from a crate.

22. An alternative account also discussed in chapter 9 turns progressive sentences into ones in which states are quantified over; 'Mary is leaving' says that a certain state (the state of Mary's being leaving) holds. That alternative account raises the same problems when it is combined with the analysis of causatives and inchoatives as the simpler version discussed here.

Chapter 7

1. When I say "derived from" I am not referring to an historical process, or necessarily to a syntactical one, but just to a regularity in contemporary English. No commitment is involved to the idea that the derived thing is in any sense posterior to the thing from which it is said to be derived.

2. Apparently following the terminology of Chomsky (1970). When the language contains a derived nominal, the use of the nominal gerund is often avoided, perhaps as a case of the phenomenon of "blocking" mentioned earlier

(see Dowty 1979). It is awkward to use 'inventing of the automobile' instead of 'invention of the automobile', and terrible to use 'destroying of the city' instead of 'destruction of the city', but 'the stabbing of Caesar' is quite natural since there is no alternative. I assume that this is merely a matter of style, and that no special grammatical constraints are needed to weed out the unnatural uses of nominal gerunds.

3. See, e.g., Cresswell 1985. Some few irregular constructions also seem to have the same meaning relations to each other, such as 'well' and 'good'.

4. I should like, however, to reiterate the point from Parsons 1970 that in these cases the adjective and adverb also contribute the same predicates to logical form. That is, both 'allegedly' and 'alleged' yield the same predicates *of propositions*. This is also true of 'necessarily' and 'necessary' (in the relevant uses).

5. Many other constructions are not well understood. For example, 'five feet' in 'A jump of five feet', or in 'A five foot jump'. (Why 'foot' instead of 'feet'?) I think that 'five feet' is actually a name of a distance, as argued in Parsons 1968. This gives 'five feet' the proper form to be the object of the preposition 'of', which in turn suggests that 'five feet' might be related to 'jump' as direct object. This seems exactly right as a treatment of 'Mary jumped five feet' and would yield all of the correct relationships between that sentence and 'A five foot jump by Mary occurred', as discussed below.

6. What we really have inside the brackets of the abstract is the *translation* of the English phrase displayed there. The treatment adopted here of the logic of relative clauses is common in the Montague Grammar tradition.

Syntactically, in "school grammar" the 'who' becomes 'whom' if the "missing" NP is in a position in which a pronoun would be in the accusative. If the missing NP is the object of a preposition, then the whole prepositional phrase may move to the front of the clause, producing, for example, 'with whom', and if the NP is a possessive then the relative pronoun becomes 'whose', and it brings its object with it, as in 'the man whose book was stolen'. Various restrictions on the formation of relative clauses are discussed in the linguistics literature.

7. It is debatable whether the form inside the abstract, 'e hurt Cynthia's ears', is a causative; if so it receives a special treatment with event subjects.

8. I am describing here the net effect of combining the constituents with each other, without saying *how* this takes place. For example, in the Montague Grammar tradition, the various conjuncts might be applied one at a time, recursively, to the head noun, with lambda abstracts being yielded at each stage of the process. Lambda reduction then yields the conjunction that I have mentioned. In earlier grammars, it was assumed that adjectives and prepositional phrases modifying nouns are actually "reduced relative clauses," so that 'the loud singing' would be produced from 'the singing that is loud' by "WHIZ DELETION," which yields 'the singing loud', followed by "FRONTING" the adjective. This too would yield the required conjunction. There are too many

modern theories to cover in any detail here, but I know of no difficulties in accommodating this idea in any of them.

9. Of course, some of the individual conjuncts have more detailed forms than are indicated here. E.g., 'e is by the choir' has the form 'By(e, the choir)', and 'e hurt Cynthia's ears' will have an underlying form that quantifies over hurtings. In displaying 'e hurt Cynthia's ears' I am as usual employing lambda elimination; the actual conjunct that is produced by the rules indicated so far is 'λe[e hurt Cynthia's ears](e)'.

10. The idea that the nominal gerundives really contain nouns and that the others do not is reinforced by trying to combine the structures of the verbal gerundive with words that go only with nouns, such as 'every'. An example of this is the clearly ungrammatical *'Every singing the song . . .' or *'Every singing sweetly . . .'.

11. I myself am not sure that 'the death of Caesar' and 'the murder of Caesar' denote the same event; this is a particularly difficult case to decide.

12. It is not true that there is a nominal gerundive correlated with *every* verbal gerundive, but the exceptions do not have eventive readings. There is no way to read 'Mary's having sung the song sweetly' as referring to an event. We cannot say, for example

*Mary's having sung the song sweetly hurt my ears.
*Mary's having stabbed Caesar killed him.

13. A "full" eventive nominal gerundive construction will contain all the ingredients of the associated sentence with the exception of the tense and the Culmination or Holding relation that relates the event to time. E.g., 'Brutus's stabbing of Caesar' will have the form

(The e)[Stabbing(e) & Agent(e,B) & Theme(e,C)],

whereas the full sentence, 'Brutus stabbed Caesar' will be

PAST($\exists$e)[Stabbing(e) & Agent(e,B) & Theme(e,C) & Cul(e)].

This fact will be useful below when I discuss the interrelations of the gerundives and the sentences.

14. Except that if the verb 'occur' is in the progressive, then I use 'Hold(e)' instead of 'Cul(e)'; see chapter 9 regarding the progressive.

15. Supposing that 'flight' is equivalent to the nominal gerund 'flying'. (For simplicity, both forms are displayed without tenses; they need 'PAST' added to their fronts.)

16. This symbolization ignores tense. It is not apparent so far how to combine the past tense with 'in 1926' so as to get the times of the flights right; this issue, regarding the proper treatment of tenses when combined with quantified NPs and temporal adverbials, takes some careful formulation and is discussed in chapter 11.

17. This embodies the traditional wisdom (= dogma?) that 'cause' stands for a relation between events, and so it is not a sentence operator.

Chapter 8

1. I have employed special styles of variables in these sentences to quantify over events and states, but they are dispensable. For example, I typically use the variable 'e' to quantify over events, as in

Mary ran = (∃e)[Running(e) & Agent-Theme(e,Mary)].

This is for heuristic purposes only; the real work is done by the predicate 'Running', interpreted as 'is a running', which is true of runnings and of nothing else. An unrestricted variable could be used here in place of the 'e' with no effect on the semantics.

2. This was the goal. In Frege's original formulation the reduction failed because the logic employed was inconsistent. Later attempts were more successful, though limited.

3. Actually, much more needs to be done than this, since the example eliminates only the apparent reference to fictional characters from a single context: the use of their names in contexts of the form '_____ is a fictional entity'. I do not mean to minimize this problem; I skip over it only for simplicity of exposition. (I also skip over the problem that the account won't do even for the displayed contexts, since it does not extend to true claims such as 'The main character of Dickens' most famous novel is a fictional entity'. My purpose here is not to engage in such enterprises but to describe their goals.)

4. This is not quite sufficient, since the reverse reading of the definition does not address the matter of applying 'sees₂' to sets that do not underlie ordinary objects. That may or may not be a problem, depending on how the rest of the reduction goes.

5. I believe that this enterprise began early in this century as an attempt to provide definitional reductions, and that eventually philosophers began to feel that actually providing the definitions was not all that important. As for whether having the definitions is important, that depends on what you intend to make of the success of the enterprise. Since there are many different things one might make of it, the enterprise is often carried out without addressing its importance.

6. Montague constructs events out of properties of moments of time, and Taylor constructs them out of states. Bennett's view is that events are *tropes*, that is, particularized instances of properties of individuals, such properties residing in agents or themes. For example, Bennett suggests that Brutus's stabbing of Caesar is a specific instance of the property of stabbing Caesar that resides in Brutus. Technically, this is consistent with the underlying event view, and it has many of the same consequences for event identity (given that one and the same trope can be an instance of many different properties).

7. Although commonly associated with Kim, these examples are not necessarily ones endorsed by him. See Bennett 1988 chapter 5.

8. The theory allows for exceptions to occur when verb-phrase-sensitive terminology is present, though whether the exceptions really do occur depends on how that new terminology behaves. E.g., the present theory is neutral

about the relation between 'Caesar was obviously shot by Brutus' and 'Brutus obviously shot Caesar'.

9. This argument is independent of whether the two uses of 'play' are synonymous.

10. Lombard adds two more clauses to the analysis: that Caesar is the subject of e, and that Caesar is the subject of s. These do not bear on the discussion that follows.

11. It may indeed be possible to find such objections if 'action' is meant to include only actions of purposeful agents. The switch/prowler example can be changed to one in which a falling rock flipped the switch and thereby alerted the prowler. Since rocks are not purposeful agents, the notion of agenthood is not appropriate.

12. The main differences are that, where Lombard has 's is a being-stabbed of y', I should have 's is a state of being stabbed & Theme(s,y)', and where he has 's terminates e', I should have 'e is a becoming of s'.

13. Taylor (1985, 26) discusses a related case (which he attributes to Christopher Arnold). Presumably, Oswald pulled the trigger, thereby shooting Kennedy dead, and thereby killing him. The shooting him dead is, I think, the same event as Oswald's killing him, and since he shot him dead with a gun he killed him with the gun. Likewise, his shooting Kennedy is also identical with his shooting him dead. But his pulling the trigger cannot be identical with the shooting, since he shot him with a gun, but he didn't pull the trigger with the gun. (This last point is the one attributed to Arnold.)

14. Dowty's issue is whether all *accomplishment* event verbs are causative-inchoative; the discussion does not extend to *achievement* verbs, as in 'reach the summit'. I finesse this qualification by limiting myself to accomplishment verbs in the examples.

Chapter 9

1. This chapter is a revised version of Parsons 1989; I am indebted to the editors of *Linguistics and Philosophy* for permission to reuse this material here. It is based on work that originated in a seminar I had the good fortune to teach jointly with Emmon Bach in the spring of 1979 at the University of Massachusetts. It was also discussed in two subsequent seminars at the University of California at Irvine. I wish to thank all of the participants for their attention and criticisms. I also wish to thank David Dowty for comments on earlier drafts. Some of the criticisms of alternative accounts of the progressive in this chapter are found in Vlach 1981.

2. The inertia world proposal has a formal part and a substantive part. The formal part says that Prog(S) is true at t iff S becomes true in every world that is an I-world at t. The substantive part says what an "I-world" is. I have suggested that Dowty's initial proposal for an explanation of I-world in terms of compatibility with the past produces an implausible account. The challenge

for the I-world theory is to provide a better account of what an I-world is. Here are some constraints on that task.

First, it seems plausible that at any given time in the history of the world some progressive sentence is true even though its nonprogressive counterpart does not become true in the actual world. If so, the formal part of the I-world theory requires that the actual world must *never* be an I-world. There must, however, be I-worlds among the possible worlds for every time t, since otherwise the formal part of the analysis would make all progressive sentences vacuously true at that time.

Second, the I-world account cannot possibly be the whole story about the progressive. In many cases we feel that we are in a position to make inferences from progressives to nonprogressives. Suppose, for example, that 'The stars are moving' is true for an extended period of time (perhaps forever, to take an extreme case). We then naturally infer that at some time in the future 'The stars have moved' will be true. Yet this is not valid on the I-world account if the actual world is never an I-world. So some notions in addition to that of I-world will be required for a complete account of the progressive.

Additional problems for any "operator-like" approach to the progressive are discussed in section 9.3.3 below.

3. See Vlach 1981 for similar critique of the inertia worlds approach. Vlach suggests that what needs to be taken into account is not what would be the case *in general* in other inertia worlds but what would be the case *involving the state and actions of the subject of the sentence*. I suspect that something like the following might be correct, using 'cross' as an example:

x is crossing the street iff x is doing something that is such that, were *it* to culminate, x would thereby cross the street.

(The "something" that x is doing is, of course, the crossing.) The inertia worlds analysis gets its plausibility from being understood in this manner. I see no way to retain the plausibility while eliminating the implicit reference to the crossing.

4. This incorporates the idea, prominent in linguistic folklore, that progressives themselves are automatically stative. There must also be added to the rule a special provision for "percolation" of the state reading down into the objects of perceptual statements. For example, the sentence

I was watching Mary build a bookcase

entails that Mary was building a bookcase, not that she built one. Putting the verb 'watch' into the progressive has the same effect on 'build', even though this does not show up syntactically.

5. This is easy to verify for the logic of modifiers; verifying the others depends on details of the formulation of explicit reference to events and the treatment of perception sentences; these are discussed in chapters 7 and 13.

6. Actually, the variant proposal needs a slight modification in order for it to work the same (in the absence of temporal modifiers) as the simpler version. Something like the variant is needed to combine properly with temporal modifiers; see chapter 12 section 12.8 for discussion.

7. The problem about building a house would disappear if 'build' and similar verbs were themselves intensional words, such as 'imagine' or 'seek'. But they are not. If Mary built a house, then there is no way to read this so as to avoid the conclusion that there was a house that she built.

8. For ways to analyze such constructions see Partee 1976 and Thomason 1976.

9. If the progressive morpheme in the inertia world analysis always has scope over the verb alone, then there is no obvious incompatibility between the inertia world analysis and the underlying event approach—although the approaches are so different in spirit that their equivalence would be surprising.

10. The intuition behind the second principle is that if Mary is painting a house then *that painting* is not yet over with. This explanation, as Bach points out, requires the assumption of underlying events.

11. Bennett 1977 makes a similar proposal in terms of interval semantics.

12. Actually, to claim that 'Mary ran' entails 'Mary was running' involves the assumption that the hold-time of an event extends through its time of culmination, if there is one. This might be doubted for so-called "achievement" phrases, such as 'reach the summit', which supposedly do not have true progressives and perhaps have no hold-times at all (though the claim that they do not have true progressives is far from obvious). If this is so, 'Mary ran' does not entail 'Mary was running' as a matter of logical form, and an additional principle is needed for nonachievement verbs such as 'run'. The required principle seems to be that there are no instantaneous isolated runnings; runnings can be runnings only if they go on (hold) for a while.

13. In conjunction with a prohibition on isolated instantaneous runnings it would also entail 'Mary ran'.

14. The assimilation of process sentences to event sentences solves a certain problem that arose in Parsons 1985 regarding tenses. A process sentence in the past tense seems to imply that the present tense version is not true, though the natural rule for the past tense did not require this and instead typically made the past tense sentence true in virtue of a process that is still going on. For example, the rule makes 'Mary ran' true while Mary is still running. But once process sentences are treated as event sentences, there is a different consequence. The past tense sentence must be made true by a process that has already culminated, and the usage principle that when we use a process sentence we implicitly limit our quantifiers to maximal processes yields the implication that no other process of the same kind is still going on. This means that 'Mary ran', though true, will have a false implication if it is true in virtue of the initial part of a running that is still going on.

Chapter 10

1. Portions of this chapter are further developments of Parsons 1987/88. I thank the officials of the Aristotelian Society for permission to reuse this material.

2. Tests for state sentences are discussed in chapter 3, Section 3.6.

3. In this example, the predicate is true of an event, not a state. I see no reason to suppose that it is a different predicate in these various uses. I do, though, suppose that 'under the tree' has different meanings when it is used as an adverbial of location and as an adverbial of motion or direction.

4. Because of 'ran' the actual form is more complicated: $(\exists x)(\text{Giraffe}(x)$ & $(\exists e)[e$ is a running & Agent-Theme$(e,x)])$.

5. I can get a reading of the conclusion that follows from the premises by reading it with a pause between the modifiers: 'The TV sits on the desk . . . by the computer'. I think this is a way of expressing two different assertions, namely, the premises.

6. The copula under discussion here does not include the 'be' of activity.

7. There remains a puzzle that is worth exploring. Why is it that the adjectives that most easily form such examples happen to be homonyms of past participles? (This relationship is discussed further in chapter 12.)

8. I have not dealt with comparatives, although they seem to form state sentences:
Mary is taller than Kim.
I take for granted that comparatives have fairly complex analyses, complex enough to defer their treatment to a later stage of the theorizing. For example, a natural treatment of the displayed sentence is something like this:
The degree to which Mary is tall exceeds the degree to which Kim is tall.
This introduces the notion of degrees of tallness, a topic that falls beyond present discussion. Since various proposed accounts differ substantially from one another, I doubt that much evidence can be obtained at this stage of investigation about underlying events and states.

9. These sentences are not acceptable English on their state readings; one can force an event reading using the 'be' of activity, in which being under the tree or being naked is something that John is doing. In such a case we get an acceptable reading—but an event reading, so not a reading that is relevant to assessing the underlying state analysis.

10. This doesn't explain the presence of 'be' in 'Mary will be home soon'. More needs to be said on this point. Fortunately, the proposal in question does not depend on the details of the syntactic analysis.

11. Some of these adjectives are "degree" words whose uses seem parasitic on the nouns that they modify. My discussion in section 4.2 that such degree modifiers can indeed be treated logically as predicates is relevant here.

12. I am passing over the issue of times here. An extra conjunct should be included to indicate when the state in question holds. Nouns also need to be temporally indexed, since something can be, for example, a child at one time and not later. Presumably the time of holding of the state indicated by the adjective should be the same as the time that the noun applies to its argument, so 'x was a red book' should have a form such as '$(\exists t)[t<\text{now}$ & $(\exists s)[s$ is a state of being red & Theme(s,x) & Hold$(s,t)]$ & Book$(x,t)]$'.

13. The situation envisaged is one in which IBM has several branches, one in a hilly region not in Paris, and one in a non-hilly part of Paris. This example is patterned after one of Barry Schein's (personal communication).

14. It will not do to analyze (J) as
J' Mary saw IBM & IBM is *entirely* in Paris,
since now (J) could be true without (J') being true.

15. This condition is written in English and therefore, according to the theory under consideration, has a form that is interestingly more complex than might appear on the surface. Since "higher-order" talk about events and states has a simpler form than other talk, and since the hypothesis under consideration attributes complex forms to talk of individuals, in logical notation the condition (*) becomes
** $(e)[In(e,R) \equiv (x)(xPe \rightarrow (\exists s)[Theme(s,x)$ & $In(s,R)])]$,
where 'e' ranges over all events and states, and where 'xPe' means that x is a participant in e.

16. In keeping with the previous footnote, this argument is fairly complex. In logical notation it goes as follows, using condition (**) from the previous footnote:
(**) $(e)[In(e,R) \equiv (x)(xPe \rightarrow (\exists s)[Theme(s,x)$ & $In(s,R)])]$,
and ignoring times:
1. Mary was in the park [Premise]
2. $Theme(s_M,Mary)$ & $In(s_M,park)$, for some s_M. [by analysis]
3. $In(s_M,park)$ [from 2]
4. $(x)(xPs_M \rightarrow (\exists s)[Theme(s,x)$ & $In(s,park)])$ [by (**)]
5. $MaryPs_M$ [from 2, assuming Themes are participants]
6. $(\exists s)[Theme(s,Mary)$ & $In(s,park)]$ [from 4,5]
7. Mary was running [Premise]
8. $Running(e_R)$ & $Theme(e_R,Mary)]$, for some e_R [by analysis]
9. $(x)(xPe_R \rightarrow x=Mary)$ [From 8, by the assumption that runnings have only their themes as participants.]
10. $(x)(xPe_R \rightarrow (\exists s)[Theme(s,x)$ & $In(s,park)])$ [from 6,9]
11. $In(e_R,park)$ [from 10 and (**)]
12. $(\exists e)[Running(e)$ & $Theme(e,Mary)$ & $In(e,park)]$ [from 8,11]
13. Mary was running in the park [by analysis]

17. See chapter 7 for discussion. Some state gerundive clauses are clearly propositional in nature, since they create opacity. From 'The butcher's being clever impressed everyone' and 'The butcher is the king' it does not follow that the king's being clever impressed everyone—or, at least, there are readings of these sentences on which it does not follow. If we take the existence of opacity to be evidence for the propositional character of clauses, then we might make a case for the existence of nonpropositional gerundive state clauses by noting the absence of opacity—on any reading—in constructions such as 'The king's being heavy made the throne collapse'. I think that this is exactly the right view of things, but I am reluctant to press this as an *argument* for the state analysis since so many other analyses of these constructions are possible. (For example, all such constructions might be propositional in nature, and the presence or lack of opacity might be blamed on the "containers": 'impressed everyone' and 'made the throne collapse'.)

18. Examples of the latter sort are due to Dorothy Edgington, and also to students in my UCI seminar on events.

19. One simple but extravagant hypothesis that would provide the additional information needed for such hypotheses is the following. We suppose that there is a special kind of state N such that any noun picks out a state of kind N. We then add the hypothesis: $Theme(s_1,x)$ & $Theme(s_2,y)$ & $x=y$ & $N(s_1)$ & $N(s_2)$ → $s_1=s_2$.

20. There is an interesting type of construction in which an adverbial appears to modify the noun, as in: 'There goes a monster with a knife'. It is pretty clear that the 'with a knife' does not modify the verb here, any more than in 'Never trust a monster with a knife'. This seems to be a reduced relative clause, meaning either 'There goes a monster that is with a knife' or 'There goes a monster that has a knife'. In both, the adverbial does not modify the noun. In the latter, it modifies the verb 'has'. In the former, the relative clause construction produces the logical form 'x is a monster & x is with a knife' for 'x is a monster which is with a knife'. This leaves the adverbial in predicate construction, which is similar to that in 'Brutus is under a tree', discussed above.

21. Since the 'be' of activity is an event verb, 'Henry is being clever again' is an event sentence using the event verb 'be', not a state sentence.

22. I am being sloppy here for purposes of exposition. "Going from zero to infinity" should really be reconstrued as something like, "No matter how far you go, starting from zero and going upwards," and "get closer to 4.9" is literally quite inaccurate (since it is true if you sum to 3.9 from below); reconstruing this accurately is complex. Informally, we need to say something like: "you can get as close as you like to 4.9 if you go far enough." This nicely introduces (hypothetical) desire and goal-achievement into the discussion, thus illustrating the difficulty of finding some systematic way to reconstrue the informal discussion in a formal mold.

Chapter 11

1. I have in mind work such as Heim 1983, Kamp 1981, Kamp and Rohrer 1983, Partee 1984. The ingredients for embedding the theory into accounts of context and discourse are the free variables over periods, instants, and events/states.

2. The present tense is also used for atemporal statements ('Two plus two is four') and for eternal statements (some readings of 'Dogs chase cats'). For simplicity I ignore these options.

3. These include what Bellert (1977) calls "domain" adverbs; I am indebted to her article for ideas on this topic.

4. One might suggest that the past tense sentence is true (on the relevant reading) because it is the past tense version of the *habitual* reading of the present tense sentence 'G.W. eats with a wooden spoon'. But this is incorrect, since the present tense sentence read habitually can be true even if Washington

has recently developed the habit and will soon lose it. There *is* a past tense sentence corresponding to this; when discussing a particular time in Washington's life, for example, one might produce the sentence with that meaning. But the past tense sentence also has a broader interpretation, something akin to 'G.W. always ate with a wooden spoon'. This is the reading that the standard PAST operator cannot capture. The issue is even clearer when a frequency adverbial is explicitly present; there is no obvious way to represent the meaning of 'George Washington *always* ate with a wooden spoon' by combining some meaning of 'always' with a past tense operator meaning 'at least once in the past'. (The formula '¬PAST¬(G.W. eat with a wooden spoon)' is not correct since it requires that he ate continually, 24 hours per day.)

5. This claim needs amplification. I regard the "narrative present" as a form of speech in which there is a feigned shift of utterance time throughout the past. This leaves the logical forms untouched; they are just the ordinary present tense versions. One must also be sensitive to the use of the present to indicate the future. In some cases this is an explicit part of the sequence-of-tense rules of English grammar. 'Leaves' in 'When Agatha leaves, Bill will be unhappy' indicates the future, not the present; the use of tenses in subordinate clauses is discussed in section 11.6. In other cases, context indicates a future use of the present tense, as in 'The Lakers play tomorrow'.

6. One interesting issue to be disentangled is the interaction of tenses with relative clauses that modify nouns within the scopes of such tenses. In 'Every child that is still alive was infected there' it appears that 'every child' must come within the scope of the past operator, since the sentence may be discussing persons who are at present no longer children. But both the meaning and the occurrence of the present tense 'is' seem to indicate that the relative clause is not within the scope of the past. If relative clauses modify nouns (as opposed to NPs), as in standard Montague Grammar, then a way must be specified to exempt the relative clauses from the scopes of the main clause tenses. (The problem, of course, is not how to find forms that will do this, but how to relate them systematically to English sentences.)

7. This proposal is found in Dowty 1979.

8. The question 'How long did Agatha X?' is a request for an answer containing a durational adverbial. As we have just seen, such answers with process verbs are not anomalous, nor are those with state verbs, but answers with nonprocess event verbs are anomalous. This explains the efficacy of the "how long" test for distinguishing events from processes and states that I discussed in chapter 3.

9. There is a reading of 'for three years' that implies purpose and differs from the constructions I have discussed so far. In 'Robin Hood was in jail for three years, but he stayed only three days', 'for three years' clearly applies to the state of being in jail—it was a state that was *intended* to last for three years. You can then say without anomaly, 'Robin Hood was in jail for three years, but he was in jail for only three days'. Since the meaning is different, the use of this "purpose" reading does not shed light on the temporal reading.

The construction 'The Sheriff jailed Robin Hood for three years' was debated in the Generative Semantics tradition. It appears to be a causative construction in which the Sheriff does something causing there to be a state of Robin Hood's being in jail. 'For three years' is a "tag" that modifies this state, similarly to 'flat' in 'hammer the metal flat'. (See section 6.8.)

10. In expanded form, without the abbreviated quantifier '($\exists 2t$)', this is '($\exists t_1$)($\exists t_2$)[$t_1 \neq t_2$ & ($\exists I$)[I<now & At(I,t_1) & ($\exists e$)($\exists t$)[$t \in I$ & Stabbing(e) & Agent(e,Brutus) & Theme(e,Caesar) & Cul(e,t)]] & ($\exists I$)[I<now & At(I,t_2) & ($\exists e$)($\exists t$)[$t \in I$ & Stabbing(e) & Agent(e,Brutus) & Theme(e,Caesar) & Cul(e,t)]]]'.

11. In expanded form, without the abbreviated quantifier '($\exists 2e$)', this is '($\exists I$)[I<now & ($\exists e_1$)($\exists e_2$)[$e_1 \neq e_2$ & ($\exists t$)[$t \in I$ & Stabbing(e_1) & Agent(e_1,Brutus) & Theme(e_1,Caesar) & Cul(e_1,t)] & ($\exists t$)[$t \in I$ & Stabbing(e_2) & Agent(e_2,Brutus) & Theme(e_2,Caesar) & Cul(e_2,t)]]]'. This makes the events different, but it leaves open whether they occur at the same or different times.

12. In several examples here I indicate restricted quantification by means of a quantifier-like locution followed by two formulas separated with a comma. For example, I use the form '(Most x)[Ax,Bx]', which is true if and only if a majority of the things that satisfy 'Ax' also satisfy 'Bx'. The semantics of similar locutions should be obvious from this paradigm.

13. If we had decided that nouns contained underlying states in logical form, we might be tempted to construe this instead as a quantification over states: (Most x)[x is a state of being a quadratic equation, x is a state of having two roots].

14. I assume, contrary to Parsons 1980, that a sentence such as 'Before the singing, she was unhappy' is elliptical for 'Before the singing occurred, she was unhappy'. This means that subordinating adverbials always operate semantically on clauses, in spite of the fact that they sometimes take explicit (eventive) NPs (such as 'the singing') as syntactic objects.

Chapter 12

1. For help on this paper I am indebted to Steve Barney, Roger Higgins, Barbara Partee, Bruce Mitchell, and a *Linguistic Inquiry* referee for remarks on earlier drafts. They have all made this better, but none of them is responsible for it.

2. The relevance of adverbs to the relation between the simple past and the perfect is discussed in McCoard 1978.

3. I return to the issue of the relation of the tenses to temporal modifiers in section 12.8. The theory explored here is consistent, I think, with the "extended now" theory of McCoard 1978.

4. Kamp and Rohrer use a more complex system of tense-references than I, because they study the interactions among sentences in texts. I can get along with a simpler symbolization because I focus on isolated sentences. I see no

difficulty in embedding the theory I give within their more complex framework, but doing so here would distract from my main theme.

5. In the examples in this chapter, the subject of a transitive verb always stands for an Agent, and the direct object stands for a Theme; the subject of a copula-plus-adjective sentence or an intransitive verb is a Theme. The theory can be reformulated without depending on the use of thematic relations, but the resulting account is considerably more complex.

6. This is the "variant" treatment of the progressive mentioned in chapter 9, section 9.2. The "main" proposal discussed there holds that for a progressive sentence to be true the event in question must hold at the time in question. The version articulated here says that it is not the event itself but rather its associated In-Progress state that holds. I believe that with a slight modification (discussed in section 12.8 below), the two treatments are equivalent, at least until we take account of complex adverbial modifiers; the one given here more closely resembles that of the perfect.

7. McCoard (1978, 227) seems to argue against the existence of such states, saying that it is nonsense to speak in terms of being in a telephoned state. For him, 'He keeps me telephoned all the time' is nongrammatical. On my account the sentence is well-formed, but it says something anomalous, not nonsensical. It is anomalous because the state of having been telephoned is one that nobody could possibly *keep* anyone in; once in it you're automatically in it forever.

8. The analysis yields resultant states for all events; if an event does not culminate, then its resultant state never holds. It would be more natural to require that nonculminating events *lack* resultant states. This change is easily made, though it complicates the formulation of the account.

9. In the example given, my present tense sentence is to be interpreted as the reportive present, not as the generic. Reportive readings of present tense event and process sentences are unusual, but they exist. If we use the past tense, the example reads more naturally; its analysis is

Simple Past:	Past Perfect:
Mary ran =	*Mary had run* =
For some event e:	For some event e:
e is a running,	e is a running,
the theme of e is Mary, and	the theme of e is Mary, and
e culminates before now.	e's R-state holds before now.

I have illustrated the analysis with a "process" sentence. In my opinion, processes are composed of homogeneous events, and process verbs pick out the events that compose them. Therefore, no special logical forms are needed for process verbs as opposed to event verbs; process verbs just *are* event verbs that, when they apply to a culminated event, also typically apply to culminated subevents of that event. This, I believe, explains most of the special properties of process sentences. (See chapter 9, section 9.5.)

10. Actually, the analysis produces the following "infinitesimal" nonequivalence: 'I have eaten the apple' becomes true the instant the apple is eaten, whereas 'I ate the apple' becomes true immediately after that instant. It is

difficult to see how to gather evidence on this matter. If both should become true immediately after the apple is eaten, then the words 'at or' should be deleted from principle (2).

To illustrate the data discussed in section 12.1, I introduce explicit notation for the tenses, as in chapter 11. With this notation, the examples become

Mary has eaten the apple =	*Mary ate the apple =*
For some period **I:**	For some period **I:**
I = now, and:	**I** is before now, and:
For some event e:	For some event e:
e is an eating	e is an eating
the agent of e is Mary	the agent of e is Mary
the theme of e is the apple	the theme of e is the apple
e's R-state holds in **I**	e culminates in **I**

The introduction of a temporal modifier such as 'yesterday' then destroys the equivalence, by producing the forms:

Mary has eaten the apple =	*Mary ate the apple =*
For some period **I:**	For some period **I:**
I = now, and:	**I** is before now, and:
I is during yesterday, and:	**I** is during yesterday, and:
For some event e:	For some event e:
e is an eating	e is an eating
the agent of e is Mary	the agent of e is Mary
the theme of e is the apple	the theme of e is the apple
e's R-state holds in **I**	e culminates in **I**

11. If this account were to be fully developed for Modern English, it would have to be distinguished from other special constructions, such as 'the writing desk'.

12. In both the passive and the past-participle-used-as-an-adjective I ignore the "implied agent." That is, I ignore the claim that 'The soup was cooled' means that it was cooled *by someone* and the claim that 'the cooled soup' means something like 'the cooled-*by-someone* soup'. Contrary to most theorists, I believe that the implied agent should not be included in the analysis of these constructions (see chapter 5, section 5.7). However, if the implied agent should be included in one of these constructions, it should appear in the other as well, so this does not undercut their equivalence. It is not a trivial matter to include the implied agent in a systematic way, for reasons that I discuss in section 12.6.

13. My focus is thus different in spirit from Lightfoot's 1979 studies of "radical re-analyses."

14. Strictly, I would like to define Conservative Restructuring as a change in which the forms of the words themselves do not change at all. With this strict wording, the loss of adjectival inflections would make the cases under discussion imperfect examples of Conservative Restructuring. This is in the *spirit* of Conservative Restructuring since the inflections were not used consistently during the period of change, and they were used less and less in all contexts

during that period. Nonetheless, a better theoretical formulation of Conservative Restructuring is needed.

15. I call this the "standard account" because it is the account most frequently given by those who attempt to trace the historical development of the perfect. The standard account can be seen as having a syntactic part, which sees a verb form originating from an adjectival one, and a further hypothesis that attributes differing semantical significance to the two readings. Some commentators state the purely syntactic claim:

> When a past participle is used with the auxiliary verb **habban** it is sometimes inflected and sometimes not. The use of the inflected form is the older construction and goes back to a time when the participle was regarded not as part of the verb but as an adjective agreeing with the object of **habban**. (Brook 1955, 90)

> Examples in which the participle is adjectival are *he us hafað þæs leohtes bescyrede* 'he has us deprived of that light' (where the present tense of *habban* is followed by *bescyrede* a past participle acc. pl. strong, agreeing with *us*) and *ac hi hæfdon þa heora stemn gesetenne and hiora mete genotudne* 'but then they had their term of service finished and their food used up' (where a past tense of *habban* is followed by two participles both of which are declined acc. sg. masc. strong, agreeing with *stemn* and *mete*, the objects of *hæfdon*). These are clearly the ancestors of the MnE perfect and pluperfect respectively.

> But examples also occur in which there is no such declining of the past participle to agree with the object, e.g. *Eastengle hæfdon Ælfrede cyninge aþas geseald* 'The East Anglians had oaths given to King Alfred' and *Hæfde se cyning his fierd on tu tonumen* 'The king had his army divided in two'. . . . This was, of course, a necessary stage in the development of the MnE perfect and pluperfect tenses. (Mitchell & Robinson 1982, §200)

Possibly semantic claims are involved in the following quotations:

> Where the participles agree—in the one case with the object, and in the other case with the subject—we have a survival from the time when they had predicative adjectival function rather than a tense function . . . *hi hæfdon þa heora stemn gesetenne and hiora mete genotudne* 'they had finished their tour of duty and used up their food', *(lar) wæs oðfeallenu* '(learning) had declined'. (Quirk & Wrenn 1958, 78)

> With forms of *habban*, the participle is normally invariable (*hæfdon . . . aþas geseald* '(they) had given oaths'), but sometimes it agrees with the object: *hie hine ofslægenne hæfdon* 'they had slain him'; here, no doubt, we see a survival of the normal use of this construction before it came to be used as a 'pluperfect tense'. . . ,—'they had him dead'. (Quirk & Wrenn 1958, 75)

Others clearly see the constructions as having significance for the attribution of states:

> Both sets of perfective auxiliaries [with "be" and "have"] were genuine OE constructions that go back to our earliest records. They coexist with, and in certain cases, are ambiguous with, two rather different constructions from which they were derived.

> The origin of the segmentalized *be* perfects . . . is to be found in adjectival constructions . . . for example, *we wæron gecumene* "we were (in the state of having) come," where *gecumene* is an adjectival form of the verb *cum-*, agreeing in number, case, and gender with the subject *we* . . .

> The development of the other perfect auxiliary, *habb-* + PP, is more complex, but also involves adjectival participials. As might be suspected from the form *have*, structures with Possessors like *I have a book* were also originally involved.

> In earliest OE we do not find *habb-* + PP in perfective constructions, only in possessive ones like *Ic hæfde hine gebundenne* 'I had him in-a-state-of-being-bound', where *gebundenne* is an adjectival form of the verb with the accusative masculine singular adjectival inflection *-ne* agreeing with *hine* . . .

Just as the *He wæs gecumen* construction split into two giving an adjectival and a perfective construction, so the sentence type *Ic hæfde hine gebundenne* split into two. *Habbe-* was reinterpreted as a marker of perfectiveness and the adjectival nature of the participial was lost. (Traugott 1972, 92–94)

And others identify the nonstate reading with an action reading:

Originally *have* in colligation with a past participle was a notional verb denoting possession, while the past participle was a complement or attribute to the object and had a good deal of adjective force, *teste* its being (in the beginning) inflected in agreement with the gender and number of the object: *I have my work done = I possess or have my work in a done or finished condition.* From this state as a result antecedent action was inferred, so that the colligation came to be used to denote completed action, as e.g. in O.E. Gospels, Mk. 8, 17, '*gyt ge habbaþ eowre heortan geblende?*' In Present-Day English the word-order in independent syntactical units usually clearly indicates whether state or action is meant, so that *I have my work done* implies the former, and *I have done my work* the latter. (Visser 1973, §2001)

16. The ending '-ende' is the standard uninflected form of the present participle. I am disconcerted by the fact that commentators do not give examples of 'be' + Present Participle in which the participle has overt adjectival inflection.

17. Actually, the analysis works well for 'hit is scinende', and also for 'þa wæs se cyning andettende', assuming that each of these has an adjectival reading. However, if the full 'þa wæs se cyning openlice andettende þam biscope' has an adjectival as well as a progressive reading, the theory so far stated does not capture it, because the role of the additional material, namely 'openlice' and 'þam biscope', is not discussed until section 12.6.

It might be argued that the conditions for Conservative Restructuring are not met even in the simplest examples, since it is arguable whether the later syntactic form (the Progressive or the Perfect) *already existed* in the language. I have supposed that treating 'be confessing' as a VERB with a normal verbal use counts as an appeal to a syntactic form that is already present in the language. But this is obvious only if we refuse to count the substructure of the new *complex* VERB as part of syntax. Certainly, by the time we get to Modern English, the helping verbs have developed special autonomous behavior; 'be confessing' is a VERB only at a level of analysis very close to the surface, and a complete account of its syntax involves forms (INFL or AUX) that have developed considerably since Old English. A full account of the transition from Old English to Modern English would have to include a discussion of changes in the helping verbs subsequent to the conservative restructuring under discussion; this is beyond the scope of this book.

18. The meaning of the past participle is a tricky issue. My analysis assumes that the past participle in Old English, when used adjectivally, had a "past" aspect to its meaning, as found in the Modern English 'cooled soup', meaning *previously* cooled soup. This is a matter of controversy among OE scholars. The issue is complicated by the fact that the past participle and the passive participle are identical in form in both Old and Modern English. This raises a methodological issue: are we to assume that there is only one participle (Mitchell 1987 calls it the "second" participle), or two? If there is only one, we shall look for a single meaning that can be used in both the perfect and

the passive; calling it "past" or "passive" will simply call attention to which use we have in mind. This approach begs the theoretical issue of whether the meanings differ in the two constructions. If there are two participles, then I am free to give independent accounts of their meanings, though I shall then need to explain why they are always spelled the same. In either case, there are difficulties with evaluating the data. The construction 'I am loved' (discussed in Mitchell 1987, §768 ff.) has at least three construals: (1) 'am' is the copula and 'loved' is an adjective, (2) the construction is a passive, and (3) the construction is a perfect with 'be' (as in 'He is risen'). The first makes 'loved' an adjective, the second makes it a passive participle, and the third makes it a past participle.

This sort of issue makes it difficult to evaluate Campbell's (1959, 295) claim: ". . . [the passive participle] expresses pure passivity, not necessarily passivity in past time." If there is no past aspect to the *past* participle, then either 'beon' was used with more content than the mere copula, or else the change from the adjectival form to the verbal form of the perfect involved the introduction of a past aspect. Since the form with 'beon' was eventually taken over by another form with 'have', it is conceivable that the OE construction 'beon+PP' never meant the same as the Modern English perfect. In that case, a more complex account is needed, one that includes the introduction of a past aspect (and so a change of meaning) in the transition from the adjectival to the verbal construction.

Another OE verb also occurred in these constructions: 'weorþan', which meant something like the Modern English 'become'. If you determine the meaning of the construction using 'become' instead of 'be', it turns out not to matter whether you attribute pastness to the past participle or not—the meaning is just about the same in either case. So far as time is concerned, this is illustrated in Modern English by the practical equivalence between 'the soup became cooled' and 'the soup became cool', if 'cooled' is interpreted as the participial form of the *intransitive* verb 'cool'.

On these issues I distinguish the participles. I assume that the *passive* participle has the same meaning as the activè verb from which it is formed, and that the use of the passive form indicates that, e.g., the subject of the sentence is to be given the same thematic role as the object of the active sentence (see chapter 5 for details). I do *not* assume that the Modern English passive is derived from Old English adjectival participles in active sentences; I do not address the issue of the origin of the passive at all.

19. These perception constructions existed in Old English.

20. The use of 'have' with this implication may not have occurred in Old English; see Mitchell 1987, §704.

21. The idea I am pursuing here is stated in the last sentence of the following quotation:

Originally *have* in colligation with a past participle was a notional verb denoting possession, while the past participle was a complement or attribute to the object and had a good deal of adjective force, *teste* its being (in the beginning) inflected in agreement with the gender and number of the object . . . From this state as a result antecedent action was inferred, so that the colligation came to be used to denote completed action . . . (Visser 1973, 2189)

22. Although I promised not to speculate about the causes of the Restructuring, Neil Elliott pointed out to me that once 'have'+PP begins to be seen as a complex event verb, the surface subject of this verb inevitably begins to be seen as the agent of the event in question. This gives us part of the needed additional conditions; the special meaning of 'have' comes almost automatically with the change in syntax.

23. In isolation, the dative ending on *Craccuse* could be translated differently; it could be interpreted as the BENEFACTIVE (the "dative of interest"), illustrated by the use of 'him' in the Modern English 'We threw him a party'. This alternative translation raises the same theoretical issues as are raised by the translation that treats *Craccuse* as a motion adverbial: *to Craccus*.

24. Cf. discussion in Mitchell 1987, §§695–701 and §724.

25. My main source for this speculation is Lehmann 1980.

26. On the interpretation given, past participles (of transitive verbs) used as adjectives always express "passivity in past time," but the autonomous adjectives that are spelled the same do not "express past time." So an amalgamation of the two forms could naturally lead to the present controversy over whether, in Campbell's words, ". . . [the passive participle] expresses pure passivity, not necessarily passivity in past time."

On the other hand, it is not clear whether the autonomous adjectives express passivity at all. If passivity is interpreted as the modern thematic role of "patient" or "theme," then all the adjectives indicate passivity. But if passivity is interpreted as requiring that a thing be acted on by an agent, then the autonomous adjectives do not indicate it.

Also, for past participles of process verbs, the pure passive will practically imply the passive in past time—since a process is a spread-out homogeneous thing, and if it is going on at present, it will also have gone on in the past. If a building is, at a certain time, engulfed by flames, it will typically have been engulfed for some time before.

The issue is complicated further by the fact that the past (= passive?) participle is used to form passive sentences as well as perfects. The passive sentence almost always indicates passivity in both senses noted above. (There are apparent counterexamples in Modern English, such as 'John is pleased by roses', but these forms did not exist in OE.)

27. I can not explain why the former suggests (although it does not require) that I still live in New York. In this example the perfect seems to suggest "recency" or "relevance to the present," much discussed in the literature. I do not see how to account for these elusive data. Nor can I account for the supposed oddity in saying 'Einstein has lived here' when Einstein is dead. (I do not find it odd, but others do.)

28. This still does not achieve the desired result, since it produces a sentence that is true if Mary has been building a house for more than three years so far. This appears to be a phenomenon more intimately related to the notion

of "exactly" than to the perfect, since the same difficulty arises with the simple past. ' . . . exactly three years . . .' seems to mean something like ' . . . three years . . . & ¬ (. . . more than three years . . .)'. The "repair" suggested in the text is still needed; together with the principle just suggested, it solves the problem.

Chapter 13

1. See Higginbotham 1985a for some work along these lines.

2. Actually, only two functions symbols are appealed to (those associated with the Perfect and the Progressive) and lambda abstracts are used very little. There is, in addition, one (nonextensional) predicate operator, 'BECOME#', which operates on predicates to produce other predicates.

3. That is, the template shows how to produce a string of morphemes in the right order. A sophisticated syntactic theory would also attribute a refined syntactic structure to this string. Any attempt to expand this fragment to more complex pieces of language would require combination with such a syntactic theory.

4. Transitive verbs and double-object verbs may appear without their objects: 'I gave to United Way' (missing direct object), 'I gave $5' (missing indirect object), 'I gave at the office' (missing indirect and indirect objects). Nonlinguistic principles might require that any giving event has both a Theme and a Goal, even when these are semantically unexpressed.

5. Recall that resultant-state is different from "target" state. The "target" state for 'throw the ball onto the roof' is the state of the ball's being on the roof; the resultant state of 'throw the ball onto the roof' is the state of the ball's having been thrown onto the roof. The target state is a possibly temporary state; the resultant state is a permanent state.

6. As discussed in section 12.8 of chapter 12, this is probably not the best form for the progressive. An event should have not only a "whole" in-progress state, it should also have in-progress states that are substates of the "whole" one. This means that 'p' is relational, but not functional. Accuracy is achieved by replacing 'OCCUR$(r(p(\alpha)),t)$' everywhere by '$(\exists s)[s$ is an in-progress state of α & OCCUR$(r(s),t)]$'. I leave the simpler inaccurate form in the text throughout the chapter for readability.

7. For reasons discussed in section 11.4 of chapter 11 we may want to conjoin with the 'OCCUR$(r(p(\alpha)),t)$' an additional conjunct written 'α incl I' meaning that all of the times at which α holds or is in progress are included in the period I. Again, I omit this clause throughout the chapter in order to increase readability of the formulas.

8. The process I have described is inaccurate in at least this way: the tense already appears in the logical form for the block, as a quantifier over and a condition on intervals of time (typically of the form: '$(\exists I)[I \blacklozenge$ now & . . .]'). This should really enter the picture much later, after the subject variable is put back on. That is, the block should be generated *without* the '$(\exists I)[I \blacklozenge$ now

& . . .]', and this condition should come into play after VPs are formed and the subject variable is put back on. This is because the tense can interact, as regards its scope, with quantified NPs whose scope is the entire atomic formula. Forcing the tense constraint to be part of the original block in effect constrains its scope to be narrower than any of these NPs, which is only one of the possible options. This is easily corrected by anyone who wishes to expand the fragment.

9. Generally, this is the moment of utterance of the sentence, though there are exceptions, as in the "narrative present."

10. Actually, the form should involve a lambda abstract, so that the subject appears only once: $(\exists I)[I < now \ \& \ \lambda x[(\exists t)(\exists \alpha)[t \in I \ \& \ Agent(\alpha,x) \ \& \ Cul(\alpha,t) \ \& \ Driving(\alpha) \ \& \ To(\alpha,store)] \ \& \ (\exists t_2)(\exists \beta)[t_2 \in I \ \& \ Agent(\beta,x) \ \& \ Cul(\beta,t_2) \ \& \ Driving(\beta) \ \& \ To(\beta,laundromat)]](Kim)]$.

11. It is unclear whether this template should be expanded to apply to certain "motion adverbials" such as 'onto u', as in 'She hit the ball onto the roof', where the logical form of the tag 'onto the roof' would be the same as the logical form of 'on the roof'.

Bibliography

Åqvist, Lennart. 1977. On the analysis of some accomplishment and activity verbs. In Rohrer 1977.

Åqvist, Lennart. 1978. Fundamentals of a theory of aspect and events within the setting of an improved tense logic. In Guenther and Rohrer 1978.

Arnauld, Antoine, and Claude Lancelot. 1660. *Grammaire Generale et Raisonnee*. Translated by James Rieux and Bernard Rollins as *The Port-Royal Grammar*. The Hague: Mouton, 1975.

Aronoff, Mark. 1976. *Word Formation in Generative Grammar*. Cambridge, Mass: MIT Press.

Bach, Emmon. 1981. On time, tense, and aspect: An essay in English metaphysics. In Peter Cole, ed., *Radical Pragmatics*. New York: Academic Press, 63–81.

Bach, Emmon. 1986a. The algebra of events. *Linguistics and Philosophy* 9, 5–16.

Bach, Emmon. 1986b. Natural language metaphysics. In Ruth Barcan-Marcus, Georg J.W. Dorn, and Paul Weingartner, eds. *Logic, Methodology, and Philosophy of Science VII*. Amsterdam: North Holland Press, 573–95.

Bartsch, Renate. 1976. *The Grammar of Adverbials*. New York: North Holland Press.

Barwise, Jon. 1981. Scenes and other situations. *Journal of Philosophy* 78: 369–97.

Barwise, Jon, and John Perry. 1983. *Situations and Attitudes*. Cambridge: MIT Press.

Bäuerle, Rainer, Christoph Schwartze, and Arnim von Stechow, eds. 1983. *Meaning, Use, and Interpretation of Language*. Berlin: de Gruyter.

Bäuerle, Rainer, Urs Egli, and Arnim von Stechow, eds. 1979. *Semantics from Different Points of View*. Berlin: Springer-Verlag.

Bellert, Irena. 1977. On semantic and distributional properties of sentential adverbs. *Linguistic Inquiry* 8: 337–51.

Bennett, Jonathan. 1988. *Events and their Names*. Indianapolis: Hackett Press.

Bennett, Michael. 1977. A guide to the logic of tense and aspect in English. *Logique et Analyse* 20: 491–517.

Bennett, Michael. 1981. Of tense and aspect: One analysis. In Tedeschi and Zaenen 1981, 13–30.

Bennett, Michael, and Barbara Partee. 1978. *Toward the Logic of Tense and Aspect in English*. Indianapolis: Indiana University Linguistics Club.

Brook, G. L. 1955. *An Introduction to Old English*. Manchester: Manchester University Press.

Campbell, A. 1959. *Old English Grammar*. Oxford: Clarendon Press.

Castañeda, Hector-Neri. 1967. Comments. In N. Rescher, ed., *The Logic of Decision and Action*. Pittsburgh: University of Pittsburgh Press.

Chomsky, Noam. 1970. Remarks on nominalization. In Jacobs, R., and P. Rosenbaum, eds., *Readings in English Transformational Grammar*. Waltham, Mass.: Ginn and Co. Reprinted in Davidson and Harmon 1975.

Clark, Romaine. 1970. Concerning the logic of predicate modifiers. *Nous* 4: 311–35.

Cooper, Robin, and Terence Parsons. 1976. Montague grammar, generative semantics and interpretive semantics. In Partee 1976b.

Cresswell, Max. 1985. *Adverbial Modification*. Dordrecht: Reidel.

Dahl, Östen. 1981. On the definition of the telic-atelic (bounded-nonbounded) distinction. In Tedeschi and Zaenen 1981.

Davidson, Donald. 1967. The logical form of action sentences. In N. Rescher, ed., *The Logic of Decision and Action*. Pittsburgh: University of Pittsburgh Press. Reprinted in Davidson 1980.

Davidson, Donald. 1980. *Essays on Actions and Events*. Oxford: Clarendon Press.

Davidson, Donald. 1985. Adverbs of action. In Vermazen, Bruce, and Merrill Hintikka, eds., *Essays on Davidson: Actions and Events*. Oxford: Clarendon Press.

Davidson, Donald, and Gil Harman, eds. 1972. *Semantics of Natural Language*. Dordrecht: D. Reidel.

Davis, Steve, and Marianne Mithun, eds. 1979. *Linguistics, Philosophy and Montague Grammar*. Austin: University of Texas Press.

Dowty, David. 1979. *Word Meaning and Montague Grammar*. Boston: D. Reidel.

Dowty, David. 1989. On the semantic content of the notion 'thematic role'. In Gennaro Chierchia, Barbara Partee, and Ray Turner, eds., *Properties, Types and Meaning*. Vol. 2. Dordrecht: Kluwer, 69–130.

Dowty, David, Robert Wall, and Stanley Peters. 1981. *Introduction to Montague Semantics*. Dordrecht: D. Reidel.

Fillmore, Charles. 1968. The case for case. In E. Bach and R. Harms, eds., *Universals in Linguistic Theory*. New York: Holt, Rinehart and Winston.

Fodor, Jerry. 1970. Three reasons for not deriving 'kill' from 'cause to die'. *Linguistic Inquiry* 1: 429–38.

Frege, Gottlob. 1892. On sense and reference. In P. Geach and M. Black, eds., *Translations from the Philosophical Writings of Gottlob Frege*. Oxford: Blackwell, 1960.

Frege, Gottlob. 1918. The thought: a logical inquiry. Translated by A. M. Quinton and M. Quinton. *Mind* 65, 1956.

Goldman, Alvin. 1970. *A Theory of Human Action*. Englewood Cliffs, New Jersey: Prentice-Hall.

Groenendijk, J., T. Janssen, and M. Stokhof. 1981. *Formal Methods in the Study of Language*. Amsterdam: Matematisch Centrum.

Gruber, Jeffrey. 1976. *Lexical Structures in Syntax and Semantics*. Amsterdam: North-Holland Press.

Guenthner, Franz, and Christian Rohrer, eds. 1978. *Studies in Formal Semantics: Intensionality, Temporality, Negation*. Amsterdam: North-Holland Press.

Guenthner, Franz, and S. Schmidt, eds. 1979. *Formal Semantics and Pragmatics for Natural Languages*. Dordrecht: Reidel.

Heim, Irene. 1983. File change semantics and the familiarity theory of definiteness. In Bäuerle et al 1983.

Hendrix, Gary. 1978. *Encoding Knowledge in Partitioned Networks*. Menlo Park, Calif.: SRI International.

Higginbotham, James. 1983. The logic of perceptual reports: An extensional alternative to situation semantics. *Journal of Philosophy* 80: 100–127.

Higginbotham, James. 1985a. On semantics. *Linguistic Inquiry* 16, 547–93.

Higginbotham, James. 1985b. Linguistic theory and Davidson's program in semantics. In LePore and McLaughlin 1985.

Hintikka, Jaakko, Julius Moravcsik, and Patrick Suppes, eds. 1973. *Approaches to Natural Language*. Dordrecht, Boston: Reidel.

Jackendoff, Ray. 1972. *Semantic Interpretation in Generative Grammar*. Cambridge: MIT Press.

Jackendoff, Ray. 1976. Toward an explanatory semantic representation. *Linguistic Inquiry* 7: 89–150.

Kamp, Hans. 1975. Two theories about adjectives. In Keenan 1975.

Kamp, Hans. 1980. Some remarks on the logic of change. Part I. In Rohrer 1980.

Kamp, Hans. 1981. A theory of truth and semantic representation. In Groenendijk et al 1981.

Kamp, Hans, and Christian Rohrer. 1983. Tense in texts. In Bäuerle et al 1983.

Keenan, Edward, ed. 1975. *Formal Semantics of Natural Language*. Cambridge: Cambridge University Press.

Kenny, Anthony. 1963. *Action, Emotion and Will*. New York: Humanities Press.

Keyser, Samuel. 1968. Review of Sven Jacobson, *Adverbial Positions in English. Language:* 357–74.

Kiparsky, P., and J. F. Staal. 1969. Syntactic and semantic relations in Panini. *Foundations of Language* 5, 83–117.

Kisbye, Torben. 1971/72. *An Historical Outline of English Syntax*. Aarhus: Akademisk Boghandel.

Lehmann, W. P. 1980. The reconstruction of non-simple sentences in proto-Indo-European. In Paolo Ramat, ed., *Linguistic Reconstruction and Indo-European Syntax*. Amsterdam: John Benjamins.

LePore, Ernest, and Brian McLaughlin, eds. 1986. *Truth and Interpretation*. Oxford, New York: Blackwell.

LePore, Ernest, and Brian McLaughlin, eds. 1985. *Actions and Events: Perspectives on the Philosophy of Donald Davidson*. Oxford: Blackwell.

Lewis, David. 1975. Adverbs of quantification. In E. L. Keenan, ed., *Formal Semantics of Natural Language*. Cambridge: Cambridge University Press.

Lightfoot, David W. 1979. *Principles of Diachronic Syntax*. Cambridge: Cambridge University Press.

Lightfoot, David W. 1980. On reconstructing a proto-syntax. In Paolo Ramat, ed., *Linguistic Reconstruction and Indo-European Syntax*. Amsterdam: John Benjamins.

Lombard, Lawrence. 1985. How not to flip the prowler: Transitive verbs of action and the identity of actions. In LePore and McLaughlin 1985.

Materna, Pavel, and Petr Sgall. 1984. Optional participants in a semantic interpretation. In P. Sgall, ed., *Contributions to Functional Syntax, Semantics, and Language Comprehension*. Amsterdam: John Benjamins.

McCawley, Noriko. 1976. On experiencer causatives. In Shibatani 1976.

McCoard, James. 1978. *The English Perfect: Tense-Choice and Pragmatic Inferences*. Amsterdam: North-Holland Press.

McConnell-Ginet, Sally. 1982. Adverbs and logical form: A linguistically realistic theory. *Language* 58: 144–84.

Mitchell, Bruce. 1987. *Old English Syntax*. Oxford: Clarendon.

Mitchell, Bruce, and Fred C. Robinson. 1982. *A Guide to Old English*. Toronto: University of Toronto Press.

Montague, Richard. 1970. English as a formal language. In Montague 1974.

Montague, Richard. 1973. The proper treatment of quantification in ordinary English. In Hintikka, Moravcsik, and Suppes 1973. Reprinted in Montague 1974.

Montague, Richard. 1974. *Formal Philosophy*. New Haven: Yale University Press.

Mourelatos, Alexander. 1978. Events, processes, and states. *Linguistics and Philosophy* 2: 415–34. Reprinted in Tedeschi and Zaenen 1981.

Panini. B. C. *The Ashtadhyayi*. Edited and translated by Srisa Chandra Vasu. Delhi: Motilal Barnarsidass, 1962.

Parsons, Terence. 1970. An analysis of mass terms and amount terms. *Foundations of Language* 6, 362–88. Reprinted in J. Pelletier, ed. *Recent Work on Mass Terms*. Dordrecht: Reidel, 1979.

Parsons, Terence. 1969. Essentialism and quantified modal logic. *Philosophical Review* 78, 35–52.

Parsons, Terence. 1970. Some problems concerning the logic of grammatical modifiers. In Davidson and Harmon 1970.

Parsons, Terence. 1980. Modifiers and quantifiers in natural language. *Canadian Journal of Philosophy*. Suppl. Vol. 6: 29–60.

Parsons, Terence. 1985. Underlying events in the logical analysis of English. In LePore and McLaughlin 1985.

Parsons, Terence. 1987/88. Underlying states in the semantical analysis of English. *Proceedings of the Aristotelian Society* 88, 13–30.

Parsons, Terence. 1988. Russell's early views on denoting. In David Austin, ed. *Philosophical Analysis*. Dordrecht: Kluwer, 17–44.

Parsons, Terence. 1989. The progressive in English: Events, states and processes. *Linguistics and Philosophy* 12: 213–41.

Parsons, Terence. Forthcoming. *Atomic sentences as singular terms in free logic*.

Partee, Barbara. 1973. Some structural analogies between tenses and pronouns in English. *Journal of Philosophy* 70: 601-09.

Partee, Barbara. 1976a. Some transformational extensions of Montague grammar. In Partee 1976b.

Partee, Barbara, ed. 1976b. *Montague Grammar*. New York: Academic Press.

Partee, Barbara. 1984. Nominal and temporal anaphora. *Linguistics and Philosophy* 7: 243–86.

Partee, Barbara, and Michael Bennett. 1978. *Toward the Logic of Tense and Aspect in English*. Indianapolis: Indiana University Linguistics Club.

Perry, John, and Jon Barwise. 1981. Semantic innocence and uncompromising situations. *Midwest Studies in Philosophy*. Vol. 6: 387–404.

Perry, John, and Jon Barwise. 1983. *Situations and Attitudes*. Cambridge: MIT Press.

Plato. 366 B.C. *Sophist*. In Harold North Fowler, trans., *PLATO: Theaetetus and Sophist*. Cambridge: Harvard University Press, 1961.

Quirk, Randolph, and C. L. Wrenn. 1958. *An Old English Grammar*. New York: Holt, Rinehart and Winston.

Ramsey, Frank P. 1927. Facts and propositions. Reprinted in *The Foundations of Mathematics*. Paterson, New Jersey: Littlefield, Adams and Co., 1960.

Reichenbach, Hans. 1947. *Elements of Symbolic Logic*. New York: Free Press.

Rohrer, Christian, ed. 1980. *Time, Tense, and Quantifiers*. Tübingen: Niemeyer.

Rohrer, Christian, ed. 1977. *On the Logical Analysis of Tense and Aspect*. Tübingen: TBL Verlag Gunter Narr.

Rohrer, Christian, and Hans Kamp. 1983. Tense in texts. In Bäuerle et al. 1983.

Russell, Bertrand. 1903. *Principles of Mathematics*. London: Cambridge University Press.

Russell, Bertrand. 1905. On denoting. *Mind* 14: 479–93.

Russell, Bertrand. 1912. *The Problems of Philosophy*. New York: Henry Holt and Co.

Ryle, Gilbert. 1931–32. Systematically misleading expressions. *Proceedings of the Aristotelian Society* 1931–32.

Ryle, Gilbert. 1949. *The Concept of Mind*. London: Barnes and Noble.

Schachter, Paul. 1985. Parts-of-speech systems. In Timothy Shopen, ed., *Language Typology and Syntactic Description. Vol. I: Clause Structure*. Cambridge: Cambridge University Press.

Sgall, Petr, and Pavel Materna. 1984. Optional participants in a semantic interpretation. In P. Sgall, ed., *Contributions to Functional Syntax, Semantics, and Language Comprehension*. Amsterdam: John Benjamins.

Shibatani, Masayoshi, ed. 1976. *Syntax and Semantics 6, The Grammar of Causative Constructions*. New York: Academic Press.

Siegel, Muffy. 1979. Measure adjectives in Montague grammar. In Davis and Mithun 1979.

Staal, J.F., and P. Kiparsky. 1969. Syntactic and semantic relations in Panini. *Foundations of Language* 5, 83–117.

Stalnaker, Robert, and Richmond Thomason. 1973. A semantic theory of adverbs. *Linguistic Inquiry* 4: 195–220.

Stockwell, R., P. Schachter, and B. Partee. 1973. *The Major Syntactic Structures of English*. New York: Holt, Rinehart and Winston.

Taylor, Barry. 1985. *Modes of Occurrence*. Oxford: Blackwell.

Tedeschi, Philip. 1981. Some evidence for a branching-futures semantic model. In Tedeschi and Zaenen 1981.

Tedeschi, Philip, and Annie Zaenen, eds. 1981. *Syntax and Semantics. Vol. 14, Tense and Aspect*. New York: Academic Press.

Thomason, Richmond. 1971. Logic and adverbs. *Journal of Philosophy* 68: 715–16.

Thomason, Richmond. 1976. Some extensions of Montague grammar. In Partee 1976b.

Thomason, Richmond, and Robert Stalnaker. 1973. A semantic theory of adverbs. *Linguistic Inquiry* 4: 195–220.

Thomson, Judith J. 1971. Individuating actions. *Journal of Philosophy* 68: 771–81.

Traugott, Elizabeth Closs. 1972. *A History of English Syntax*. New York: Holt, Rinehart and Winston.

Vendler, Zeno. 1967. *Linguistics in Philosophy*. Ithaca, New York: Cornell University Press.

Vendler, Zeno. 1984. Agency and causation. *Midwest Studies in Philosophy* 9: 371–84.

Visser, Fredericus. 1963, vol. 1, 1966, vol. 2, 1969/73, vol. 3. *An Historical Syntax of the English Language*. Leiden: Brill.

Vlach, Frank. 1981. The semantics of the progressive. In Tedeschi and Zaenen 1981: 271–92.

Vlach, Frank. 1983. On situation semantics for perception. *Synthese* 54: 129–52.

Wallace, John. 1966. On what's happening. Dittograph.

Wheeler, Samuel III. 1972. Attributives and their modifiers. *Nous* 6: 310–34.

Wik, Berit. 1973. *English Nominalizations in -ing*. Uppsala: Universitatis Upsaliensis.

Zimmerman, Thomas Ede. 1987. Transparent adverbs and scopeless quantifiers. In Jeroem Groenendijk, Dick de Jough, and Martin Stokhof, eds., *Foundations of Pragmatics and Lexical Semantics*. Dordrecht: Foris, 87–99.

Index